Gerrit Pool

Modern Rugby

The essential concepts and skills

Tafelberg

To Chester for his dedication and perseverance.
Fame has not changed him.

28 Wale Street, Cape Town 8001

Set 10 on 12 pt Plantin
Printed by National Book Printers,
Drukkery Street, Goodwood, Western Cape
First edition 1997

ISBN 0 624 03274 4

Contents

Preface

Coaches and players throughout the rugbyplaying world are battling every day to master this great game - one that can so easily become complicated. Coaches not only want to know what to teach their players, but also how their players can put the theory into practice. Often the search is for the short-cuts in coaching and for solutions to the many problems that can crop up so quickly during play.

It is not only the inexperienced coaches who struggle at times; even those with experience still encounter problems. They are permanently under pressure because they are expected to keep up the name or proud records of their school, college, university or club. The frustration of seeing their team struggle to get going but not knowing how to turn things around is all too familiar to them.

The players have similar problems. How many props, for example, suffer unnecessarily in the scrum for many seasons not because they are not strong enough, but because of sheer ignorance?

The coach does not have time to read through pages and pages searching for answers to his problems. This is why the information is presented schematically, so that the solutions can be found quickly.

Modern Rugby has been written in everyday rugby-idiom, the ordinary language used by the players. It deals with the various facets of the game, from the very basics right through to its complexities.

Many beginner-coaches, however, have difficulty seeing the game as a whole. The close bond between forward and back-line play and how they influence one another, is therefore strongly emphasised. It is to be hoped that this will enable the coach to see how the different facets fit into the broader context of the game. When line-out possession, for instance, is discussed, the advantages and limitations of possession at No. 2, 4 and 6, and the way it affects the backs are discussed too.

Modern Rugby is much more than simply a reworked version of *Wenrugby*. The latter, aimed mainly at the daily problems experienced by every coach - from the beginner to the specialist - was received favourably. Subsequently just about every coach asked for the inclusion of specific aspects in any new publication: the persona of the coach, preparing for and planning matches, analysing them, selecting a team, forward and back-line play, contact, dealing with the player on a personal level, psychological preparation, refereeing and the laws of rugby, and in particular how to correct mistakes.

What is the origin of this new approach?

KEY TO ILLUSTRATIONS

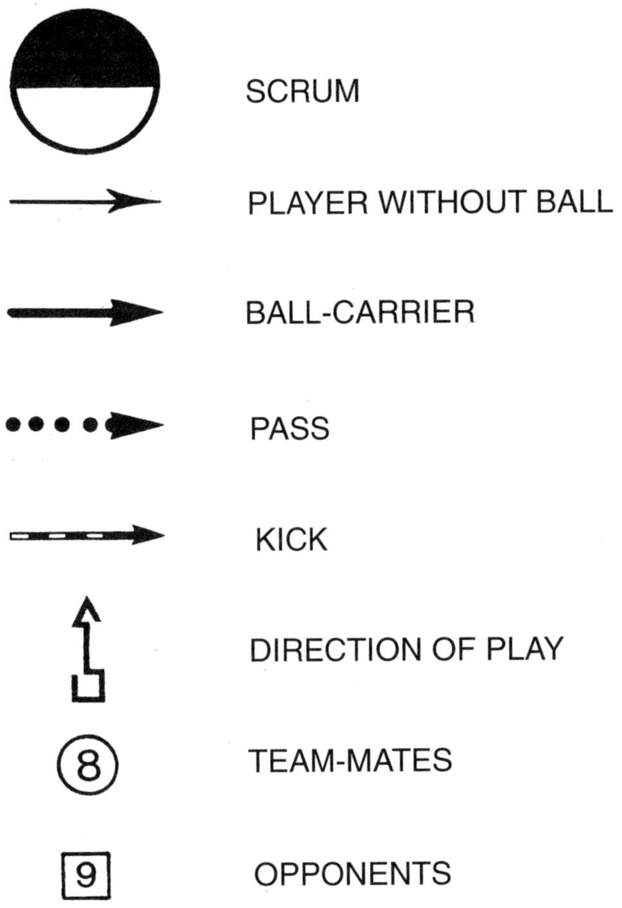

The introduction of the World Cup competition in 1987 and the money and prestige involved have had a profound effect on every rugby-playing nation. The honour of qualifying for it and possibly even winning it has put tremendous pressure on the top playing nations such as England, France, Wales, Scotland, Ireland, Australia, New Zealand and South Africa to perform well and win.

Nowadays the end of one World Cup competition signals the run-up to the next. Coaching techniques and styles of play are constantly being evaluated and long-term planning has become an integral part of the successful teams. The direction taken by the two previous winners - especially New Zealand and Australia - as regards their preparation and different styles of play has been carefully studied and, in most cases, imitated.

Rugby as a sport cannot free itself from the influences of other competing sports or the community within which it is played. In the case of Australia, rugby is constantly waging a battle against Australian Rules and Rugby League. In New Zealand, the Home Unions and France, the opponent is Rugby League and, of course, soccer, where the big money lies. It should therefore come as no surprise that aspects of the Rules and particularly the League game have been incorporated into Rugby Union. This is discussed in the chapter on the approach to, or philosophy behind, *Modern Rugby*.

South African rugby has, up to 1992, when it returned to the fold of international rugby, remained only a spectator on the sidelines of this process. As regards the game itself, most provincial coaches have clung to obsolete methods of practice and styles of play, which have indeed given them local victories but which would not necessarily give them the same success internationally. The same applies to the referees' interpretation and application of the rules; during the years of isolation they lost touch with international practice. Here it is not a matter of who is technically "right" or "wrong", it is rather a case of what is being done internationally. And to complicate matters further, our game on the administrative level has been, and still is to a certain extent, caught up in the throes of the political transition process.

The Springbok tour to France and England in 1992 shocked us out of our complacency and caused a headlong rush to indiscriminately copy the methods of practice and styles of play of international teams. In the process, two basic mistakes were made.

Firstly, we forgot to take account of the essential nature of the South African rugby player. As impossible as it is for the Frenchman's game to be taken as a blueprint for the New Zealander's, so it is for the South African's to be a blueprint for, say, the Frenchman's.

Secondly - and this generally arises from the first mistake - we strove to "catch up with international standards". This is an error in perception, because international teams are constantly developing and such an attitude therefore implies that we will always lag behind the rest of the world. Our thinking should focus on innovation and on taking the lead in the development of rugby.

At national level, it is a fact that no team has ever retained the World Cup. This simply indicates that the level of play that won South Africa the 1995 World Cup, has to be raised considerably if the next cup is to be won too.

The level of play in the southern hemisphere's Super 12 Competition, for example, has already risen to and above levels formerly only reached by internationals.

It was with this in mind that I studied and personally discussed the approaches of several internationally successful coaches: Pierre Villepreux and Pierre Berbizier (France), Alec Evans, Bob Templeton and David Clarke (Australia), John Dawes and Alun Davies (Wales), Jim Greenwood (Scotland) and Don Rutherford, Rodger Uttley and Dick Best (England). Especially interesting were the advanced approach and methods of practice of New Zealand coaches such as Lee Smith, Jim Blair and John Hart. In the process one had to be careful not to forget the truths taught by our own maestro at Stellenbosch, Doc Danie Craven.

Modern Rugby is bound to be invaluable to the inexperienced coach, and it will stimulate the more experienced coach to even greater heights.

Gerrit Pool
October 1996

1. The coach

As a man thinketh, so is he

Characteristics of a good coach

Every coach should strive to remain true to his own personality in the way he coaches. Just as personalities differ, so do coaches. Despite all differences, however, the ideal coach is someone who:

☐ loves the game;
☐ is enthusiastic about the game;
☐ knows the game and is always innovative;
☐ can convey his knowledge of the game to other people;
☐ enjoys working with people;
☐ is a realist; and
☐ upholds his own rugby code.

Few coaches can boast all these characteristics, but those who are successful usually have most of them. The perfect coach, however, has yet to be born!

Love of the game

Rugby is the only game I know in which almost anyone can take part, irrespective of physique, strength, speed or intellectual ability.

Rugby is a way of life. Players experience true enjoyment only when they have learnt to play for each other, in other words, when they create opportunities for each other. This and the camaraderie that flows from it, create the platform from which the talented player can develop his abilities while benefiting the team as a whole.

The genuine coach is prepared to give more than just his time and his knowledge of the game to the players. The way in which he introduces young players to the game and the codes he upholds can influence young people's lives permanently.

Enthusiasm

Without enthusiasm a coach achieves nothing. The good coach probably began his career with little knowledge, but definitely with a lot of enthusiasm. An inspired teacher quickly recruits ardent followers!

Knowledge of the game

A coach must be a student of the game. He must be prepared to listen to the advice of everyone - players, ex-players, people with an interest in the game, armchair critics, yes everyone - and separate the wheat from the chaff. An attitude of "I know it all" is a sign of arrogance, inexperience and immaturity. With such an attitude the players will lose out.

Every coach improves with experience. Ex-players who coach usually lament the fact that they did not have the knowledge in their playing days that they now have as coaches!

This is precisely the purpose of this manual: to help the player understand what rugby is about, i.e., not just being taught how to pass, but also learning the *when* and *where* of passing the ball. In this way the greatness of the game is discovered by the player.

To summarise

The coach must know the following:

☐ What each *position* requires of a player, and how to teach him the basic techniques and to let him practise them.
☐ How the various individuals function as *units* both as backs and as forwards, i.e., how each section works.
☐ How and when a *team* must play to be truly effective, i.e., he must be able to "see" how the game will develop under various circumstances.

Conveying knowledge

The ability to convey knowledge is generally the difference between the coach who succeeds and the coach who fails. There is a world of difference between the ability to do something yourself and the ability to teach it to someone else.

This is where many ex-players fall short. Because a player respects his coach first and foremost for what he learns from him, the coach's achievements as player will only have a short-term impact, after which it will quickly become less important if the coach is unable to convey his knowledge.

Although knowledge can be conveyed in various ways, the following points should always be kept in mind:

☐ A player learns the quickest from what he sees.
☐ A coach should start with the simplest and gradually progress to the more difficult things.
☐ The correct practice methods speed up the learning process.
☐ The criterion is whether the method succeeds on the field of play.

Ability to work with people

A coach should never be carried away by his enthusiasm for, and interest in, the game to the point where he forgets he is working with people.

In this respect coaches would do well to remember the following:

☐ Most people play rugby for pleasure, i.e., they want to enjoy it as a game. Players really enjoy the game only when they run with the ball. Keep this in mind when you work out practice sessions.

☐ Players do not take the field with the intention of making mistakes, especially not in front of hundreds or thousands of spectators. But mistakes are made. Players make mistakes because they:

- do not know how to do something, i.e., they have not yet mastered a technique;
- do not know when to carry out a movement, i.e., they do not yet understand what the game is about;
- are not concentrating.

☐ Always be positive with your players - even when you criticise them. They must believe at all times that you have their interests at heart.

☐ Choose your words carefully when the players are tired. Tired players do not have much patience, especially in the dressing room after a hard match that has been lost!

☐ Keep a close eye on your players. Every player has personal problems from time to time. It doesn't help to rant and rave at someone when he is dejected or depressed.

An encouraging word at the right moment can earn you a lifelong disciple. When students write exams, for example, they are emotionally drained. It may seem like a contradiction, but you should then plan practices so that they are invigorating and recreational. When planning matches during these periods, expect and allow for a higher percentage of errors.

☐ Don't misuse players to enhance your image as coach, and always be sincere in your actions. Players respect a coach who is honest, and they accept his shortcomings. Large clubs sometimes have the problem of the opportunistic or mercenary coach who uses the talent of the club's players to increase his own prestige and market value. He usually stays at a club for a year or two at the most and follows a short-term-maximum-own-advantage approach after which his role is played out. Then he has to look for greener pastures again. Be careful of the coach who changes clubs every two to three years!

☐ If you don't know something, admit it to the players, thus maintaining your credibility.

Realism

Set attainable goals. It is important to win and everyone wants to win, but this should not be the only objective. Therefore choose your goals in such a way that, even if your team loses a match, the players will still feel that it wasn't all for nothing. This will help to build up your team on a constant basis, and success will follow.

Upholding a rugby code

☐ Play the ball, not the man.

☐ Where it is possible to run with the ball, do so.

☐ Every player who wins possession creates the potential for a try.

☐ The player's mind-set should be to create opportunities for fellow team members.

☐ Foul play is not part of the game; hard play is.

☐ The referee is always right.

☐ There is no place in the team for a rugby thug.

☐ The coach is in the privileged position of helping to shape his club's history.

The methodology of coaching

Basic principles

Coaching is based on the following principles:

☐ Teach players new movements when they are not tired. Tired players find it difficult to concentrate.

☐ Show/demonstrate. Players learn more quickly with their eyes. Let players who can carry out a movement correctly, demonstrate it.

☐ Explain. In other words:

- indicate the key players for a specific movement, i.e., who must nominate (when the movement should be initiated); carry it out (who must break the defensive line); support (who must help and round off, and where); and cover (in case an error is made).

Remember: Tell each player initially only what he needs to know in this position.

☐ Practise movements step by step, i.e., from an oversimplified situation to a real one.

☐ Practise movements first without opponents:

- Let the players walk when they practise a movement for the first time. This gives them a chance to talk about it.
- Bring in the supporting players. Show them exactly where help is needed. Make sure there is always support behind the ball-carrier both to the left and to the right.
- Show where cover is needed. Gradually increase the speed with which the movement is carried out.

Remember: The coach must concentrate on the core aspects throughout.

☐ Then practise with opponents (first only the players' immediate positional opponents):

- Tell the opponent exactly what to do (otherwise he will spoil things because he knows what is going to happen).
- Have the movement carried out against the opposing back-line and loose forwards.

☐ Create the opportunity for new movements to be carried out during practices. Let the players first practise repeatedly in sections during warm-up (only backs or forwards separately).

☐ Match practice: Allow players to carry out new movements during a match where and when the risk is smallest, e.g., in the opponents' half and/or when they have a comfortable lead.

Remember: As the skill and confidence of the players increase, the risk inherent in the movements decreases.

The coach's position on the field

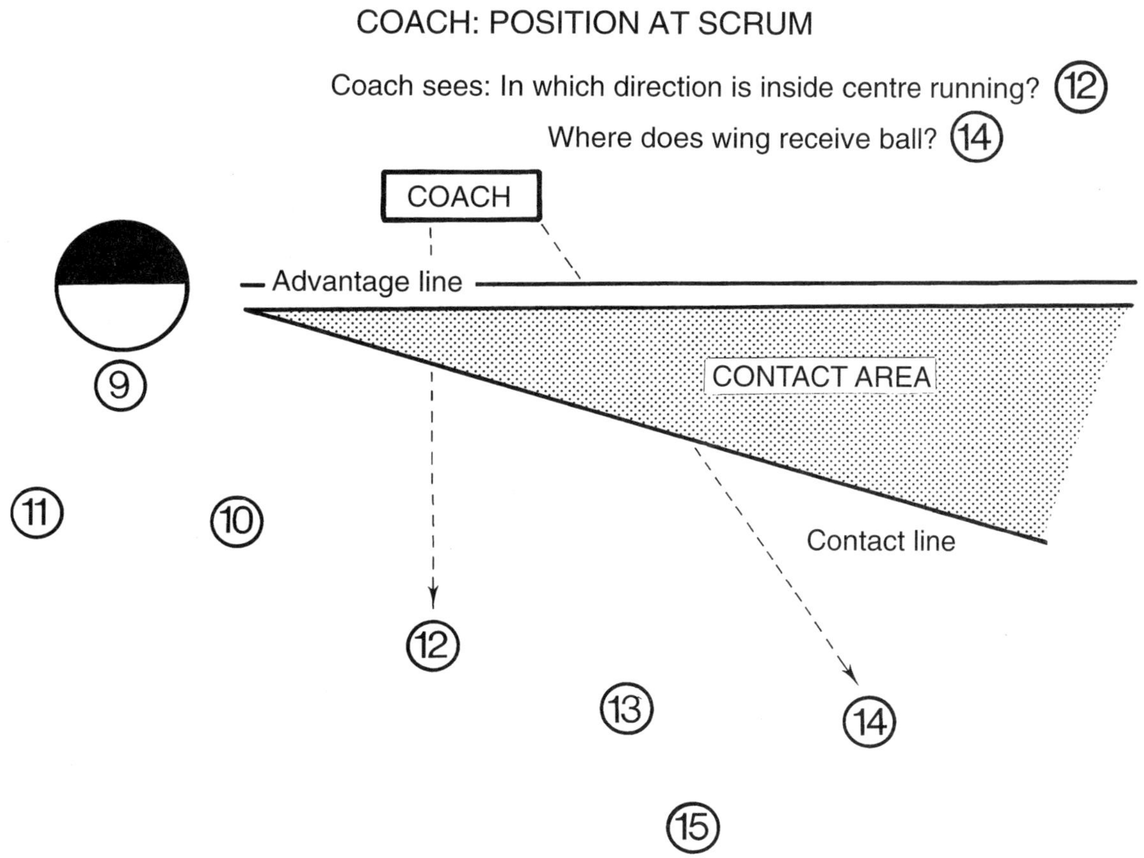

During practices

WITH THE BACKS

Remember: The biggest mistake is to stand where play starts.

☐ Use the lines on the field:
- as markers to see how far the backs move forward; and
- to make clear to the players the concepts of the advantage line and particularly the tackle or contact line.

☐ Face the back-line to see whether they run straight or across the field.

☐ Stand opposite the point where:
- the key player is in the line movement to see whether he plays correctly;
- the tactical manoeuvre is going to be executed so that you can judge the movement as a whole.

☐ Stand at the specific point on the field where a movement is normally carried out to assess (in conjunction with the players) the possibilities and problems of the movement at that spot.

WITH THE FORWARDS - BEFORE THEY GO DOWN

☐ Stand in front of the hooker:
- to observe how the first row binds; and
- to check hip and shoulder positions.

WITH THE FORWARDS - WHEN THEY GO DOWN

☐ Stand next to the front row to observe:
- whether the front row goes down in a forward position; and
- whether the second row goes down in a pushing position (note the position of the knees - straight knees cannot push).

☐ Stand behind the eighth-man to see whether there are gaps between the forwards' bodies: are the hips of both props inwards, are the shoulders and hips of the locks close against each other, are the flanks pushing forward?

☐ Note the following when the pack of forwards goes down against a scrum machine:
- A sledge (a dead weight): The players must push immediately.

☐ Because a sledge does not push back, players tend to go down first and then gradually get into a pushing position. This is a bad habit! The push must be explosive, not slow.
- A scrum machine with springs (that responds to pressure): The pressure must be applied immediately. The players should not relax after the first push, but keep up the pressure after the first explosive shove.

WITH THE FORWARDS - IN A LINE-OUT

☐ Stand in front of the line-out to see:
- whether the jumpers at the front (prop and/or first lock) jump forward and diagonally in and, after they land, take up a powerful position (feet hip-width apart with the front

foot about half a metre in front of the back foot and buttocks thrust towards the opponents); and
- whether the supporters on either side of the jumper bind forward.

☐ Stand next to the line-out on the side of the team throwing in to see:
- whether the players who cover do not overrun the ball;
- whether the players close the gaps in the line-out with their arms and legs;
- whether the players go in from behind when they form a driving maul; and
- whether the first player in a peel off from the line-out gets the ball on the field side of the catcher or deflector so that he can move forward instead of across field.

☐ Stand on the opponents' side of the line-out opposite the point to which the players are going to peel off or form a driving maul to see:
- whether they protect the ball in such a way that the opponents cannot see it and therefore block it, and whether the supporters come in from behind and come in straight.

WITH THE FORWARDS - IN A MAUL

☐ Stand behind the maul to see:
- whether the ball-carrier has moved the ball back to the last player on his side of the maul;
- whether the supporters isolate the ball-carrier on the sides from the opponents;
- whether someone goes for the ball if the ball-carrier is prevented from passing; and
- whether the rest of the ball-carrier's team-mates join from behind in a pushing position.

☐ Stand on the opponents' side of the maul and look:
- whether you can see the ball, which means your team is going to lose possession;
- whether you can see gaps between the ball-carrier and the first supporters where the opponents can squeeze through and slow down possession; and
- whether the supporters are binding those opponents on the sides (according to the rules, of course), who are trying to edge past the maul as far as the referee allows.

Remember: The referee cannot see both sides of the maul at the same time.

WITH THE FORWARDS - IN A RUCK

☐ Stand behind the ruck to see:
- whether the ball-carrier keeps the ball available on his team's side;
- whether the first two supporters go in on either side of the ball-carrier;
- whether the other supporters enter the ruck in a scrum formation; and
- whether the forwards bind onto one another.

☐ Stand to the side of the ruck to see:
- whether the players stay on their feet and go over the ball, i.e., whether the ruck has forward momentum.

☐ Stand on the opponents' side of the ruck and look:
- whether you can see the ball (if so, you are going to lose possession); and
- whether the spearhead of the ruck is right behind the ball (in this way you immediately spot the "vultures" who are fringing on the sides).

During kick-offs and drop-outs

When the opponents kick-off

☐ Stand behind your forward who catches the ball
- to see whether the catcher turns in time;
- to see whether the first two supporters shield in time;
- to see whether the designated player makes the ball safe;
- to see whether your players are firmly bound to the maul that has developed; and
- to listen whether your players are communicating.

☐ Stand behind the opponents to see:
- whether your forwards move towards the ball in time; and
- whether the sides of the maul are tightly bound.

WHEN YOUR TEAM KICKS OFF

☐ Stand behind your forwards to see:
- whether two players are nominated to go for the ball;
- whether the rest move in behind the ball; and
- whether those who defend on the sides of the maul are in position.

☐ Stand behind the opponents to see:
- whether your first two players keep their eyes on the ball;
- whether one of your players goes past the ball in case of the opponents deflecting it to their side; and
- whether your team's defensive pattern (this includes the backs) shows weak spots.

During matches

ON THE PAVILION (I.E. ON THE TOUCH-LINE)

☐ It is a good position to see:
- whether the forwards move ahead in set play and support in depth;
- whether the backs play shallow or deep and move forward aggressively or not; and
- whether those who cover are in the right position or whether they stand too deep or too shallow.

☐ It is a bad position to see:
- whether the forwards scrum too loosely, whether they close up and support in the line-outs and whether they drive straight towards the opposing try-line in the tight-loose;
- whether there are gaps in the opponents' defence or whether gaps develop; and
- whether the backs run straight.

BEHIND THE GOAL POSTS

☐ This is an inconvenient position, but nevertheless ideal to assess the following:
- whether the forwards move in close cohesion when they drive, go into the rucks and mauls from the back, go down firmly in a scrum and support in the line-outs and during kick-offs and drop-outs;

COACH: POSITION AT LINE-OUT

PEELING OFF IN FRONT

Coach looks at: Hooker
6 & 7
Direction of ball-carrier - forward?

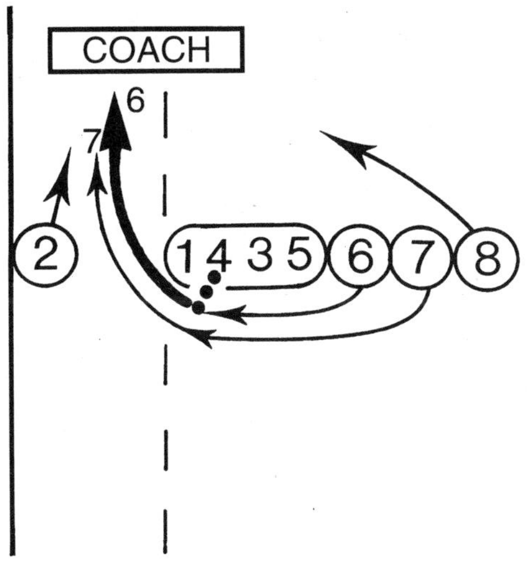

PEELING OFF AT THE BACK

Coach observes: Player peeling off forward
Support
Centres

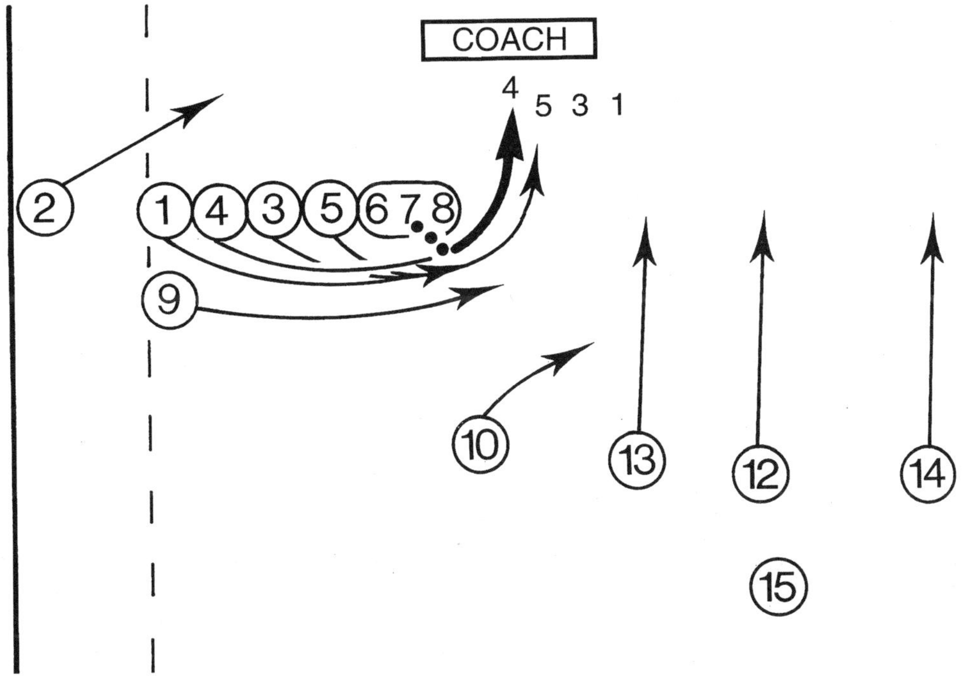

- whether the backs run straight, vary their starting positions, vary the length of their passes, change the direction of attack and spot and create gaps in the opponents' defence; and
- whether your team as a whole concentrates on the weak spots in the defence.

□ Here you cannot see:
- to what extent your individual players and your team as a whole play forward.

Remember: The higher your seat, the better you can "read" the match.

The coach's relationship with his players

The game centres on the player, not the coach. Rugby can be played without coaches but not without players. Although a coach is not essential in rugby, good coaching can enrich the game and heighten the enjoyment of the player. In other words: the coach is the conductor of the rugby orchestra.

The player has certain expectations of his coach:

□ He wants to respect and trust his coach as a person.

□ He expects his coach to know the game and to be able to convey that knowledge.

□ He wants his coach to help him achieve and develop as an individual player. Most players see their coach's personal achievements as neither here nor there, and they soon build up an aversion to a coach who constantly refers to his own accomplishments. Players sometimes refer to this as "The older I get, the better I was" syndrome!

□ He wants to know what his coach wants to achieve with the team and is prepared to work hard for it. As soon as he gets the impression that the coach is using him, and the team, only to improve his own image, he begins to distrust him. The coach who takes credit for victories but blames the players for defeats quickly runs into trouble. When the team wins, everyone wins, and when the team loses, everyone loses.

□ He wants his coach to set certain norms. Practices must be disciplined, thoroughly planned and challenging.

□ He wants to enjoy his practices to such an extent that he can forget his problems. The last thing he wants during practice is frustration. He does not want to know beforehand what he is going to do on a specific day except that his coach will be satisfied with nothing less than his best. Players who have built up a good sweat do not complain at the end of a practice - players who are idle do! A player will, given the chance, waste the coach's time without any qualms, as long as his own time is not wasted!

A coach is continuously confronted with an imminent clash of interests between the team and individuals. As coach, he is responsible for the team's welfare, and every player should be important to him. The player, on the other hand, has a much narrower view of the game. He puts his own interests first. What is important to him is how well he does. Successful coaches manage to reconcile these two seemingly conflicting approaches.

A coach also has to contend with his share of "difficult" players. They are usually the ones who feel their role in the team's success is not recognised or appreciated and then there are those who are bored. The solution to this is simple:

□ In the first place, every player must feel he is important to his team-mates and to his team's success. To the coach this is not a big problem, because to him every player is important. The ordinary player, however, does not always have the insight to appreciate the true value of his team-mates. A coach must therefore not fail to give credit where it is due to players such as the tight forwards, who are seldom in the limelight. The same goes for the creative but inconspicuous player. At the end of the day, the try that was scored from the line-out by the wing originated with the hooker, who threw in well so that his lock could take the ball. The tight forwards therefore played as big a part in the try as the wing.

□ Secondly, always keep an eye on the talented player, because he is the one who becomes bored first. Give him responsibility, and your "problem child" will become an asset!

No team can achieve success in the long run if the players take no interest in each other. This is what team spirit is all about. The relationship amongst the players (and with management) off the field will, in one way or another, be reflected on the playing field. The coach who builds up team spirit around the tight forwards rarely goes wrong. These five players are, because of the demands of their positions, used to creating opportunities for others rather than themselves. They are used to taking physical punishment without complaining; in fact, most of them enjoy it! These are the men who keep the team together when things go wrong.

The coach's team will, in the final analysis, do only as well as he, as a person, gets on with his individual players. Conversely, the coach is not the player's buddy. Familiarity quickly breeds contempt, especially when a criticism is made by the coach. The coach must always maintain a distance between himself and his players without breaking down the communication they have with him.

The way in which a coach criticises a player is of the utmost importance to their relationship and, ultimately, to team spirit. Criticism must be positive, frank and restricted to the shortcomings in the player's game, not his personality. Offensive remarks get you nowhere. Knowledge of the game, particularly the specific position of the player, helps you to understand the player's actions and to discuss them with him accordingly. The hooker, who is in the midst of the scrum and is being pushed from the front and from behind, is much less tolerant towards criticism than the flank on the side of the scrum. Therefore criticise only what is essential, and rather talk with the player after the practice about his other shortcomings - then he will listen. A player will accept criticism if he feels the coach

means it sincerely. This is why he also expects the coach to tell him when he is playing badly. Remember, a player generally knows when he is not pulling his weight. A passing or tongue-in-cheek remark achieves much more than a tirade in front of team-mates.
Remember: If it is at all feasible, involve an injured player in the team's activities. He wants to feel his coach takes an interest in him as a person and not only when he needs him as a player.

Before a match

During preparation

Set realistic and attainable goals for the team and the individual before the time, ones they can reach even if they lose the match. The coach who measures success only by victories and defeats doesn't have a chance of building up a team in the long run!

The players' confidence for a match must already be built up during practice the preceding week, and not during a pep talk on the day of the match. Modern aids such as a video of a previous match can be used to show good play and make the players feel positive.

Players need not be motivated for important matches. Such matches motivate the players. Here the coach should rather concentrate on technique and strategy. In the case of an "easy" match, however, the coach has to watch his step and keep his players on their toes.

Excessive tension before a match could be very draining especially in the case of the inexperienced player. It results in that well-known "lame" feeling. A good antidote to this is to guide the player to keep to his daily routine before the match. In his thoughts about the match, he should concentrate on his primary task, i.e., on what he should do, rather than on his opponents.

Players should see their opponents as people of flesh and blood. The coach should particularly guard against emphasising the opponents' strong points in such a way that his own players see them as being virtually invincible. He should resist the temptation to whip up his players to the point where they hate their opponents. Subsequently they may have to play together for their province or even for their country! The coach should teach his players to play the ball mercilessly, yet within limits. No match is so important that a team should feel they deliberately have to injure the most dangerous opponent or, as the rugby player puts it, play the opponent off the field.

Explain to the players beforehand the feelings they are going to have during the different phases of the match. Remind them of the feeling of tremendous exhaustion within the first five minutes of a game, and the second half that just won't end! It helps to know your opponent feels the same way. They should look out for signs of tiredness in their opponents, such as getting to a scrum or line-out slowly.

Players can overcome the psychological battle against fatigue more easily if they remember the following points: A canoeist prefers competing on a winding river with rapids and other obstacles, and does not feel nearly as tired as during a race over the same distance on flat water on a straight river. Why? In the first instance, he does not have time to think about how tired he is; he is paddling from one bend to the next, from one obstacle to the other. In the second, the course is monotonous, and he has more than enough time to think about how tired he is and to feel sorry for himself! The rugby player who simply plays and plays until the match ends will find himself in the same position as the second canoeist. The player who plays from scrum to scrum and from each new facet to the next, i.e., who always has an immediate goal, concentrates on the game so much that he forgets about himself - like the canoeist on the winding river. He is the player who still gives his all in the last minute of the match.

At top level, talent is usually distributed quite evenly. The team that capitalises on its opportunities and that gets to grips with exhaustion, pain and setbacks best is the team that wins. It is the team that, in rugby idiom, is emotionally hard! Mistakes are part of rugby. In toplevel rugby a player cannot afford to worry about mistakes he has already made. What is done, is done. The important play is the one which comes up next.

The coach must teach his players how to deal with being behind in points during a match. The only score that really counts is the one on the scoreboard when the final whistle blows. When his team is behind in points it is imperative that a player must know not to panic but to concentrate on his basic task instead. The scoreboard will reflect this composure or the lack of it.

Ensure a positive attitude towards the referee. If the referee has conspicuous weak points, rather emphasise how the team can avoid situations in which he may give a dubious ruling. Players should under no circumstances concentrate on the referee. Remember, the referee is always right. Rather sort out uncertainties and any dissatisfaction after the match, not on the field.

In the dressing room

All the players must be in the dressing room at the appointed time. In this regard, the coach must be relentless, because players who arrive late cause unnecessary tension and stress.

The coach must see to it that his players do not become too tense. He must go through their joint and individual tasks for the last time and he must ensure they warm up properly. Establish a specific routine according to which this is done every time. It helps to calm the players down.

The players are already tense enough; the coach should therefore be careful what he says. If you know your players, you should know who needs to be calmed down or who needs extra encouragement. Now is not the time to come up with innovations or to show signs of panic yourself. Rather lie low if you are also tense. Strangers, of course, should be nowhere near the dressing room.

During a match

Try not to shout at your players during a match. Apply the same self-discipline on the sideline as you expect of your players on the field. Be particularly careful of offensive remarks. The player usually doesn't hear them, but his friends and family do!

Acknowledge good play. Come to an arrangement with your captain and other leaders on the field beforehand about signals you will give if tactical adjustments become necessary. In this way you can eliminate unnecessary confusion and reproaches afterwards. When things go wrong, it is no use yelling at the top of your lungs what the team should be doing. Rather wait for a break in play and then ask the players to concentrate more than ever on the basic aspects. Even the best coach, at times, has to witness his team being thrashed. This is the ideal opportunity for him to show the stuff he is made of.

After a match

When your team wins, let them enjoy their victory. You, as coach, may know that the team may have won by a wider margin if it had made fewer errors. But this is neither the time nor the place to point this out.

When your team loses, go to the dressing room. At least one positive thing must have happened during the match. Look for those highlights and point them out to your players. This is the start of the rebuilding process for the next match. You won't gain anything by emphasising all the errors now.

Rather say too little in the dressing room than too much! Analyse the match critically and distinguish between the major factors that led to poor play and the individual mistakes that resulted from it. Decide beforehand how to convey this to the team at the next practice.

The players, who in the meantime have thought about the match themselves, expect their coach to give his opinion about it. When he does, he should remember that criticism and humour are a much more effective combination than criticism and sarcasm. After all, when the post-mortem is over, everyone must be able to look one another in the eye again and continue with the game.

Preparing for a match

General

One of the biggest deficiencies in our rugby coaching is the lack of planning. Too many coaches try to get their teams ready for action with a stirring pep talk just before a match instead of preparing the players systematically in the course of the preceding week.

Planning is essential because:

☐ it is a prerequisite for success;

☐ it calms the players down and strengthens their belief in their own abilities; and

☐ it neutralises many of the opponents' strong points.

The framework given below is an example of what a coach should take into account over a period of a week, when he prepares the team for a match.

The objective is relaxed but determined players who know what to do, because:

☐ Excessive tension is detrimental to a team. Before a match it drains the players. During a match it causes poorer observation (the tense player's field of vision narrows), it causes slower and jerky movements, and it causes taut muscles that work against one another instead of in unison.

☐ Self-confidence leads to better performance. The players know what to do and they know they can do it because it has been spelt out to them in advance; their tasks are simple and they have already practised them again and again, and they know their opponents are only human:

Remember: Tension goes hand in hand with:

- lack of experience;
- the importance of the occasion; and
- the players' self-confidence and belief in their own abilities.

What you should know beforehand

Your own players' strengths and weaknesses

☐ Use your players' strong points to:

- breach the defence, e.g., with a fly-half who sidesteps well; and
- fool the opponents, e.g., by skipping your attacking full-back.

☐ As far as your players' weak points are concerned:

- hide them, e.g., if you have a slow left wing, encourage him to cut in and feed supporting players on his outside, or take a switch pass from the outside centre and try to cut through; and
- cover them with other players, e.g., if your fly-half is nervous in the first few minutes of the match and inclined to make handling mistakes, have the blind-side wing up in close support.

When the match takes place

☐ Early in the season more errors are made; limit the risky movements and have the players cover the whole time.

☐ Late in the season the players are stale; create new challenges.

☐ In exam time:

- the players react more slowly; and
- the players make more errors; choose simple movements and restrict risky movements close to your own goal-line.

The opponents

The following are some characteristics that may be found in an opposing team. Decide what you must plan for and make provision for possible adjustments:

☐ Their pattern of play:

- They concentrate on their forwards.
- They play the ball to the wings.

- They run from their own goal-line.
- They favour counter-attacks.
- They run from free/penalty kicks.
- The halves kick often.
- They are a disciplined team.
- They play very negatively (they hog the offside line).
- They play an intimidating game.
- They soon give up when they fall behind.

☐ Dangerous individuals:
- e.g., a noted provincial or an experienced player with a well-known strong point;
- whom your players know (when teams play one another often, the players get to know the finer points of their opponents' game).

Remember: Work out how to counter the opponents without presenting them as being invincible.

The field

☐ Where it is situated?
- At the coast: The players do not become as tired and the ball does not travel as far.
- At altitude: Where is the team from? Players from the coast become very tired. The ball travels far, it rolls faster, and it bounces higher and more often.

☐ The surface:
- Soft: What does the ball do? Can the players get a firm footing?
- Hard: What does the ball do? Injuries (abrasions).

The referee

The coach should plan in such a way that his team is not at a disadvantage.

☐ Every referee has a characteristic approach, priorities in what he looks for, and a style of interpretation, particularly in respect of:
- mauls and scrums;
- line-outs;
- the tackle situation;
- offside;
- high kicks (10 m circle);
- inadmissible (unacceptable) play, and
- in discipline/backchat on the field.

Remember: As far as the players are concerned, the referee is always right!

The weather

☐ Sun:
- What time of day does the match take place (in the morning, afternoon, late afternoon)?
- What direction does the field lie? (If it lies east-west, and you win the toss, you should play into the sun in the first half of an afternoon game.)

☐ Wet weather:
- It is raining but the surface is good.
- It is wet and muddy.

☐ The wind is blowing:
- across the width of the field;
- diagonally across the field;
- along the length of the field.

☐ Hot and humid weather:
- Intake of fluids before and during the match as well as clothing are important.

☐ A sudden change of weather during a match:
- Let the players adjust to this calmly.

☐ Floodlights:
- Are the players used to playing under floodlights?
- What is the quality of the lights?
- Will dew make the ball slippery?

Working out a strategy

☐ First work out a strategy on your own:
- Make provision for an alternative.
- Keep long-term objectives in mind.
- Simplify the strategy as far as possible.

☐ Then finalise it with the team:
- Put it clearly and concisely to your leaders. Incorporate their knowledge.
- Discuss it with the whole team and make adjustments.
- Define every individual's task (do not give more than three simple tasks; a tired player quickly forgets!)
- Emphasise especially what you are going to do if you lose or win the toss; losing the toss should not upset the players.

Practices

☐ Concentrate during the week on:
- the specific match, practising strategy without overemphasising the match; and remind yourself of
- your long-term objectives for the team (you know what you want to achieve by the end of the season).

☐ Concentrate the warm-ups on:
- strategy (movements, etc) so that the players can start the practice with a task in mind; and
- the code words for specific plays which save time.

A match practice

☐ Always start with the basics and then teach something new every time. Players should not be expected to learn too much at a time.

☐ Now concentrate on expected match situations, e.g.:
- where you are going to attack; and
- strategies to counter the opponents' attacks.

The match

Before the match

GENERAL

☐ Keep to a specific routine. This calms the players down.

PEP TALK

☐ Is this still necessary after a week's preparation? If so, go low on the emotion!

☐ Preferably a brief rather than a lengthy pep talk.

IN THE DRESSING ROOM

☐ A fixed warm-up routine including all the players prevents individuals from becoming too tense.

☐ Let the players warm up in groups (the forwards and backs separately). Each group should go through their own tasks, codes, tactical manoeuvres and defensive patterns.

☐ Calmly move among the players for a short while and:
- focus individual players on their tasks
- reinforce self-confidence; and
- check strategy and possible adjustments one more time with the leaders.

☐ Say exactly what the team is going to do after the toss so that every player can give his all from the very start.

During the match

THE FIRST 15 MINUTES

☐ Nerves! Restrict risks (not necessarily through kicking!) by playing:
- safe, e.g., to the blind side close to the forwards;
- tight, so that the forwards/backs are in close contact with one another; and
- in the opponents' half.

☐ Severe pressure. Deal with it and use initiative. Look at:
- The scrum: Who puts in the ball (i.e., who is making mistakes)? Who gets good/bad balls? We are under pressure: avoid scrums.
- The line-out: Who gets good/bad possession? We are struggling to gain possession: keep the ball away from the touch-line.
- The ruck or maul: Who retains/loses possession? We are losing possession: think why. If nothing works, avoid it.
- Back-line play: Who has the initiative? If we are struggling, play blind side. Keep the ball behind their backs.
- Defence: Behind or in front of the advantage line? If they break the line: which individual made the mistake? Cover defence?
- The opponents: Are they deviating from their expected pattern of play? In which respect? How can we counter this? Don't panic, we have made provision for this.

10 MINUTES BEFORE HALF-TIME

☐ The tired stage. Everyone is making an effort to concentrate:
- attack and exploit mistakes.

HALF-TIME

☐ Let the players drink liquids before any discussion takes place.

☐ The coach gives advice and addresses key problems. Captain and pack/back-line leaders talk.

10 MINUTES AFTER HALF-TIME

☐ Everyone is refreshed; be alert to the need to counter the attacks the opponents may have up their sleeve.

THE NEXT 20 TO 25 MINUTES

☐ Time passes slowly.

☐ Concentration lapses.

☐ Many more mistakes are made.

THE LAST 10 MINUTES

☐ Talk to one another and consciously give it your all.

☐ If you are leading by only a few points, play lower-risk attacking rugby in the opponents' half.

☐ If you have a big lead or if you are far behind, keep the ball alive and attack from everywhere.

Immediately after the match

☐ Rather say too little than too much.

☐ Do not start criticising (the players are tired).

☐ First allow yourself a day or two to get perspective on the match.

Post-mortem

☐ Analyse the match rationally. Measure progress according to long-term objectives.

☐ Be positive. Give constructive criticism: the players still have to play until the end of the season!

Motivation

Many coaches are permanently on the look-out for expressions, tried and tested in matches, that will encourage their players - often themselves, too. Beware. This is a specialised and complex field. The saying: a little knowledge is a dangerous thing, applies. If you are going to get involved in this aspect of the game, first familiarise yourself with some of the vast literature compiled by sport psychologists.

However, beware of the "professionals" who only want to be seen and associated with a winning team. They normally disappear when the going gets tough.

The bottom line remains: When a player has serious problems, call in the true professional! In the meantime have a look at:

☐ William E. Warren: *Coaching and winning*, and

☐ Harris & Harris: *The Athlete's guide to sports psychology: mental skills for physical people.*

2. Approach towards the game

We have met the enemy; he is us

The coach's approach to the game determines how he capitalises on the skills of his players to defeat the opponents.

In reality rugby is a complicated game that requires a variety of skills. It is therefore the task of each coach to simplify and clarify the game for the player. The player must understand what it is about. In accordance with this point of view - to convey the essential points to the player in a simple way - winning rugby is:

Aim	Meaning
☐ Gaining possession.	Primary possession is therefore essential.
☐ Attacking the weak points in the defence and, if there are none, creating them.	To do this the player's vision and perception and ability to evaluate correctly and make the right decisions must be developed; he must perceive the weak points before he gets to the ball.
☐ When the first attack fails:	
- Retaining possession.	Continuity.
- Summing up the new situation quickly.	Observing and deciding.
- Reorganising.	Communicating and positioning in time.
- Attacking the new weak points.	The more skilled, the easier.
☐ Moving the ball as fast as possible.	That is, keep the ball on the move: forward until it is slowed down and then sideways until it can be taken forward again at a fast pace.
☐ Moving forward - with or without the ball.	Only when play goes forward is space created on the sides; when the attacking team does not move forward after three passes, it can no longer run off the ball.
☐ If the opponents have the ball, put them under pressure so that they lose possession through handling/kicking errors.	The importance of pressure in the primary facets; good defence.

In this approach primary possession, i.e., scrum and line-out possession, is of cardinal importance.

Scrumming remains the basis of primary possession

One of the major changes in modern rugby is fewer scrums and generally faster play. This is the result of the influence of rugby league and the insistence on more spectacular and safer rugby. Consequently the laws (explained in chapter 3) were changed accordingly. Scrums are suddenly regarded as being of lesser importance, and coaches have begun concentrating more and more on line-outs and retaining possession. Athletic forwards with ball skills and agility, for example, are deemed a more fashionable asset than those with brute strength.

This approach is short-sighted. No team can come out on top without a powerful scrum. Strong tight forwards remain a prerequisite for success, and the approach should be to develop their other skills. Even though nowadays there are only 20 to 25 scrums per match (or more in bad weather) instead of 35 to 40 in seasons gone by, a powerful scrum still has the following advantages:

☐ It is a major source of good possession for the backline.

☐ The loose forwards come into play more quickly and make it easier to retain second-phase possession.
☐ It puts the opponents at a disadvantage because:
- it enables you to wheel the opposing scrum and keep it under pressure as it suits you;
- it puts the halves under great pressure and makes it difficult for them to cross the advantage line; and
- it drains the opponents physically and gradually takes their forwards out of the game.

Line-out possession forms the basis for most attacks

☐ Three, preferably four, athletic jumpers ensure possession and create possibilities for attack in the form of:
- driving, mauling and peeling off by the forwards; and
- a fast ball for the back-line.

Possession gained from the opponents is a bonus that must be exploited immediately

Possession is usually gained from:
☐ Set play:
- own scrums and line-outs; and
- tight-heads or ball taken from the opposition's throw-in at line-outs.
☐ Mistakes by the opposition:
- errors in the handling of the ball;
- contact situations in which they lose control of the ball; and
- being weak in the tight-loose.
☐ Good defence:
- creates loose balls;
- forces the opponents to kick away possession.

When possession is gained, the weaknesses in the opponents' defence should be attacked immediately. These weaknesses, which are illustrated in chapter 5:
☐ usually arise because of bad alignment or because the opponents are out of position through an error of their own; and
☐ can be created by misleading the defenders about where a breakthrough is going to be attempted.

Who can attack?

☐ The ball-carrier:
- by attacking the space in front of him; and
- by going through the weak spot himself or committing or drawing his opponent and passing the ball sideways to team-mates adjacent to the weak spot.

☐ The supporter:
- by positioning himself opposite the weak point in time.

Attacking the space

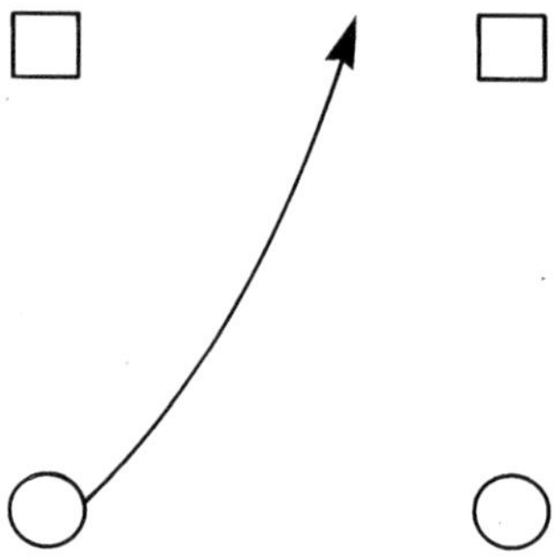

Drawing an opponent

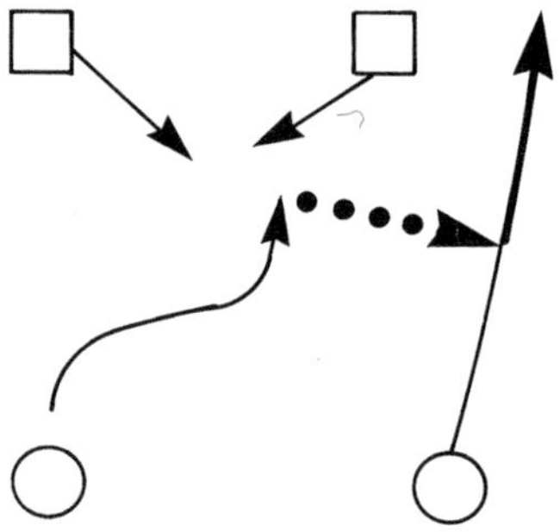

This means not waiting until he has received the ball and only then starting to run towards the gap (in this case he usually runs diagonally and is therefore less effective); and
- by playing in the same direction until there is no more room to manoeuvre;

WRONG

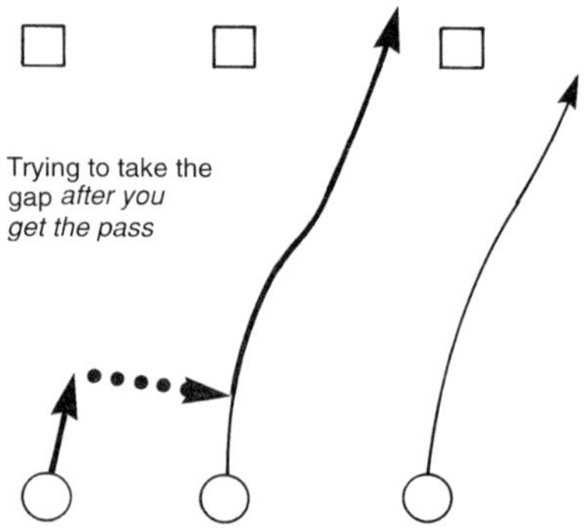

CORRECT

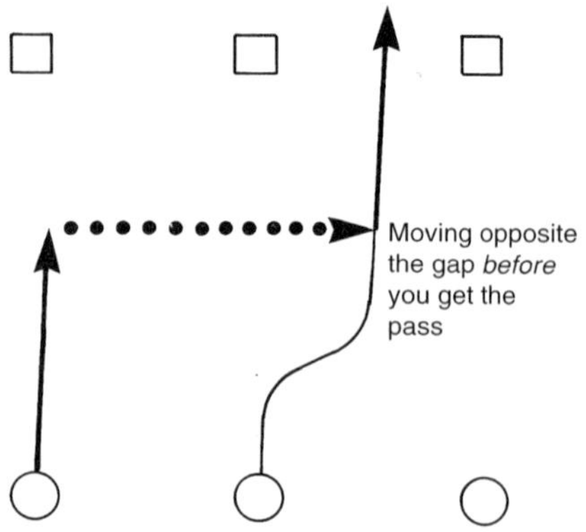

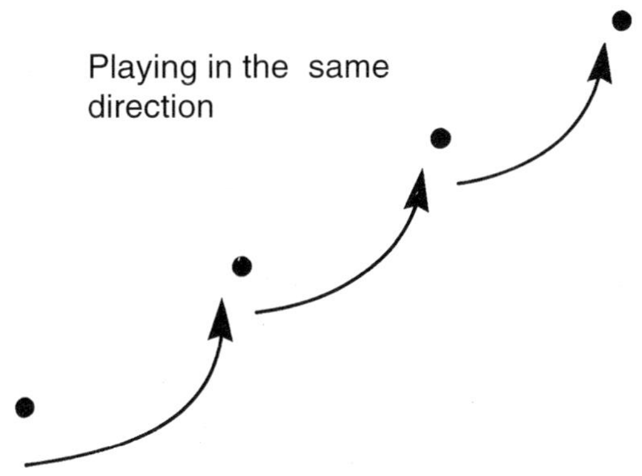

- by the last player with room to manoeuvre deciding whether he can beat his opponent on the inside/outside or whether he should deliberately move to the inside to make the ball available to his team-mates by passing to them.

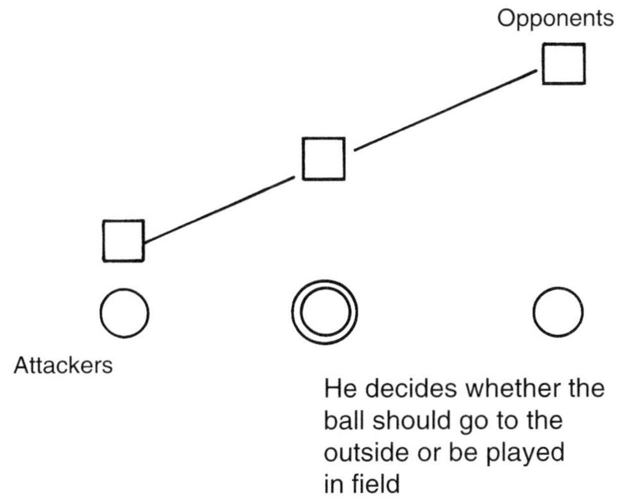

- The backs therefore make contact only when it is unavoidable because of pressure.

The contact situation

As the level of competition rises, it becomes increasingly difficult to break the defensive line at the first attempt, which obviously results in increased contact. It is of the utmost importance that every player should know how to react in such a contact situation. The backs should be coached in such a way that they can fill the role of loose forward if this is required by the situation.

In a contact situation retaining possession is a prerequisite for the launching of a second-phase attack. Two different contact situations can be distinguished:

☐ Those that occur because the ball-carrier, e.g., a back, fails to break the line. If this happens:
- the ball-carrier must make sure the ball is not tackled and made static, i.e., he must try to distribute the ball before contact;
- the ball-carrier must either place his team-mate in the gap or give him enough space and time to decide on his best option; or
- the closest players must carry on the movement as fast as possible. This should take place with the minimum contact and preferably without mauls or scrums so that maximum speed and momentum is maintained.

☐ Those that are created deliberately to form a base from which the next attack can be launched:
- The defence is disorganised and a weak spot(s) is created for a renewed attack.
- Unless a ruck is formed quickly, this type of possession is usually slow and the opposition therefore has time to reorganise its defence.

Deliberate contact by the backs should be the last option because it slows down the speed on the ball.

Although a player should always try to distribute the ball before contact, during a match contact is unavoidable. It usually takes place when the defenders are organised and well distributed over the field.
- In such a case the ball-carrier should move towards the strongest point in the defence - to concentrate the opponents even more - and then, before contact, move the ball away to the weaker spot, where his team-mates are organised. This can be done effectively if the principle of running angles is applied.

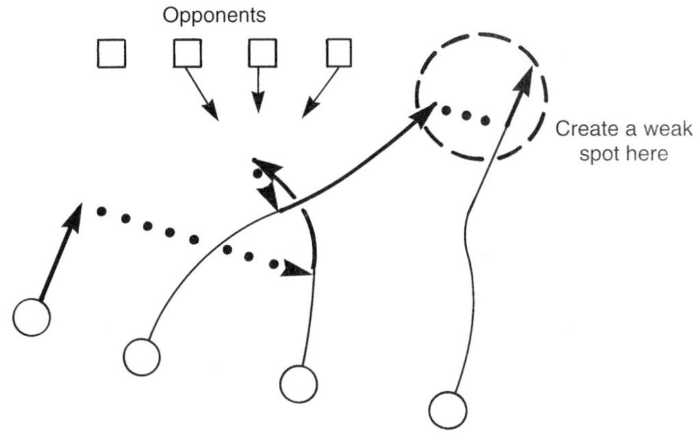

When contact does take place:

☐ The ball-carrier must ensure that the point of contact is in his favour and on the defender's weak spot (for example his arm rather than his shoulder): He can achieve this by, before contact:
- sidestepping (thus shifting the contact point from the defender's shoulder to his outstretched arm);
- giving a dummy pass (putting the defender off balance); or
- slightly shortening his strides (thus creating timing problems for the tackler).

☐ This enables the ball-carrier to retain control - and therefore possession - of the ball more easily, and:
- quickly make the ball available to his team-mates; or
- as a last option, go down with it and form the basis for a quick ruck.

Remember:
☐ The objective is still to launch the best possible first-phase attacks.
☐ All second-phase play slows the ball down.
☐ Continuous and deliberate second-phase play is a sign that the team lacks confidence in its ability to attack from the first phase.
☐ The more skilful the players, the less it is necessary to make deliberate contact to create a second-phase platform from which to launch a fresh attack.
☐ The faster the players sum up the new situation after contact and reorganise themselves, the more effective the attack.
☐ Deliberate contact does have a place in rugby, but it should, like primary possession, be practised thoroughly beforehand.
☐ It should also not become a goal in itself. If it comes to be regarded as the only way to score a try, rugby will degenerate into the unimaginative approach of Rugby League. The days of the highly proficient and agile backs who are not big and heavy will then be numbered. The answer lies in variation.
☐ It is important that the opponents' forwards who stay out on the sides in the tight-loose are drawn into it by your team driving through the middle in a maul or after a ruck. In this way the hangers-on or loiterers are forced to defend. When they are drawn in, the ball can be played short by the scrum-half from the ruck to one/two of your team's forwards, who are now driving onto the opponent's back-line. In such a case your team's backs can play shallow together with the forwards. The situation where forwards drive onto forwards after a maul is thus avoided.
☐ No team or player can beat the touch-line! It kills play.

The dynamic play that arises from this approach can be applied only if specific principles are followed in practices.
☐ The length of time of the practices may vary, but they should all be intensive.
- Intensity is something that has to be learnt.
☐ Every player must understand that the team plays a 15-man game, requiring communication between forwards and backs, and with the emphasis on:
- gaining and retaining ball possession;
- always playing forward, with or without the ball;
- shifting the target constantly to the weak spots until you are through; and
- keep moving the ball as fast as possible.
☐ The skills of all 15 players should be developed to the full.
- Handling forms the basis, and the ball should therefore be used in all practices.
- Forwards must learn to think and react like backs.
- Backs must be able to play like loose forwards.
☐ The players must be taught to communicate with one another constantly, especially in respect of:
- weaknesses in the defence;
- the direction in which the team should play; and
- the speed at which the ball should be made available.
☐ A lot of attention should be given to the alignment and realignment of the forwards and backs, i.e., they must learn to get into the right starting positions in time.
☐ A player's vision must be developed and he must learn:
- to sum up situations and take up the correct position before he gets to the point of breakdown; and
- to make the right decision on how, i.e., with which skills, to play from there.
☐ Particular attention should be given to the fly-half's vision and decision-making ability, because he is the one who determines:
- the direction of play;
- where penetration should take place (flat and close by or deep and wide); and
- the defensive pattern (man on man, or out tackling).
☐ Drills should take place - just like in a game - in short explosive sessions of 10 to 15 seconds with:
- maximum speed;
- emphasis on quality; and
- emphasis on quantity while maintaining quality.
☐ Players should learn to handle stress, and practices should therefore take place:
- in small restricted areas;
- against opponents; and
- with controlled contact.
☐ A player should learn to shake off the emotional consequences of mistakes quickly to prevent them from negatively influencing subsequent play. Mistakes are part of being human, and they are therefore part of the game. The more you fear making mistakes, the more mistakes you'll make.
☐ Drills should have a purpose and they should be specific.
- They should teach and/or improve individual skills.
- They should teach and/or sharpen specific facets of the game in preparation for a match.
- They should correct errors made in the previous match, i.e., they should be remedial.
☐ Ultimately, the game itself should be used as much as possible to teach the players to take the right options on the field.

The French coach Pierre Villepreux in a lecture at an international conference on coaching, summed it up as follows:

"In a dynamic game the mobility of the 30 players and the ball produces continuous action (the passing game) and even though each situation is changing players have the ability to cope. The players are obliged to adapt their game to the actions and reactions of their own team but above all to the ones of the defending team.

"It is the distribution of the defending players which guides the decision of the ball-carrier and consequently the movement of his support players. The players have to re-adjust their actions depending on their comprehension of the situation.

"To coach 'decision making' it is necessary to use the game itself and for the coach to be able to manage the situation with opposition.

"Coaching is not about telling players what they have to do but a way of using the reality of the game to permit the players to find the best solution; to give the best answer depending on the present capabilities of the player and/or team. In this dynamic game the aim is to link constantly (as quickly as possible and as well as possible) the penetrating moves and the driving round moves. The players have to react to the speed of the action, to the situations they know and naturally to the new situations. The game's situations have to be as close to the real situation as possible and you must know and anticipate what will happen next.

"In rugby the difficulty is to play when the game is static (scrum, line-out and ruck) but also in the long maul phase which gives time to the defence to arrange an efficient organisation or to find an organisation (if none was originally present).

"The capacity to play in a dynamic way which links backs and forwards and vice versa, presents the following problems:

- ☐ When to penetrate the defence.
- ☐ When to run wide with the ball round the defence.
- ☐ Useless mauling which stops the dynamic flow.
- ☐ Playing flat in the right occasions (but above all playing the game over the advantage line)."

3. Laws

Don't give the referee the opportunity to interfere

Before the basic laws are discussed, first some points about refereeing that remain in force irrespective of how the laws may change.

These points are of the utmost importance because a referee's interpretation of the laws determines the direction in which a game develops. In fact, the quality of the referee determines the level to which the game can develop during a match. The previous interpretation by South African referees of the tackle law illustrates this. They allowed the tackler to kill the ball and supported and defended players who dived onto, or beyond, the first two players, or went to ground to get the ball. This resulted in the Springboks being heavily penalised on their tour to France and England in 1992. Players cannot adjust overnight and, when they are under pressure, are inclined to fall back on old habits that were learnt over years.

☐ Good relationships with people and an understanding of a player's situation are extremely important. (A back who is offside and a prop who is being pushed from both sides in a scrum will definitely not react in the same way to a sharp reprimand from a referee!)

☐ A referee who knows the game is usually in a more favourable position and has more time to make the right decision. He positions himself in time because he knows the direction in which the team will probably play. A referee who knows the laws but not the game is often in a weak position and may interfere with possible good play because he acts too hastily. ("Don't just look at the situation; look through it." This implies insight into the game by the referee.)

☐ In all the truly classical matches in world rugby there has been a referee who has applied the advantage law brilliantly. The 1973 All Blacks vs Barbarians and the 1985 Wallabies vs Barbarians matches are excellent examples.

As far as the advantage law is concerned, however, referees should keep in mind:: "Never let the offending side gain advantage because you've played advantage."

☐ A good referee concentrates on the team playing negatively, and is not constantly on the lookout for mistakes made by the team that wants to play constructively. (Face the people who want to do the damage.)

☐ A good referee acts preventatively; he does not play the role of policeman. When he sees a player infringing a law or about to do so, he warns him in time rather than waiting for the infringement to take place and then penalising.

☐ A good referee constantly communicates with the players. They soon realise how the referee sees the game and interprets the laws, and they adapt accordingly.

☐ A good referee never allows the first offender to turn his offence to his own advantage. This applies to mistakes in both general and foul play. The referee who penalises the player who hits back because he takes the law into his own hands and lets the first offender go scot-free does not solve the primary problem. Indecision on the part of the referee often results in players taking the law into their own hands.

☐ Every good referee corps maintains discipline in respect of the way in which its members apply the laws. There are too many referees who, because of their position of authority on the field, apply their own specific interpretation of a basic law such as the tackle law. This confuses the players and is extremely frustrating to the coach, who is suddenly faced with a new interpretation.

The training of referees has changed very little over the past decades. It is still largely theoretical and makes little use of modern technology. Referee training should take place in phases. There are certain basic laws every referee should know the first time he blows the whistle. If he is in the wrong here, he will certainly lose face with the players. Then there are laws that make provision for eventualities that occur only every now and then. Very few players, if any, will hold it against the referee if he makes an error in such a case. This should be borne in mind when any training is planned.

The contention that many seasons of refereeing in minor leagues is needed before enough experience is gained, is rubbish. With the aid of modern technology, the opportunity can be created for a referee "to blow" a full season's matches within a period of a month. The way in which pilots are trained with flight simulators is an example that can be followed by referees, e.g.:

☐ Make a video of, for instance, 40 to 50 tackles that have occurred in top-level competition, both locally and overseas. Number them from 1 to 40 and insert 4 to 5 second intervals in between. The referee should look at the situation and answer immediately; this is what he has to do on the field. This in itself would be a sifting process, since it is not every individual who can react quickly and correctly to a real situation, irrespective of his theoretical knowledge.

After all is said and done, however, the coach's attitude towards his players in respect of the referee should be: There is only one referee on the field and his decisions should be respected.

Although laws change continuously, they are discussed here as they stand. They have been simplified, and are presented from the player's point of view; as such, they should contribute to increasing knowledge on the subject.

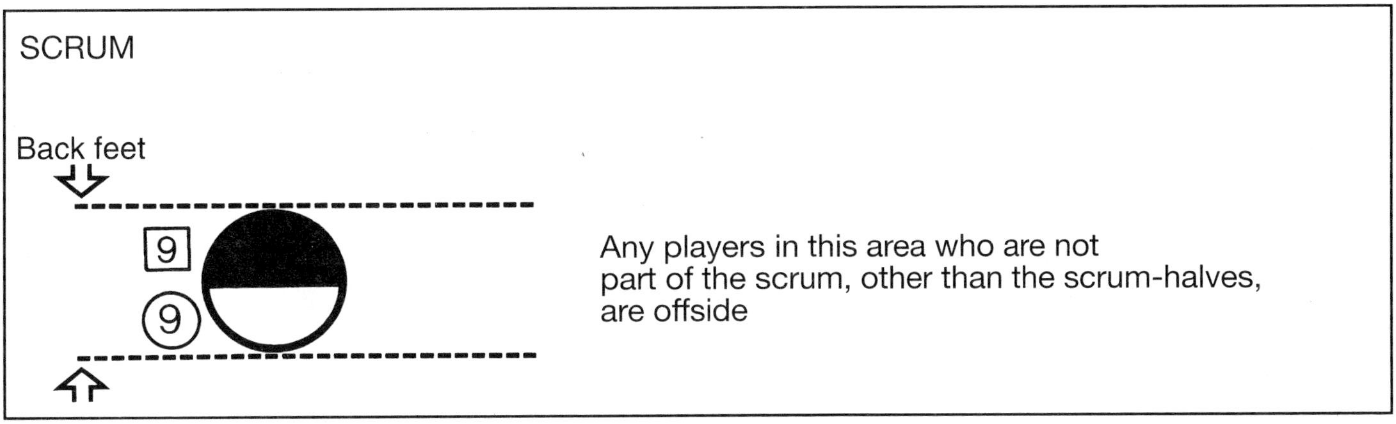

Scrum

Basic laws

☐ Eight players must go down on each side.
- No loose forward may leave the scrum before the ball is out of the scrum.
- The No. 8 of the side in possession may play the ball.

☐ The front rows may not charge at one another.
☐ No player may deliberately cause the scrum to collapse.
☐ Players must bind with at least one arm and one hand.
☐ No player may play the ball in the scrum with his hand.
☐ No player may deliberately kick the ball out of the tunnel.
☐ The ball may come out at any place except the tunnel.
☐ When the ball is out of the scrum, it may not be brought back in.
☐ The ball must be put in as soon as the scrum goes down and is set.
☐ While the ball is still in the scrum, the scrum-half may do nothing to give the opposition the impression that the ball is already out.
☐ No player may deliberately lift an opponent off his feet or force him upwards out of the scrum. (Here the referee must watch closely to see whether the player who is "squeezed" out of the top of the scrum may not perhaps be too weak. This is very dangerous because the scrum may often collapse.)
☐ The hooker may lift his foot when the ball leaves the hands of the player who puts it in.
☐ Before a scrum takes place, the referee must first indicate the spot on the field where it is to be formed. The two sets of front rows must be within an arm's length of one another before they go down. (It is extremely dangerous for the two sets of front rows to go down too close together, because they then do not have enough time to get their heads out of the way if something unexpected happens. This can result in a serious neck injury. The referee should rather err on the side of too much distance between the front rows when they go down. The contact between them looks dangerous, but is much less so because they have time to see what is coming.)
☐ When a 5 m scrum is awarded, it takes place opposite the point where the ball went dead and not where it crossed the goal-line.

Offside

☐ Everyone, except the scrum-halves, must be behind the lines that run parallel to the goal-lines and between the feet of the last player in the scrum. The defending scrum-half must stand on the same side of the scrum as his opponent who puts the ball in or, if he stands on the other side, behind the last player's feet. If he is on the same side, he must stay close to the scrum.
☐ The scrum-halves must stay behind the ball until it is out of the scrum.

When the scrum wheels

☐ Past 90°: The scrum must be reformed and the same team must put the ball in, except when the other team pushes or shoves the wheeling scrum in such a way that they gain control of the ball.
☐ The previous mentioned scrum laws apply in the usual way.

Maul

Origin

☐ A maul originates when three players, at least one from each team, are bound round the ball. They must all be on their feet.

Offside

☐ Offside is determined by the lines at the feet of the last players who are part of (i.e., bound by one arm at least) the maul. No player - not even the scrum-halves - who is not part of the maul may go beyond the respective lines. As soon as the ball comes out, the offside lines fall away.
☐ A player may join the maul only from behind his team-mate who forms the back of the maul.
☐ When the maul becomes static the side not in possession gets the put-in at the scrum (use it or lose it).

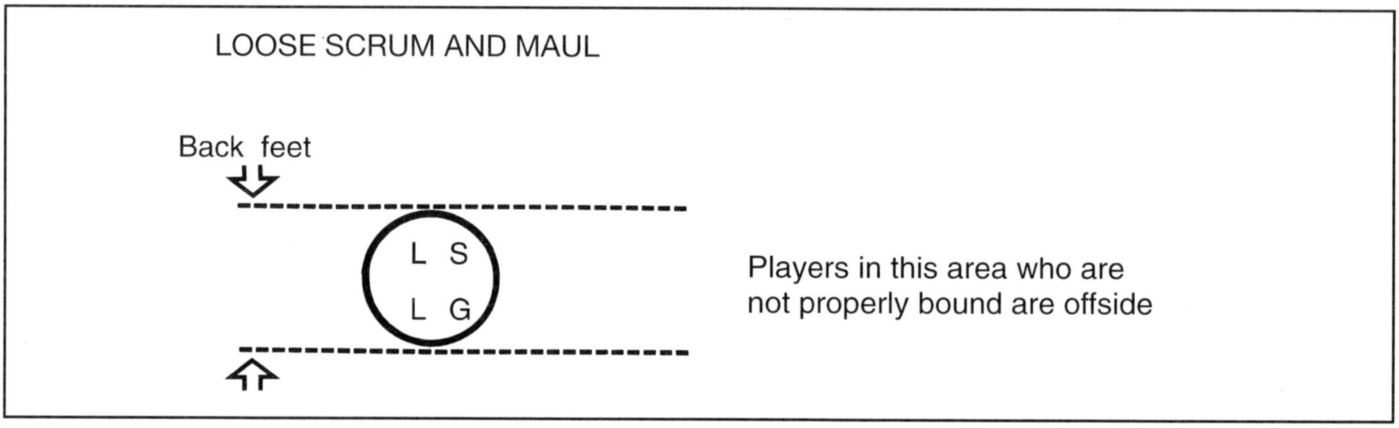

Ruck

Origin

☐ A ruck originates when two players, one from each team, make contact with one another while on their feet over the ball, which is on the ground.

Offside

☐ Offside is determined by the lines at the feet of the players who form the back of the ruck. No player who is not bound to the ruck may stand between these two lines. As soon as the ball comes out, the offside lines fall away.

☐ A player may join the ruck only from behind his team-mate, who forms the back of the ruck.

☐ If the ruck originated over a player who fell with the ball, no player may dive onto the ball.

Remember: Distinguish between this situation and one where the ball lands on the ground among players in general play. In the latter instance, they are allowed to pick it up!

☐ No player may dive onto a ruck. The players must get over the ball while on their feet. They cannot use this as an excuse to trample players who are lying trapped away from the ball.

☐ The side in possession when the ruck is blown up because the ball can't be freed, gets the put-in in the scrum.

Line-out

☐ There must be two players from each team in the line-out.

☐ The players must stand between the 5 m and 15 m lines.

☐ The line-out begins when the ball leaves the thrower's hand.

☐ Offside lines:

- For the players who take part in the line-out (the forwards, the thrower and his opponent, and the scrum-halves), it is the imaginary line through the middle of the line-out until the ball touches either a player or the ground. After that it is the ball.
- For the players who are not part of the line-out (the other backs), it is 10 m on either side of the throw-in line

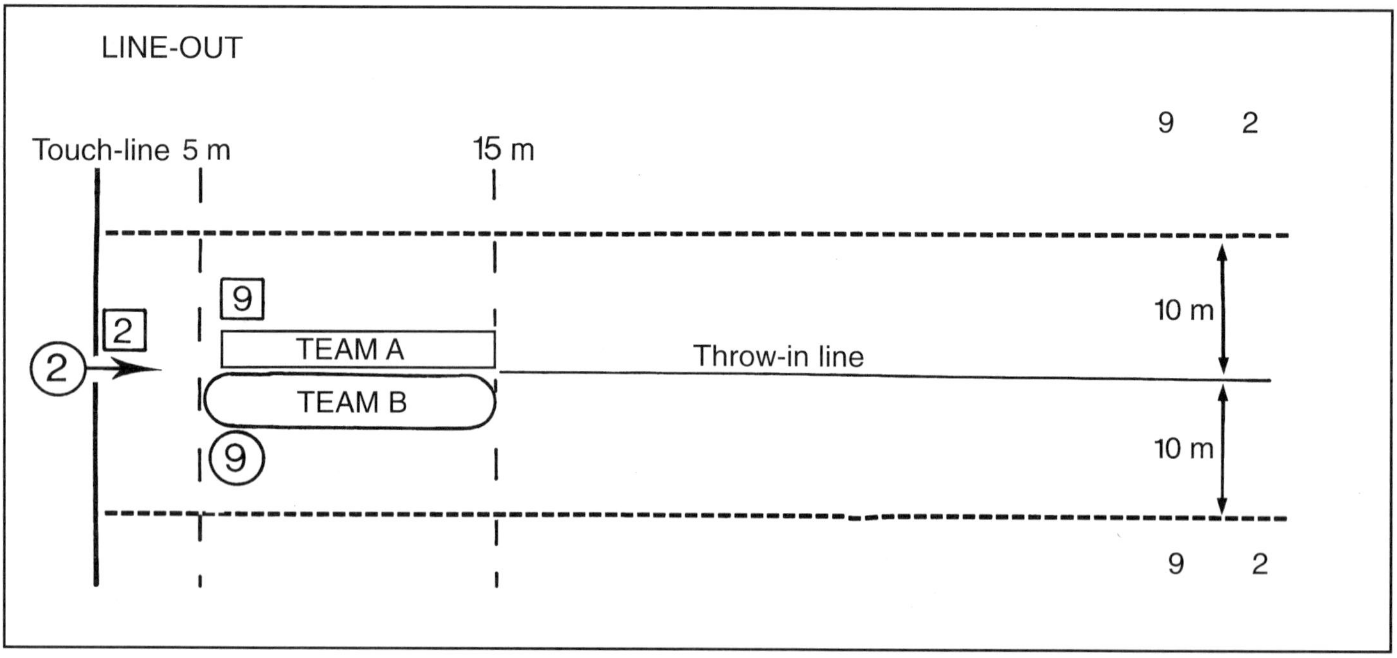

or their own goal-line depending on which is closer. They must stay behind the line until the line-out has ended.

☐ The line-out ends when:
- the ball leaves the line-out (e.g., ricochets out). (The shoulders of the outside players in the line-out are the criterion. They form the so-called box);
- the player who has the ball leaves the line-out;
- the ball is thrown beyond the 15 m mark; or
- a maul or ruck develops and moves away from the throw-in line.

☐ Peeling off from the line-out is allowed provided the player:
- starts running only after the ball has left the thrower's hand;
- stays close to the line-out; or
- goes specifically for the ball.

☐ Any player jumping for the ball, may be supported after he starts his jump regardless of where the ball is still in its flight.

☐ The players of the team that throws in may not move out of the line-out after they have formed up, even if the ball has not yet been thrown in.

☐ For short line-outs the usual offside laws apply. Players are allowed to change position in the line-out after the ball has left the thrower's hand.

☐ In the case of a quick throw-in:
- the same ball must be used;
- no outsider may have handled the ball;
- it must be straight and travel for at least 5 m - the player may throw the ball in from anywhere along the sideline closer to the defending team's goal-line on condition that he uses the same ball and fetches it himself; and
- the player may throw the ball to himself but he may catch it only after it has travelled 5 m.

Tackle

☐ This takes place when two things happen simultaneously, i.e., the player with the ball is held in such a way that he cannot run and the ball touches the ground.

☐ The ball-carrier must immediately release the ball and roll away from it, or at least try to do so. Until he is on his feet, he may not prevent another player from playing the ball.

☐ The tackler must first get onto his feet (not his knees) before he can play the ball.

☐ When the ball-carrier is brought down without the two requirements that define a tackle being present, he can:
- when the ball touches the ground but he is not held, get up with the ball and play on; or
- when he is held but the ball does not touch the ground, immediately pass the ball or make it available.

☐ After a tackle, any other player "not involved in the tackle" must be on his feet when he plays the ball.

☐ The tackler may not in any way prevent the tackled player from releasing (or placing) the ball to his own side.

☐ If the tackler falls in such a position that he blocks the ball and cannot get out of the way, the tackler must be allowed to place the ball over the tackler's body, for example, see Zinzan Brooke of New Zealand against England at Twickenham in December 1993.

Goal area

☐ All the laws apply in the goal area, except those for a scrum, ruck, maul, line-out and tackle (these apply only between the goal-lines).

☐ When the defender infringes in his own goal area, a 5 m scrum follows and it is the opponents' ball.

☐ When the attacker infringes in his opponents' goal area, a drop-out from the 22 m is given.

☐ When the defender plays the ball back across his own goal-line and any team breaks a law, a 5 m scrum follows and it is the opponents' ball.

Offside in general play

General

☐ The following concerns offside in general play (other than scrums, line-outs and mauls and scrums). Players who do not know these laws:
- cause most of the penalties to be awarded against their team; and
- forgo opportunities to exert pressure and score a try.

☐ You are not offside simply because you are in front of the ball!

☐ You are offside, however, if you are in front of a team-mate who:
- has the ball; or
- was the last to play the ball.

☐ When you are offside, you will not be penalised if you do not interfere with play.

☐ You can play when:
- a team-mate runs past you from behind with the ball;
- a team-mate kicks the ball from behind you and then runs past you;
- a team-mate who was behind the kicker runs past you; or
- you run back behind the team-mate who was the last to play the ball.

The 10 m circle law (very important)

When you are in front of a team-mate who kicks the ball ahead, and an opponent is waiting to catch it, you must put a distance of 10 m in any direction between you and your opponent. Even if you remain passive within this circle you will be penalised - you must get out of the way!

When you are outside the 10 m circle but still in front of the team-mate who kicked, you can play again as soon as the kicker or another team-mate places you on side. You can play again before this, however, if the opponent who catches the ball:

☐ passes or kicks it;

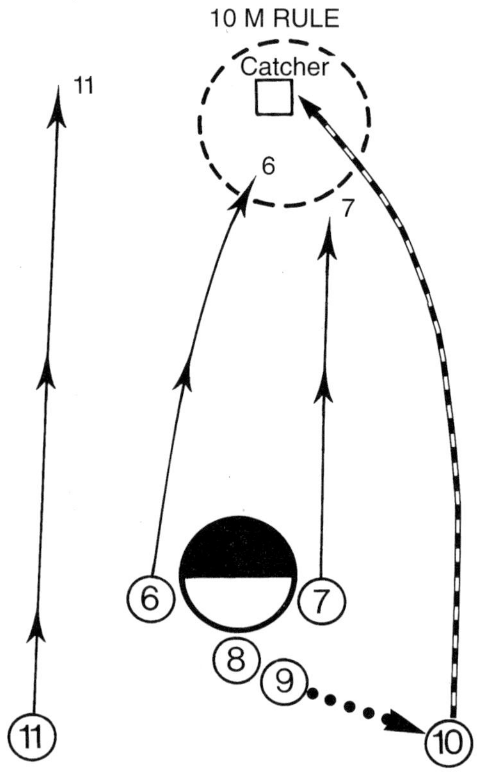

(6) must move out of circle - *nothing* can put him onside inside the circle

Although (11) and (7) are offside they can be put onside by their team-mates or the catcher of the ball

The same applies to (6) once he is out of the circle

- ☐ has run 5 m with it; or
- ☐ knocks it on.

AN IMPORTANT EXCEPTION

☐ When you are on your opponents' side of the ball and they have just won a quick ruck or maul, you can play only after they:
- have run 5 m with the ball; or
- have kicked the ball.

A pass does not place you on side in this case.

☐ Players forget that:
- when they are in front of the ball and a team-mate kicks from behind against an opponent, they are onside and can play immediately!

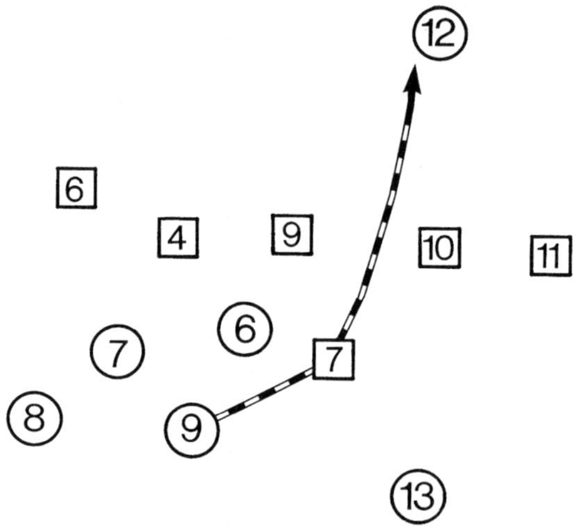

Scrum-half (9) kicks against an opponent. The ball ricochets to (12) who was in an offside position, No. (12) can play immediately because he has been put onside by [7] who touched the ball

Kicking

☐ When the ball is kicked directly into touch from outside one's own 22-metre area a line-out is given to the opposition directly opposite from where the ball has been kicked.
☐ When the attacking side kicks the ball deliberately over the dead-ball line, a scrum to the opposition is given on the spot from where the ball has been kicked.
☐ For a quickly taken kick-off from the 22-metre line, the kicking side's players don't have to be behind the ball. However, players in front of the ball have to keep to the laws regarding the offside.

Catching

☐ Any player, when in his own 22, can call a fair catch while in midair jumping for the ball.
☐ Outside his own 22, the player taking a clean catch under pressure from, say, an up and under, gets the put-in in the ensuing scrum.
☐ No fair catch is allowed from a kick-off from the halfway line.

4. Team selection

One player can make a difference, but a team can make a miracle

Following South Africa's re-entry into international rugby and the inevitable pressure to win, team selection has gained a new dimension with the search for players who can adapt to the new styles of play required at international level. Before discussing ordinary club selection, a few points on selection and coaching at international level.

☐ An international coach is under tremendous pressure to win. If his team does not produce the goods, his head is often the first to roll.

In this respect rugby-playing countries would do well to follow, or at least think about, the example of the big soccer-playing countries like Germany and Italy. Appoint the best coach available and pay him well. He must show results; or he is dismissed. Because it is his job that is on the line, he is the one who selects the team. The system in these two countries, where a lot of money and prestige are involved, is that the coach selects the team with the help of two, three or four scouts who share his vision of the game and keep him informed regarding the form, fitness and talent of the players.

☐ The adoption of a specific style of play will influence team selection.

In South Africa, as in several other countries, the sudden emphasis on "direct rugby", which, in reality is rugby league in a different form, has led to the selection of centres whose play differs little from that of loose forwards. The approach of crossing the advantage line near the set phases has led to new emphasis on first-phase possession and strong defenders. The lighter yet skilful player will fall by the wayside. Coaches who retain perspective, however, will know that the strength of a successful team lies in the way in which it can vary its game. New Zealand's performance during the 1995-World Cup is an excellent example of just that.

☐ Back to club and school level.

It is easy to say what the ideal rugby team should look like. We all know, however, that a selection committee usually only has a limited number of players to choose from. In any event an ideal team exists only in theory. Our main aim here is simply to give some practical suggestions that will be of use to any selection committee - even one with a limited number of players to choose from.

Tips

Coach

☐ The coach must have a say in the selection of his team, since the team's performance is his responsibility.

☐ A coach at a big club with a lot of players usually decides in advance what type of rugby he wants his team to play and then selects the team accordingly. In such a case a specific player is sought to fill a specific need/ position. Here the coach's opinion weighs heavily.

☐ The coach of a club with few players first assesses the attributes of the players he has at his disposal - then he decides which pattern of play will make them most effective. Team selection is then "easier" because the players who are available must play!

☐ A coach should never make his team's pattern of play subject only to the type of players at his disposal. Initially it is the players who determine the pattern. After all, you can't play 15-man rugby with players who don't handle the ball well! Every coach should, however, in accordance with his vision of the game, have a long-term approach and work to that end. In the above example, he should pay a lot of attention to ball work during practices and choose low-risk match situations during which his players can run with the ball. If you believe in 15-man rugby but your players are not skilled with the ball, expand this area of play as the confidence of your players increases. With this approach you develop the players for your type of game.

Handle the "advice" given by players carefully. With big money involved a player would hardly recommend a better player to take his place in the side!

The same applies to players who always praise you. Is this their way of ensuring they stay in the side? Surely they wouldn't risk suggesting something that might be construed by the coach as criticism - even though they might be right - if it put their place in the side at risk.

Forwards

Front row

Remember:

☐ First-rate rugby starts with first-class forward play.

☐ A team is as good as its front row:

- The number one requirement for a front row is strength.
- There is a world of difference between a loose-head and a tight-head.

☐ A loose-head is usually:
- shorter and stronger in the neck and back, because the direction of push is forward and up and he pushes with one shoulder;
- lighter than a tight-head; and
- a calmer type of person because his first task is to help his hooker and not to become involved in a personal duel with the opposing tight-head.
☐ A tight-head is:
- usually taller than a loose-head, because he pushes forward and the loose-head has to hold him up;
- usually heavier than a loose-head because his weight has to counter the natural swing of a scrum; and
- often an aggressive player (ask the psychologists why).
☐ A strong hooker is a great asset. He is:
- a tight forward who likes scrumming;
- someone who consistently throws in accurately in the line-out and is your most crucial line-out player (if your hooker cannot throw in but is your only player who can go down in the front row, let a loose forward, who can throw in, do so, and put the hooker at No. 6); and
- someone who does not flinch from contact in the tight-loose.

Locks

☐ Locks are selected because they can take balls in the line-out.
- The aggressive jumper stands in front where there is a lot of barging. This is the place for the shorter but stronger lock who likes contact. An exceptionally tall lock with a calm nature can also be effective in front.
- The true jumper and lock with ball skills is positioned in the middle of the line-out. He must be able to jump high. Good timing is essential, particularly in the case of a fast ball that comes straight at him.
☐ If your locks can't scrum, you don't have a scrum.
- The lock on the tight-head side should be the better scrummager. He is usually the hard worker (because he is subjected to the most pressure). He is also heavier, because he has to counter the natural swing of the scrum. (The scrum often wheels to his side.)
- The lock at the loose-head side is usually the weaker scrummager, the lighter of the two and a tall, good line-out jumper who, because of his lean physique, often doesn't scrum well.

Loose forwards

☐ Loose forwards form a combination.
☐ It is the loose forwards who keep the ball alive and regain possession from the opponents. The ideal combination consists of at least one strong, one fast and one tall loose forward. During the early nineties the trend was to play with one small and two big loose forwards. Nowadays one tall loose forward seems to be enough with the emphasis on strength, speed and skills for the other two. Two of these three usually play together from a set facet. The eighth-man is involved every time. Slow loose forwards who know where the game is going will, as the match develops, beat the fast loose forwards, who play purely on instinct.
☐ In the choice of flankers priority should be given to players who like to play forward.
☐ The loose-head flanker is usually:
- shorter, so that he can break away from the scrum fast; and
- an aggressive defender (because no attacker may break across the advantage line on his side of the scrum).
☐ The tight-head flanker is usually the one who:
- if necessary, can also play lock; and
- is the taller of the flankers and therefore the line-out specialist! (In modern rugby, control at the back of the line-out is crucial.)
☐ The eighth-man is in a specialist position. Of the three loose forwards, he is the one who:
- must show the best judgement (he must be able to "read" a game);
- must be faster than average;
- can scrum and control the ball behind a scrum (if the eighth-man has difficulty here, the scrum-half has problems);
- can jump well at the back of a line-out; and
- must be able to handle the ball well, because he initiates driving play rather than rucks or mauls.
☐ Several international teams prefer to play with the following combination:
- a fast, light flanker who always plays open side;
- a strong, tall flanker who always plays blind side and is good in a line-out; and
- a strong, heavy eighth-man (for scrumming and driving) who can also do line-out work.

Back-line

Halves

☐ Every successful team has a good pair of halves, one of whom must:
- be able to break, i.e., he should not be afraid of contact, otherwise your centres are always under pressure (it helps if he is strong and/or has an exceptional skill like forcing a gap);
- be able to kick (and know when to kick); and
- be fast, especially over the first 15 to 25 m.
☐ A scrum-half must be able to pass to either side relatively quickly and he must have sound judgement. If you have to choose between a scrum-half with a quick pass but poor judgement and one with a reasonable pass and sound judgement, choose the latter. The scrum-half should also know when to:
- pass;
- break;
- play with the forwards; and
- kick.
☐ A fly-half must:
- be able to handle the ball flawlessly;
- be able to make sound judgements (he must have wide vision and be able to spot the weaknesses in the defence)

and he must know, in particular, which side to play to: whether he should play shallow or deep, whether he should play wide or penetrate close;
- be able to kick well and know when to kick; and
- play ceaselessly by supporting and/or covering.

A fly-half who can defend fearlessly is a great asset.

Centres

☐ A good pair of centres:
- is better than two good individualists; the one should complement the other, e.g., a good attacker works well with a good defender; and
- should be faster than the halves over 50 m (in most cases the speed of a fly-half is adequate for an inside centre but not an outside centre).

☐ Each centre must have a specific strong point, e.g.:
- he must be able to defend fearlessly; he must "hit" his man on the other side of the advantage line (fly-halves who are moved to centre usually fall short here);
- he must be physically strong and tough because centres make contact so frequently;
- he must have a specific skill like sidestepping (usually the shorter player who is inside centre) and/or swerving (usually the taller, faster player who is outside centre); and
- he must be able to kick a grubber/chip kick.

Wings

☐ The wings must be fast! Once a fast player is away, he is seldom caught.

☐ The slower wing must have a special skill, e.g.:
- a swerve that makes his opponent hesitate;
- a sidestep to beat his opponent on the inside;
- speed variation so that his opponent hesitates; or
- a powerful hand-off.

☐ A clever wing beats his opponent before he gets the ball by looking to see exactly where he is positioned and how he defends.

☐ Wings should be fearless. By the time they are normally tackled, they are already running at considerable speed and will fall hard. A wing who learns early on in his career how to fall will have a long future ahead of him!

☐ A wing must be able to stop his opponent.

☐ A wing must be able to catch high balls. This applies especially to the left wing because the opposing fly-half often kicks to his right (most fly-halves are right-footed).

☐ A wing must be able to concentrate the whole time and stay fully involved in the game, particularly the blind-side winger, for purposes of:
- cross-defence;
- cover when the full-back attacks; and
- support in a counter-attack.

Full-back

☐ A full-back:
- should be fearless; the up-and-under is the downfall of many a promising full-back;
- must be able to stop any opponent with a tackle;
- must be able to handle the ball faultlessly (the forwards lose heart if they regularly have to fall back because of handling mistakes by their full-back);
- must be able to kick with both feet (a full-back who can place-kick and drop-kick is a great asset);
- must be able to "read" a game, i.e., when to go into the line to attack or counter-attack; and
- must be fast enough to join the attack outside the centres.

When the full-back is slower than the outside centre or winger, the following requirements for attacking full-back play should be kept in mind:

☐ The player who is the last to pass the ball to the full-back must slow the game down somewhat. He can either slow down himself or merely change his line of running. (The full-back concentrates on this player to get his timing right.) The full-back joins the back-line parallel to the touch-line.

Leadership

Captain

☐ A good captain is a prerequisite for any team that wants to win in tough competition.

☐ Schooling: There is no such thing as a "born" captain, and even the "born" leader has to be trained in captaincy. The coach should let the captain know what to look out for during a match and how to react to it.

☐ A captain must be able to assess a game and adapt his team's strategy accordingly. He is assisted in this regard on the field by players in specific positions and on the touch-line by the coach during injury, water breaks and half-time.

☐ A good captain must first and foremost earn his place in the team on merit as a player.

☐ He should know every player in his team and how to work with them as individuals.

☐ His position: In the case of an inexperienced team it is advisable to choose a captain from the forwards or scrum-half. This is because he can be close to action, rather than in a remote position. If things go wrong in the close exchanges, the entire team collapses. In an experienced team the position of captain is less important than the personality of the player in charge. There are no categorical guidelines in this respect and the coach should decide according to circumstances.

☐ Choosing or appointing a captain? A coach who knows his players can appoint a captain. A new coach or a coach with a new team can first let the players choose and then, after a trial period - which the players must know about beforehand - finalise the captaincy.

Pack leaders

☐ The thought of there being several "leaders" on the field is enough to unnerve any coach. In the case of an

inexperienced team, only a captain and vice-captain should be appointed - one from the forwards, the other from the backs. At high-level competition there should be more leaders, but each one's areas of control should be strictly defined. Such leaders can be chosen from the following positions:
- The pack: Any player, except the captain if he is a forward. He has to make sure the forwards play; he makes no tactical decisions but simply urges his team-mates on.
- The tight forwards: Usually the hooker. He is the middle of the five tight forwards and has to make sure they fulfil their basic tasks.
- The loose forwards (only at the highest level).

The backs' leaders

☐ The halves:
- The scrum-half should be in touch with his forwards. If the scrum-half is subdued, the forwards don't play!
- The fly-half should make the scrum-half's decisions easier by constantly communicating with him and, where possible, pinpointing, indicating or signalling any weak points in the defence by shouting ("Go left!", "Kick!", etc). He should also look out for his forwards falling out of the game and immediately alert the scrum-half to bring them back in.

☐ The full-back/winger combination:
- The full-back is in control of the two wingers' defensive positioning.
- The full-back is in an excellent position to detect shortcomings in the opponents' pattern of defence and attack.

5. How to use possession

Possession is golden

Hours are spent during practice on techniques and skills that are necessary to gain possession in facets such as scrums, line-outs or the tight-loose. It goes without saying that good possession is a prerequisite for good, winning rugby. Possession in itself, however, does not guarantee winning rugby. The successful team is the one which knows how to use its possession effectively.

Here are some tried and tested guidelines that will help players make the right decision when their team gains possession.

Kick-off

Kick-off by the opponents

☐ The higher the kick, the more pressure on you.
☐ Shallow and against the touch-line:
- consolidate;
+ drive towards the open side with a loose forward coming from the blind side;
+ rolling maul/drive through the middle with the pack;
+ get the ball to the halves, who decide from there.
☐ Shallow and infield:
- If you are under pressure: consolidate.
+ Your options to either side are open.
- If there is no pressure, e.g., after a bad kick:
+ Attack the gap between the forwards and backs.
☐ Deep against the touch-line:
- Get the widest angle for a touch kick.
- See whether the open-side winger is shallow; if not, a counter-attack to his side is possible.
☐ Deep away from the touch-line:
- Move the ball away from the opponents and attack.
- A back uses space and kicks for the touch-line:
+ in front of the forwards;
+ into open spaces.

Kick-off by your own team

Kick-off from the halfway line

☐ The higher the kick, the easier to deflect the ball back or catch it.
- A relatively deep kick-off should still enable your forwards to get the ball as it comes down.
- A kick against the wind can be deeper because a high ball under these circumstances tends to "float".
☐ The aim is repossession.
- Two players go for the ball (teach them to go past the ball before deflecting it back), two stay in deep in case it is deflected back or falls loose, and two go past on the sides in case the opponents cannot control the ball (they will not be offside because there is no maul).
- There should be maximum pressure across the width of the field if the opponents succeed in keeping possession.
☐ Where do you kick to?
- Close to touch so that your opponents can play only to one side.
- Alternatively shallow and into midfield to an isolated player, e.g., the hooker.
+ Blind-side defence must be good.
- Deep into the corners in front of your forwards;
+ to force a line-out in your opponents' half.

Kick-off from your 22

☐ For repossession:
- A few metres over the 22.
- High so that your players get to the 10 m line at the same time as the ball.
☐ As a surprise tactic:
- For your loose forward, 5 m over the line.
- For your back, in the centre or blind side.
☐ For distance:
- Deep into open spaces.
+ Preferably behind the opposing forwards because it is then easier to organise defensive lines.

Scrum

☐ The channel through which the ball comes through the scrum and the speed with which it does so, determines what you can do:
- Fast (any channel): All your options open.
- Slow: There is pressure on your scrum-half unless you have a solid scrum that keeps the opponents under pressure.
☐ If the scrum moves forward.
- The options of the loose forwards and halves increase.
☐ If the scrum wheels.
- It is usually easier to play in the same direction as the wheel.
☐ A skilful eighth-man and scrum-half can also, as an exception to the rule, play effectively against the wheel of the scrum.
☐ Tight-head ball:
- Here it is the speed at which and the place where the ball comes out of the scrum that determines:

+ who plays it; and
+ in which direction.

Line-out

Normal line-out

☐ Where to throw the ball:
- The deeper into the line-out, the more the options.

☐ How to win the ball:
- Deflect or catch it with both hands at the top of the jump and then pass to a player outside the line-out.
+ Play to the back-line wide of the fly-half.
+ Peel off at the back or the front.
- Take it with both hands and bring it down.
+ First consolidate to induce the opposing three-quarters to go offside (this is not a very good option because referees seldom apply the 10 m offside lines at a line-out).
+ Start a rolling maul/drive through the middle until the halves decide whether they or the forwards should take play further.
- Deflect to a forward in the line-out.

☐ Throw over to:
- the last forward, who quickly moves further back and is joined by the inside backs and loose forwards;
- an inside back, e.g., fly-half or centre; the rest of the three-quarters play shallow and close while the loose forwards support.

☐ The opponents' ball:
- On which side of the original line of throw-in do you win it?
+ On their side, the forwards play.
+ On your side, the halves decide.
- How does the scrum-half get it?
+ If it is a clean ball, all options are open.
+ If it is a bad ball, he should under no circumstances be caught behind his forwards.
- If you win it quickly:
+ The fly-half decides, depending on the position of the opposing three-quarters (if it is deep, attack; if it is shallow, skip, set up second phase or kick) and the place on the field (the risk is greater, of course, closer to your own goal-line).

Short line-out

See chapter 7 on problems in line-out play.

To summarise

☐ How to win the ball:
- Deflect or catch it at the top and pass.
+ Play to the backs or loose forwards.
- Catch and drive forward.
+ Drive close and/or begin a rolling maul before playing a fast ball back to the blind side.

Second phase

General

☐ Your aim is second-phase possession after the minimum contact, i.e., without a loose maul or scrum necessarily being formed.

☐ All second-phase play slows down the speed with which the ball is moved and should be avoided as far as possible.

☐ The more skilful your players, the more easily they break the defensive line as individuals or in sections, i.e., the less second-phase play is necessary.

☐ When the attackers outnumber the defenders and the running angle is parallel to the sideline:
- Commit the opponent and pass before making contact.
- Except when skipping is fast and across the width - not depth - and towards the second-last or last (unmarked) attacker, a skip neutralises the advantage of more attackers because the defenders simply move across following the ball.

☐ It is the ball-carrier's responsibility to retain possession. The supporters must ensure that the opponents do not interfere or kill the ball.

☐ When, in set play, there are the same number of attackers as defenders:
- one of the outside attackers moves to the inside with the ball to where the most defenders are or are coming from;
- just before contact, he passes the ball with a switch or ordinary pass away from the pressure point to a team member who has come round from the inside to the outside. (Run towards the pressure, but pass away from it - see illustrations on p. 15.)

☐ When speed can be kept on the ball by means of a rip and roll:
- When the ball-carrier makes contact with the defender so that the ball is open to the right, the closest supporter comes in on that side with his right shoulder leading, rips the ball from the ball-carrier's hands and immediately sends the next fastest supporter away.
+ It is important that the ball-carrier comes up with the ball (opens up his torso) at the last moment to facilitate the rip process.

☐ When, in broken play, the ball-carrier is on his feet immediately in front of his team-mates, i.e., he has help close by:
- He makes sure that:
+ he makes contact on the tackler's weak point by taking the initiative away from the defender at the last moment with a sidestep or dummy pass and/or by shortening his strides;
+ the ball is available (in the gap, if possible) for the first supporter, who comes through in depth and at speed; and
+ he puts pressure on his defender(s) so that he is eliminated.

- The first supporter reacts as follows:
+ If the ball is in the gap, he goes in on the ball through the gap and *plays*.
+ If the ball-carrier is tackled but still on his feet, he rips and *plays*.
+ If the ball-carrier is tackled with the ball, he goes in on the ball (remember that the ball-carrier's elbow must lift) and drives forward with the ball.
- The next supporters:
+ drive in on the sides of the ball-carrier; and
+ drive the opponents away in such a way that they at the same time form the "front row" of an ensuing maul formation.

□ When, in broken play, the ball-carrier is on his feet in front of his team-mates, *who are a few metres back*:
- He prevents himself from being isolated.
+ He takes on the opposition usually by driving with a shoulder into them and while doing so rolls the ball a few metres back on the ground away from the immediate opposition and towards his team-mates.
- He slows down the game so that his team-mates can catch up by:
+ staying on his feet as long as possible; and
- as a last option, going to ground with the ball.

□ When, in broken play, the ball-carrier is *on his feet behind his team-mates*:
- He stays on his feet and tries to retain possession until his team-mates arrive (4 to 5 seconds is usually enough) and a maul can be formed.
- After that, the options are:
+ A rolling maul or drive;
+ whatever the halves decide.

□ When the ball-carrier is tackled *with the ball (to ground)*:
- His first option is to pass the ball before it touches the ground.
- His second option is to place the ball.
- The supporters' task is determined by the position of the opponent(s).
- When there is *only one opponent* - the tackler:
+ the first supporter has the choice of either picking up the ball and playing it himself or passing to the second supporter, who then plays on. It is important that the ball goes to the supporter who is in the best position in terms of speed and depth immediately to attack the defence at the weakest point.
- When *a second opponent is relatively close to the ball*:
+ the first supporter secures the ball by stepping over the tackled player, i.e., the ball, lowering his buttocks for a powerful position and passing from that position to the second supporter.
- When *a second opponent is very close to the ball*:
+ the first supporter steps over the ball and takes the opposition away from it so that the second supporter can play the ball unhindered.

□ When several opponents are close to the ball:
+ The first few supporters form a ruck in which they drive the opposition away from the ball. The ball is then the scrum-half's, who plays either to the three-quarters or to other forwards.

Defence

□ An opposing back is tackled in a line movement.
Important: The speed at which the ball is gained determines who plays the ball and to where.

It is vitally important whether it is an inside back close to the forwards or an outside back out wide that is tackled.

Loose ball: Tackles - closer to touch or midfield

- closer to touch
  - immediately to blind side
- midfield
  - straight ahead
  - close to tackled player

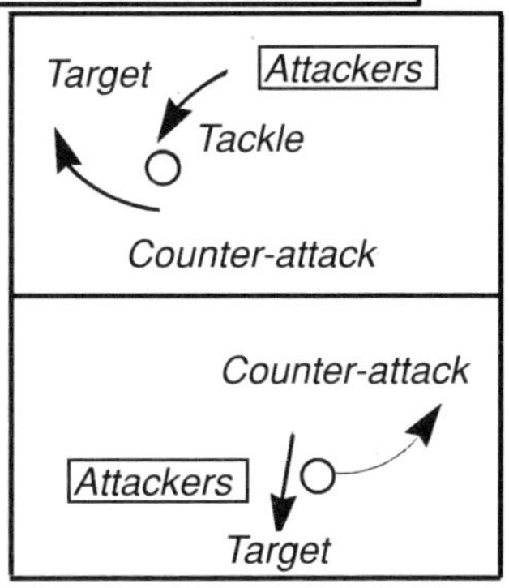

□ When an inside back is tackled and the ball bounces loose, the weak spot is within 1 to 2 m of the ball and that is where an attack is launched straight towards the goal-line.

Loose ball: Knock-ons

- immediately to the blind side
- speed

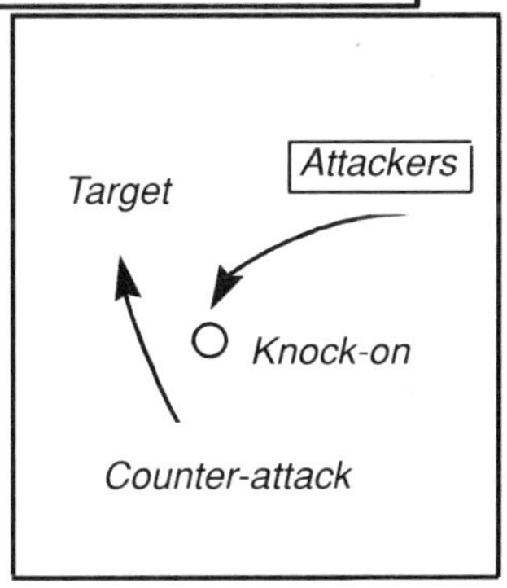

□ When the ball comes out more slowly, e.g., by means of a mini-loose maul (rip and take), the weak spot is still within 1 to 2 m from the attacker who lost the ball, or to the blind side.

☐ When the ball comes out even more slowly, e.g., after a relatively quick maul, the weak point is blind side for a fast counter-attack.

☐ After a slow maul, establish where the defence is weakest, i.e., where there are few opponents.

- This is usually the blind side.

+ The halves decide whether to run or kick (the observation of the entire back-line but particularly the wingers and full-back is important here).

- The main thing is that the ball must end up behind the opposition's first line of defence.

☐ In the case of a quick ruck, the options are:

- for the first player to drive forward straight ahead if there is a gap behind the ball; or

- for the ball to be passed quickly to the blind side.

☐ In the case of a slow ruck, the same options are available as for a slow maul.

☐ When play is mistakenly directed to the wrong side, i.e., where there are more opponents than attackers, the options are:

- When you want to retain possession, e.g., outside your own 10 m line:

+ create a second phase deliberately and draw your opponents in until they are outnumbered by your team; to achieve this it may be necessary to go beyond the second phase even as far as a fourth or fifth phase; the ball then goes out. (Just remember after third phase your chances of keeping possession and scoring diminishes rapidly.)

- When you want to change the pressure:

+ launch an up and under; or

+ kick into empty spaces.

☐ Possession from a ruck where several defenders stay out on the fringes usually falls under a slow maul except when the ball is won quickly.

From the opposition's kicks

Chip/grubber kicks in midfield

- straight ahead through the middle

  or

- ninety degrees to furthest touch-line
  - supporters running into position

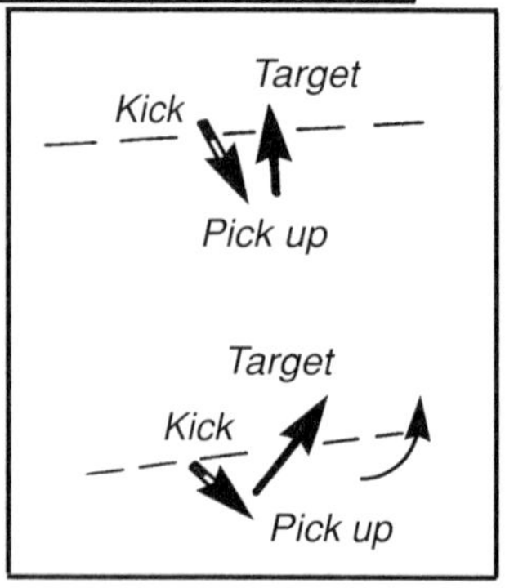

A short kick forward:

- When the catcher is static, his possibilities of attack are fewer and he must begin with a pass. (A sidestep may be the exception.)

- When the catcher runs into the ball and either catches it out of the air or scoops it up from the ground:

+ The weak point is virtually right in front of him.

+ He can break the defensive line quickly. (Examples are David Campese and Mark Ella's counter-attacks for the 1985 Wallabies against the Barbarians.)

Kicks close and parallel to touch - midfield open

- in front of attacking forwards
- long pass across field
- speed forward towards weak spot
  - uneven pressure of alignment

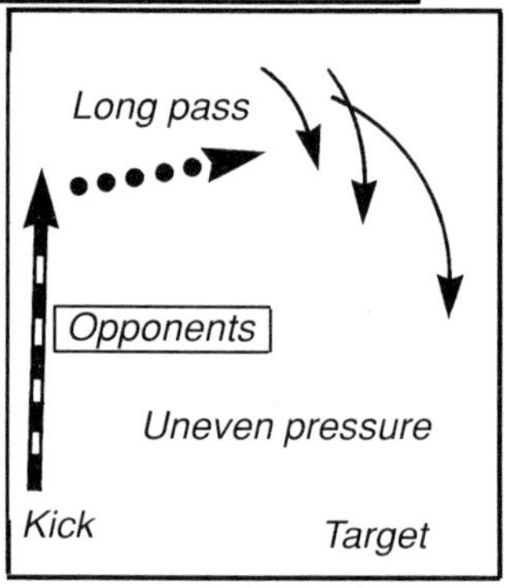

☐ A long kick forward close to touch:

- When the midfield is not under pressure:

+ Play the ball away from pressure with a long pass across the width of the field.

+ Fool some of your opponents coming up unevenly with a change in direction using a scissor pass, for instance, or a switch or dummy pass. (An example is Roger Gould's counter-attack for the 1985 Wallabies against the Barbarians.)

Kicks - up-and-unders - pressure in midfield

- immediate attack to blind side

  or

- dummy attack infield
  - switch attack to touch-line

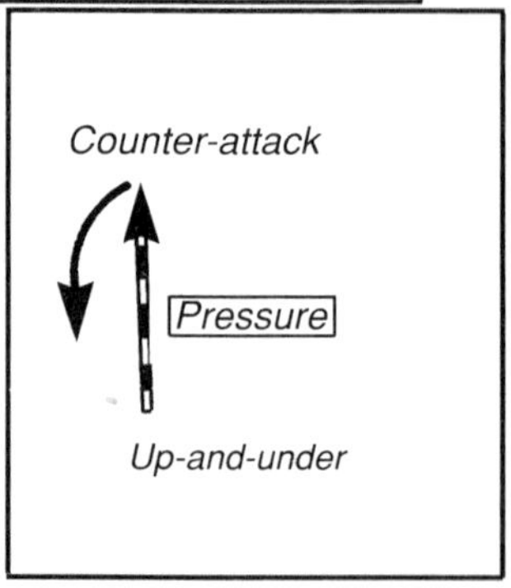

- When the midfield is under pressure:

+ The catcher runs towards midfield (runs towards pressure) and switches the direction of attack with a scissors or switch-pass back up the touch-line (pass away from pressure).

☐ A diagonal kick forward:

- When the catcher is alone without support:

+ inside your own 22, kick the ball out;
+ outside your own 22, kick the ball either deep towards your opponents' goal-line or high up and under.
- When the catcher has support:
+ the way in which the opponents come to the defence and the catcher's skills will determine the counter-attack options. (Think of Phil Bennett's sidesteps that began Gareth Edwards' remarkable try for the 1973 Barbarians against the All Blacks.) A safe option is to counter-attack to the blind side up the touch-line. (Tim Horan's counter-attack after taking an up-and-under from Rob Andrew in the 1991-World Cup final is a perfect example of this.)

Kicks across field from touch to midfield or goal

- opponents concentrated in one part of the field
- catcher has time
- space against the far touch-line
- supporters quickly in position

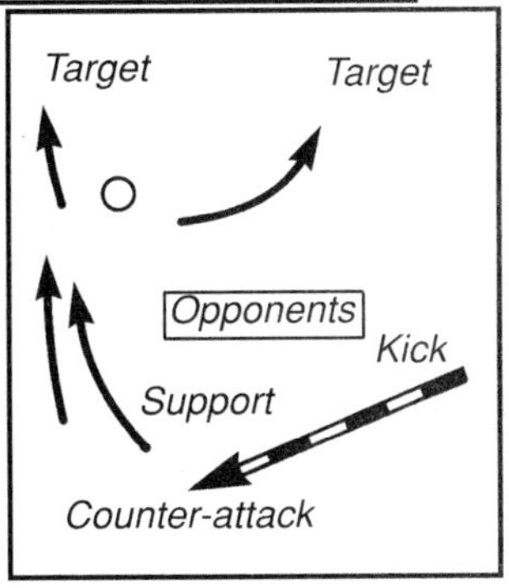

6. Problems and solutions: the scrum

Think and stay alive

Characteristics of a good scrum

☐ The players are comfortable.
☐ The scrum is immediately set and balanced.
☐ It goes down in such a way that it exerts instantaneous pressure.
☐ The backs of the players form a table top.
☐ Seen from behind, there are no gaps between the players.

The scrum tends to wheel slightly clockwise, i.e., to the tight-head side

On its own
Correct this as follows:
☐ Put the heaviest players on the tight-head side.
☐ Make sure the tight-head side is slightly in front when you go down.
☐ The tight-head prop should push off both feet.
☐ The tight-head lock and flanker should lock.
Remember: When the tight-head side goes back, your options for attack to the right are limited.

Because of the opponents' tactic
Correct this as follows:
☐ Concentrate on exerting pressure with your right shoulders.
☐ Push towards your tight-head.
☐ If all this does not help, have all the forwards take short steps towards your tight-head; the scrum will then move, crab-like, in that direction.
☐ Your last option is to help the swing on to just past 90° (at which point the referee is obliged to order the scrum to be re-formed).

The scrum does not stand still

Try the following commands:
☐ Legs wide!
☐ Pull arms!
☐ Heads up!

The ball comes out of the scrum too slowly after it has been hooked

☐ Has the ball been put in properly?
- The hooker should indicate beforehand exactly where and at what speed he wants the ball.
- The scrum-half should hold the ball so that it suits the hooker's foot when struck.
☐ Are the channels open?
- The ball usually gets caught against the loose-head's right foot and the loose-head lock's left foot.
☐ Are the tight forwards playing the ball?
- The loose-head flanker should drop his inside knee to prevent the ball from shooting out that side (he can also play the ball himself).
- The loose-head flanker should push the ball through if it gets trapped at the loose-head lock's side.
☐ The eighth-man should try to control the ball by pushing with his right leg and channeling the ball with his left foot (he must hold the pressure!). Do not be afraid to let him go down between the left flanker and lock and then play a fast channel-one ball.

The shove forward is not powerful enough

Check the following points:
☐ Whether the scrum-down is forward for the pushing position.
☐ The point of contact of the shoulders.
☐ The binding of the arms.
☐ Whether the upper backs are straight.
☐ Whether the feet are a hip-width apart.
☐ Whether the knees are bent (the front of the knee should be in line with the back of the buttock).
☐ Whether the locks' feet, on shoulder contact, move forward.
☐ The eighth-man goes down together with the five tight forwards.
☐ Whether the front row lifts slightly thus transferring the power from behind.

Problems of individual players

Loose-head

Problem	*Cause*	*Solution*
You go down to the ground.	The opponent comes down onto your neck.	Go down aggressively; don't hesitate. Go down fast. Come in with your neck underneath the opponent's breastbone.
	The opponent pulls you down with his right arm.	With your left arm stretched out, bind forward as far as possible and turn your elbow in. Bind with your left hand in the crook of his right arm.
Your head is pushed down onto your knee.	You go down with your left foot too far forward.	Put your left foot back. Bend your knees more and, with your feet back, push from below up and forward with the help of the flank and lock.
Your hips swing out to the left	Your weight is on your outside foot. You go down with your left foot too far forward. You do not bind securely enough with the hooker at the hips. You go down with your feet too close together.	Go down with your right foot slightly in front.
Your push forward is not powerful enough.	Your neck and shoulders are too low.	Go down so that your hips are lower than your shoulders and you can use the force of your legs to push slightly up and forward.
The tight-head keeps coming in hard and the referee does nothing about it.	You go down from too far away.	Move closer before you go down. Emergency measure: Quickly get out of the way to the left so that the tight head falls down between you and the hooker! (He who does not listen, must feel!)

Hookers

Problem	*Cause*	*Solution*
You cannot reach the ball near the mouth of the scrum.	You are trapped with your face down.	Go down with your upper body turned slightly to the left. The scrum-half can put the ball in more slowly and deeper, and you can then hook it slightly to your right - channel 3.

		The scrum-half can put the ball in more slowly and your tight-head can hook it - channel 3
Your opponent comes in underneath your ribs.	You go down too slowly. You go down too close.	Go down with the hard part of your right shoulder on your opponent's neck.
The opposing tight-head pushes in onto you diagonally.		Stay bound tightly against your loose-head. Your loose-head can go for the tight-head's open ribs with the help of your lock and flanker.

Tight-head

Problem	***Cause***	***Solution***
Your hips swing out.	You go down with your weight on your outside foot.	Keep your hips tight against the hooker and your weight on your left leg.
	You go down with your right foot too far forward.	Go down with your right foot slightly back.
	You bind too far below the hollow of your hooker's right shoulder.	Slip your left shoulder slightly away from your hooker so that your upper body is square to the front when you go down.
The loose-head comes in underneath your ribs.	You go down too close. You go down too late.	
Your push forward is not powerful enough.	You are not pushing from both feet. You are trying to push on your own.	The angle between your torso and hips should be about 100° to 110° so that you can transmit the locks' power forward instead of them pushing your hips down.

Locks

Problem	***Cause***	***Solution***
You push through the front row.	The loose-head's hips swing out to the left. The tight-head's hips swing out to the right. The hooker pushes diagonally towards his loose-head.	Bind firmly through the prop's legs with your outside arm and keep his inside buttock on your outside shoulder. Bind firmly before you go down. Make sure your prop's weight is on his inside leg. Look up, keep your upper back hollow and push your stomach down.

Forward shove is not powerful enough.	You push from one leg/foot.	Position your feet at least a hip-width apart. The tight-head lock's feet can be further apart to counter the swing of the scrum to his side.
	Your feet are not in a pushing position when you go down.	Bend your knees just more than 90° to push forward. Make sure your studs have a firm grip and your ankles lock.
	You change the position of your feet after the scrum has gone down.	Go down in such a way that your feet move forward after contact - definitely not back.
	You bind incorrectly.	Push your shoulders where the prop's buttock and upper leg meet. The tight-head lock should bind over the top. Make sure you bind securely.
	The flankers and/or eighth-man pulls you apart when he goes down.	

Flankers

Problem	***Cause***	***Solution***
Your shove is not powerful enough.	You are lazy and go down only after the tight forwards have gone down and are already under great pressure.	Go down before the front row goes down. Move forward together with the front row and push up immediately.
You pull the locks apart.	You go down with your feet behind one another and hang onto the locks to keep your balance.	Throw your inside hip against the lock and push with your inside foot slightly in front of your outside foot. Your feet should be comfortably apart. If you can reach, bind on the furthest lock.

Eighth-man

Problem	***Cause***	***Solution***
You pull the locks apart.	You go down after the rest of the forwards and then pull the locks' hips apart to get your head in. Your feet are too close together to balance.	Bind high against the locks' buttocks. Position your feet at least a hip-width apart right from the beginning. Go down at the same time as the locks. Make sure the locks' knees are bent enough so that you do not push their hips towards the ground.

7. Problems and solutions: the line-out

We must have it

Changes in the laws have inevitably led to adaptations in line-out techniques. The current laws, according to which there must be a metre between opposing players without a restriction on the distance players of the same team need to keep from each other, have resulted in several adaptations. For example:

☐ The players of both teams move aggressively in a line towards their opponents' side of the line-out and try to shield their jumper (a technique the British Lions applied with great success in 1971 in New Zealand, which is similar to American gridiron where you prevent your opponents from playing the team-mate with the ball). Here you are entirely in the hands of the referee for protection.

☐ The players of the team throwing in create gaps in their own line-out so that their opponents also have to move further apart. The jumper then moves forward or backward in his own line-out until he is opposite the gap in his opponents' line-out. He uses this gap to get to the ball (it sounds more complicated than it is!).

☐ Because you are allowed to support the jumper after he has started his jump, the ability to jump high is not as important as in the past to get possession.

It is common practice for players to change their positions in the line-out. This calls for good understanding between the thrower and the jumper.

Where should you aim your throw?

☐ Throw in to the jumper/position where your team has the best chance of getting the ball, since the aim is, in the first place, to secure possession.

☐ Bring in an element of surprise and vary the throw-ins in respect of:

- an ordinary line-out;
- a line-out where there are only jumpers; and
- a short two-man line-out.

Advantages and disadvantages of different positions

Ordinary line-out

Prop (No. 1 in the line-out)

WHEN TO USE HIM

☐ For variation and an element of surprise two to three times during a match.

☐ To win an important ball.

☐ To peel off in front of the line-out close to the opponents' goal-line.

☐ In wet and/or windy conditions.

ADVANTAGES/DISADVANTAGES - FOR OWN BACK-LINE PLAY

☐ It puts the fly-half under great pressure and makes it difficult for him to take the ball shallow (skip the inside centre when you pass if you want to play wide).

Lock at the front (No. 2 in the line-out)

Especially if he is physically strong or exceptionally tall.

Vary the quick jump with the lob, which is caught over the top of the second prop.

WHEN TO USE HIM

☐ In wet and/or windy conditions (safe).

☐ To peel off in front of the line-out or drive on the catcher (attack).

☐ To tire the opposing forwards (contact).

DISADVANTAGES/ADVANTAGES - FOR OWN BACK-LINE PLAY

It has the same disadvantages for back-line play as when the prop catches the ball.

LINE-OUT: DRIVING INTO BACK

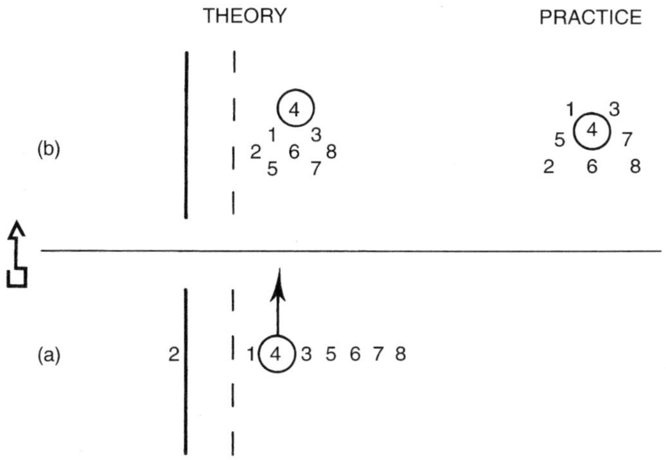

Lock in the middle (No. 4 in the line-out)
Usually the highest jumper with the best timing.

Vary a quick jump slightly across, forward and up (there is little chance of obstruction) with a lob taken slightly back.

WHEN TO USE HIM

☐ Good ball:
- To pass or deflect off the top direct to the scrum-half
- Bring the ball down first and then pass.
+ For a push drive on the opponents' goal-line or in their half.

ADVANTAGES FOR OWN BACK-LINE PLAY

☐ It has many advantages for back-line play because of the many options, e.g.:
- immediately behind the line-out;
- centre field; or
- wide.
- For the back-line to play either centre field or wide.

Tall loose forward (No. 6)

WHEN TO USE HIM

☐ For useful variation between No. 5 and No. 7,
☐ especially when the opposing No. 6 is short.
☐ See No. 7 below.

ADVANTAGES FOR OWN BACK-LINE PLAY

☐ It is a good ball for back-line play:
- All options are open.
☐ It creates the possibility of also playing blind side.

Tall loose forward (No. 7)

WHEN TO USE HIM
Particularly in an attack.

☐ Possession at the back of the line-out creates an excellent platform for attack by the forwards.
☐ It offers the back-line several possibilities of attack.

ADVANTAGES

☐ Ideal for peel off movements to infield.
☐ A good basis for a drive on No. 7.
☐ The scrum-half can break on either side; on the blind side he can play with the hooker or winger.
☐ The fly-half can take the ball flat behind the line-out in the so-called "vacuum".
☐ The forwards can easily join up with the back-line again.
☐ For cutting outside the fly-half and inside centre (the opposing forwards are drawn into the tight-loose).
☐ For playing wide with an extra man in the back-line.

LINE-OUT: DRIVING THROUGH THE MIDDLE

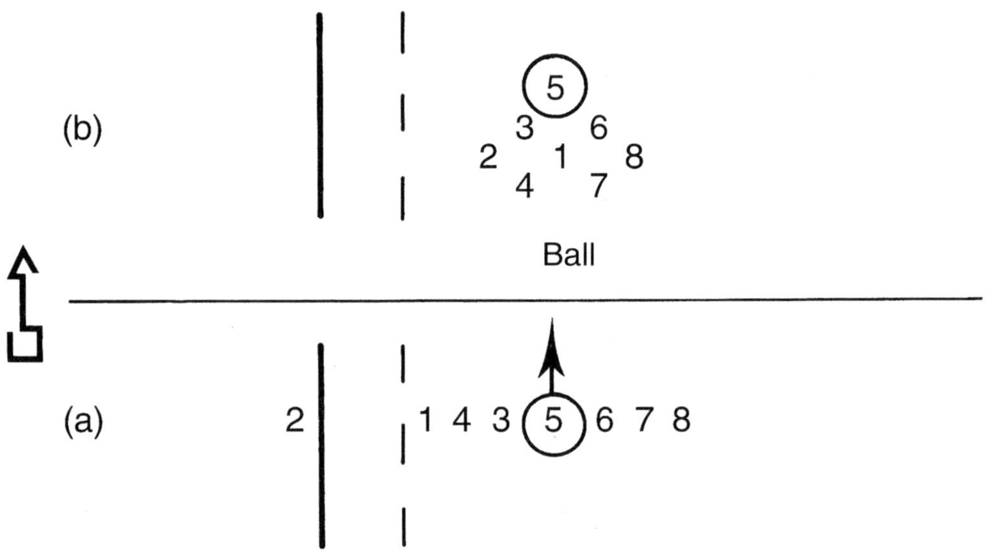

N.B. In practice the ball will be shifted immediately to (1)

LINE-OUT: DRIVING FROM THE BACK

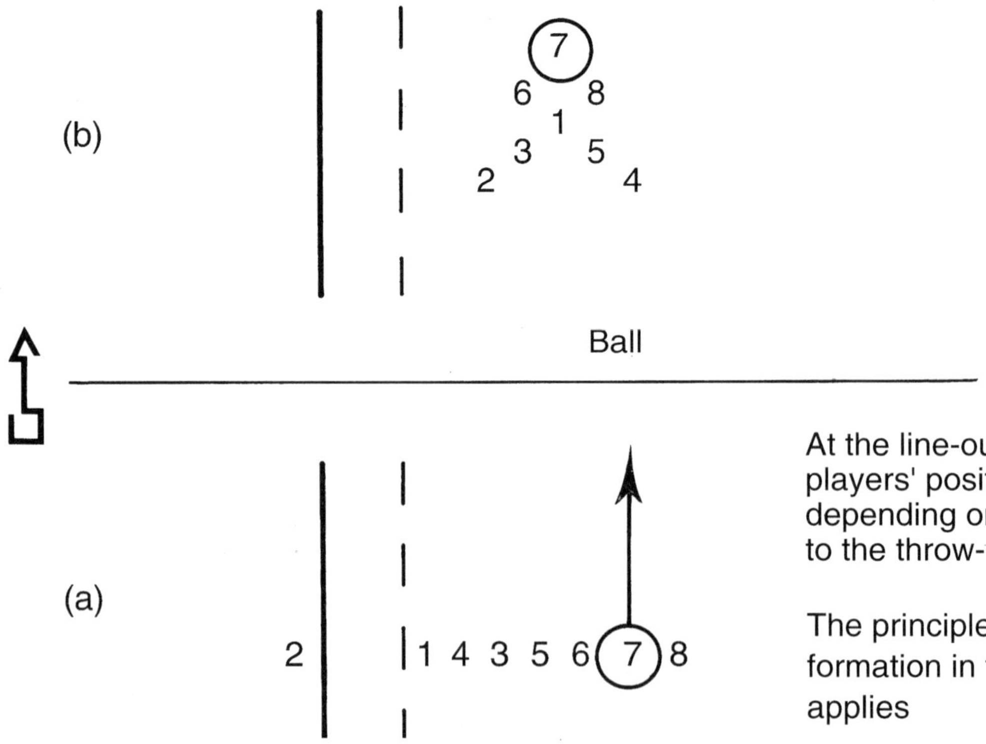

At the line-out drive the players' positions will vary depending on how they read to the throw-ins

The principle of the wedge formation in the drive always applies

Eighth-man (No. 8)

WHEN TO USE HIM

☐ A throw to the eighth-man in the line-out creates a platform for a peel by the other forwards.

☐ About 5 m over the line-out for the eighth-man.

ADVANTAGES

☐ The eighth-man plays forward himself.

☐ The other loose forwards join him on his inside for driving.

☐ The inside centre comes up quickly and takes a short pass (1 m) from the eighth-man.

Line-out where there are only jumpers (3/4/5-man line-out)

The jumpers stand as close together as possible so that the opponents cannot get through the line-out.

There are three types of throw-ins:

☐ A lob to the centre of the line-out. All the jumpers go for the ball, which is deflected to:

- the scrum-half, who quickly passes to the fly-half, who (1) plays wide (remember that, when five jumpers are in the line-out, the slowest forwards are probably outside) or (2) plays directly onto his opponent together with his forwards by driving through and creating a good second-phase ball (halves can also kick defensively to touch or attack and kick an up-and-under or kick to gain ground); or
- the last player in the line-out, for a peel off from the front. If possible, the inside backs immediately join any driving movements. If a second-phase ball develops, the scrum-half (1) breaks shallow open side, or (2) plays deep and wide open side with an extra man in the back-line or (3) plays back to the blind side.

☐ A quick throw-in to the front jumper. He:

- deflects the ball directly to the scrum-half, who, in turn, quickly passes to the fly-half, who then either plays wide or kicks (or the scrum-half himself kicks); or
- passes to one of the forwards at the back peeling off round the front. If he is stopped, the scrum-half breaks open side, sets up a drive by the forwards and then plays out to the back-line in the same direction he has just broken.

A second possibility is to play deep and wide with an extra man in the back-line.

☐ A relatively quick throw-in about 3 to 4 m behind the line-out:

- The jumper at the back moves back quickly infield to catch the ball. The rest move for the peel off.

The closest forwards or backs come up straight and take a short pass (1 m) from the catcher, drive through or create a good second-phase ball.

- The entire line-out moves back a fraction before the throw-in to where the ball will be thrown to. There is a choice of (1) deflecting to the scrum-half, (2) deflections to other players as mentioned above, (3) taking the ball and driving (thereafter the scrum-half breaks wide and cuts with either the forward or the fly-half in the gap immediately next to the maul) or (4) the scrum-half playing deep and wide with an extra man in the back-line.

Just remember, when the back-line plays deep and wide, the contact line is far behind the forwards. The backs should therefore be ready to correct any mistake immediately and play as loose forwards themselves. If they don't cross the tackle-line first time, they should stay on their feet (or pass in time) so that the team retains the ball until the forwards catch up.

Short two-man line-out

Here the key is surprise and variation and there must be a good understanding between thrower and jumper.

Surprise

☐ Opponents: Especially against opponents who play conventionally and are easily thrown when faced with something "different".

☐ Phase of the match: early in the match to take the initiative or in the "tired" stage of the match when the opponents are less alert.

☐ Place on the field: To be safe, first in the opponents' half where the risk of penalty kicks is in your favour or within 5 m of your goal-line (throw in over the line-out to the back-line).

☐ Stage of the match: If you have a comfortable lead, why not be more adventurous? If you are behind and there is little time, you have nothing to lose.

Variation (only a few examples)

☐ A throw-in to the line-out when one or both jumpers are particularly tall and/or jump high:

- The scrum-half is wide awake for a possible break himself.
- The fly-half (1) kicks an up-and-under behind the opponents' back-line and forwards to his centres and loose forwards, (2) sets up a drive or maul or ruck with his forwards on the opponents' back-line or (3) skips his centres (and the opponents' forwards!) and passes to his full-back, blind-side winger and open-side winger.

☐ The two jumpers change position:

- The player at the back quickly moves infield and catches the ball behind the line-out (the same options are open to the halves provided they start moving after the ball has left the thrower's hands).
- The player at the back quickly moves even further back and the tall loose forward in the scrum-half's position jumps into the line-out for the ball (when he catches it, he usually goes straight through the line-out).

- Just before the ball is thrown in, the two jumpers quickly change position and the ball is thrown in either behind or to the front (the same options are open to the halves).

☐ Dummies:

- The player at the back first takes two steps back and then returns to his original position for the jump (the same options are open to the halves).
- Both players quickly move back and the scrum-half catches a short throw-in at the front. (Example: Nick Farr Jones' try against Scotland.)

A good understanding

Remember: The team that throws in should win the short line-out!

☐ The thrower should know exactly when and where to throw in; he should not allow himself to be put off by the forwards' movements.

☐ It is safer to have a scrum-half in the scrum-half position on your ball but a loose forward there on the opponents' ball.

If you cannot get clean possession

Thrower

Problem	Cause
He almost always throws in inaccurately.	He does not look where he throws and he does not throw at a target.
He often throws in skew.	He is not balanced. Looks at the direction in which his elbow is pointing when the ball leaves his hand.
The jumper is uncertain.	The thrower hesitates when he throws in.
The opponents in front of your jumper get the ball.	The thrower throws in too short.
He does not concentrate first and foremost on his throw-in.	He is in too much of a hurry to join the line-out.

Jumper

Problem	Cause
He does not jump with confidence.	He does not think he can get the ball and is uncertain about either the throw-in or the support.
He jumps high enough but does not get control of the ball.	He does not keep his eye on the ball.
He can't take the ball cleanly.	His hands are too tense; he does not use a stop hand.
He loses control of the ball between the point of contact and shoulder height.	He must be fairly relaxed in taking the ball, but aggressive in bringing it down for delivery.
The front jumper does not get to the ball. The opposing prop prevents him from going forward.	He does not jump forward diagonally, he does not get his shoulder in in front of his opponent when there is a fast ball or the prop in front does not concentrate and do his job.

Supporters

Problem	Cause
Despite good throw-ins, your good jumper does not get to the ball.	The supporters on either side of the jumper do not prevent the opponents from obstructing.

The opponents break through your line-out.
The supporter doesn't know whether the jumper takes a fast or a slow ball.

The supporters do not step towards the ball to prevent the opponents from breaking through.

Tips

Thrower

□ Look at your grip on the ball.
- The point of the ball should be in the V of your thumb and forefinger and you should have two fingers on the laces.

□ Get a target and look at it when you throw in.
- The target is where the ball is to be caught.

Try to pull back as little as possible when you throw in.
- The flatter the trajectory of the throw, the less the opportunity for obstruction.

□ Rather throw in too deep than too short.
- One of your team-mates is ready for the ball if it goes beyond the intended jumper.

□ Try the two-handed throw-in, as used in basketball and netball. The way you vary the flight and the speed of the throw-in is vital. Sean Fitzpatrick of the All Blacks and Phil Kearns of the Wallabies have mastered this technique to perfection. It is very difficult for the opponents to guess where you are throwing to.

Jumper

□ What type of jump is called for?
- Forward and up so that your shoulder is in front of your opponent.
- Straight up to beat your opponent with speed.
- Slightly back and then up so that you actually jump behind your opponent (the "lob").

□ Stand the same way every time before you jump so that you do not give away the signals.

□ Take off with speed and preferably off your inside foot.

□ Keep your eye on the ball all the time so that fewer balls ricochet off your hands.

□ Keep your inside shoulder slightly in front to facilitate the turn.

□ Keep your hands relaxed so that you get control of the ball more easily.

□ Your hands should be at shoulder level before the take-off for faster reaction and less obstruction on your arms.

□ Pluck the ball out of the air.
- You lose control of the ball most often between the point of contact and bringing it down to your shoulders.

□ Land in a strong position with your feet apart to the sides and to the front.
- This immediately forms a strong base around which your supporters can consolidate.

Timing between jumper and thrower

□ What is your signal to the thrower?
- For the inexperienced, the type of jump determines the type of ball; for the experienced player it is just the other way round.

□ Maintain your rhythm even when something goes wrong.
- This will help the task of the struggling thrower enormously.

Supporters

All the players should know the position where the ball is intended to go, and what type of throw-in it will be (ex. fast or lob).

□ The supporters immediately in front of and behind the jumper:
- Step with your inside foot diagonally over the advantage line; this protects the jumper.

□ Bind on the jumper with your arms upward so that you can support him immediately after he has started his jump. If you bind on him only in a forward position, you hinder rather than support him.
- Lift your inside elbow to protect your face and prevent obstruction against the jumper.

□ The next jumper in case the ball is thrown in over the nominated jumper:
- First be ready to catch the ball when it goes over the jumper before you close up. At international level it often happens that the jumper first barges his opponent off balance before going for the ball himself.

□ In case the jumper is tackled with the ball or the ball goes loose:
- Is there always a predesignated player to help the jumper get the ball or control the ball if it ricochets?

The same players always help one another, e.g., No. 1 helps No. 5, No. 5 or 6 helps No. 4, No. 3/4 helps No. 7 and No. 5 helps No. 8 (you can use other players but the principle remains the same).
- Take the ball only if the jumper says so.
- Move in such a way that a ball that is knocked back comes towards you; cover the gap between the scrum-half and the line-out.
- Always move towards the ball; never overrun it.

□ The rest of the forwards:
- Does the signal indicate clean possession, a drive in the line-out, a peel off or deliberate deflection?
- Clean possession: The aim is to prevent the opponents from getting to the ball or pushing you back (in this case you bind only to the sides of the first three players: the jumper and two supporters on either side).
- Push drive: The aim is to go forward with the ball in between the opponents (in this case you bind in scrum formation with the first three players forming the front row).

- Peel off: The aim is to break through either behind or in front of the line-out. The ball is passed diagonally either to the back or to the front or it is deflected so that the catcher can run parallel to the touch-line as soon as possible instead of diagonally across the field. The first player who gets the ball from the jumper tries either to get away clean or to eliminate the last opponent in the line-out. The ball must be kept available at all times so that your team-mates can play it on.
- Deflection: Step closer with your inside leg to the player who is to deflect to prevent the opponents from breaking through (it is against the rules to hold onto an opponent!).
Remember: All the players should immediately move towards the point where the ball is thrown.

Opponents

☐ Look how your opponent jumps for the ball, supports or closes up:
- Now work out counter-strategies to beat him to the ball.

☐ On your own throw-in:
- Your forwards try to occupy (or utilise) the space between them and the opponents as quickly as possible.
- Shield your jumpers from the opponents.

☐ On the opponents' throw-in:
- Your forwards move in between theirs (it is then easier to catch a bad throw-in).

8. Problems and solutions: the tight-loose

Never be isolated

Over the past few seasons the spotlight has fallen on this aspect of the game, with much talk about concepts like "ball retention". There is nothing new in this since *the objective of any team should be to gain possession and then to retain the ball until points are scored.* (My view of this is set out in detail in chapter 2.) Fashionable or not, concepts like "direct rugby" and "ball retention" have again highlighted the role of the loose forward.

The task of the loose forward

Possession

☐ To help your tight forwards so that your team gets good ball from set play. The loose forward should therefore give the tight five all his support.
☐ To play the ball yourself in such a way as to put your backs in a more favourable position to score points.
☐ To support the ball-carrier when your backs attack, thereby making sure your team retains possession.
☐ Regain possession after losing the ball through aggressive defence, and to apply constant pressure to prevent the opponents from crossing the advantage line with the ball.

Scrum

Own scrum

☐ To help your front row.
- Go down with the front row and exert pressure immediately.
- On the signal, shove or lock.

☐ The left flanker controls the ball at channel 1.
- Drop your inside knee to prevent the ball from shooting out there.
- Guide the ball to the eighth-man (channels 1 and 2).

Opponents' scrum

Nowadays several countries use an open-side flanker and a blind-side flanker. The open-side flanker is fast and his main task is to put pressure on the opponents' backs on the open side, regain possession for his team and, after defensive play, get the ball off the ground again as fast as possible. The blind-side flanker player is the heavier, stronger of the two. He is used mainly in hard defence, aggressive driving and line-out possession.
☐ Lift your head to see what the back-line is planning.
☐ Shove or lock first.
☐ The left flanker:
- Slip your right shoulder slightly off the prop's buttock and be ready for the scrum-half's break (break forward and up; don't wait for the scrum-half).
- Tackle the first attacker who comes round the scrum. Stop him dead in his tracks, and even try to move him back towards his own goal-line. If he is in a low driving position, throw him over your leg to the ground in such a way that the ball is on your side of the ensuing ruck. He will either lose possession or the ruck will be delayed.
- When play moves to the other side of the scrum, first drop back deep and sum up. Close to the opponents' goal-line, break forward towards the fly-half. In your own half, however, first secure your side of the scrum and then drop back deep.

☐ The right flanker:
- When the opponents play to your side of the field with their loose forwards or scrum-half, tackle the first player with the ball back to his own goal-line. If the opponent is too heavy, turn him so that the ball is on your side.
- When the opponents use their back-line, break away across the width for the first 5 to 6 m (in this way you prevent inside breaking and reach the ball first because the opponents' backs are playing towards you).

☐ The eighth-man:
- Study the chapter on defensive patterns.
- Defend shallow open side and particularly blind side. Take your defence to the attacker, otherwise he will cross the advantage line.

Line-out

Own throw-in

☐ Where is the ball to be thrown?
☐ When the ball is caught, are you:
- the first supporter;
- the sweeper; or
- do you stay out of the line-out?

☐ If the throw-in misses the jumper
- do you go for the ball?

☐ When the ball is deflected
- do you form a barrier, using your legs to prevent them from barging through the line-out?

☐ Where do the halves play to?
- Where are they going to attack the advantage line and where will your support be needed?
- This determines, in particular, the position of the last loose forward in the line-out. When his back-line plays wide, he leaves a gap in front of him in the line-out through which an opponent can be lured so that he ends

NO. 8's POSITION AT THE BACK OF THE LINE-OUT

(a) When your side is playing to the back-line

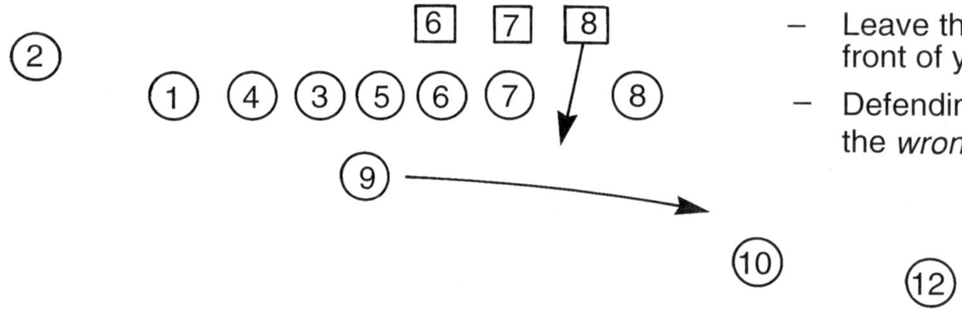

- Leave the gap in front of you
- Defending No. 8 is on the *wrong* defensive line

(b) When your side is kicking

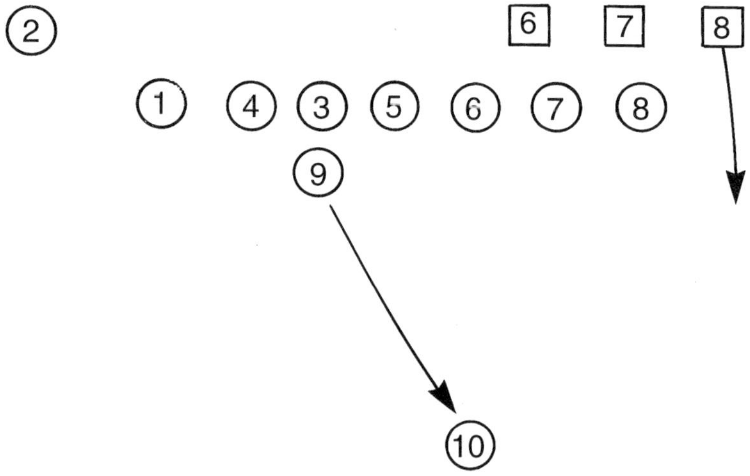

- Leave the gap behind you
- Defending No. 8 goes too wide to bother kicker

up at the wrong running angle for defence. If your fly-half intends to kick, leave space at the back to ensure the opponent is again on the wrong running angle.

Opponents' throw-in

☐ Every loose forward must know what to do when the ball:
- is thrown in to the front;
- is thrown in to the middle; and
- is thrown in to the back or over the line-out.

☐ The loose forward must anticipate where the ball is going to be thrown to:
- Where is the opposition's best jumper?
- Where is the line-out? If it is in the opponents' "22", they will probably throw it to the front; in your half, the throw-in will probably be deeper; from your "22", they may peel off either to the front or to the back; and, within 5 to 10 m of your goal-line, you can expect a drive in the middle of the line-out.

☐ The route of the loose forward is determined by the whole team's defensive pattern.

With the backs (joining)

Where does the back-line play to?

☐ Open side:
- to the wing
- movements

☐ Blind side (where no kicking takes place).

☐ Where do the loose forwards play to when the ball is passed to the back-line?
- Two loose forwards support deep, i.e., directly from behind at the point of contact. From the scrum to the right it is usually the eighth-man and left flanker. (This is very difficult to learn because it means the loose forward sometimes has to run back depending on where the contact line is. The way the All Black flanker Michael Jones plays off his backs or other forwards from rucks and mauls to score or create sensational tries, is an

LOOSE FORWARDS: SUPPORT AND BACK-LINE PLAY

(A) SHALLOW

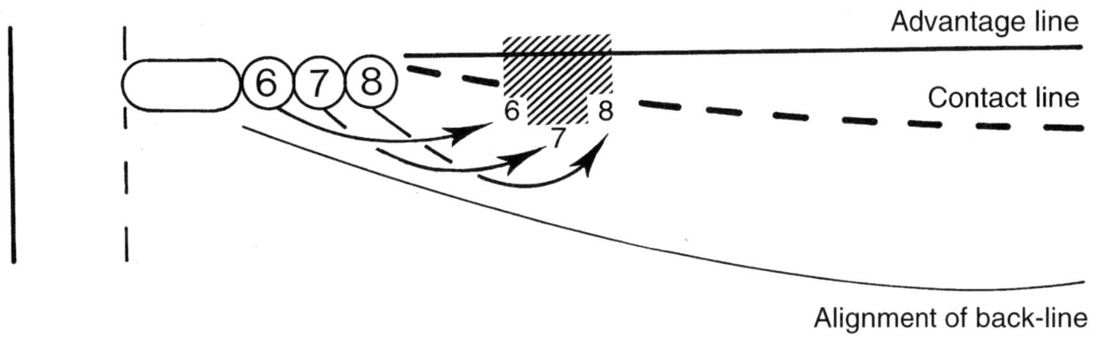

(B) MIDFIELD

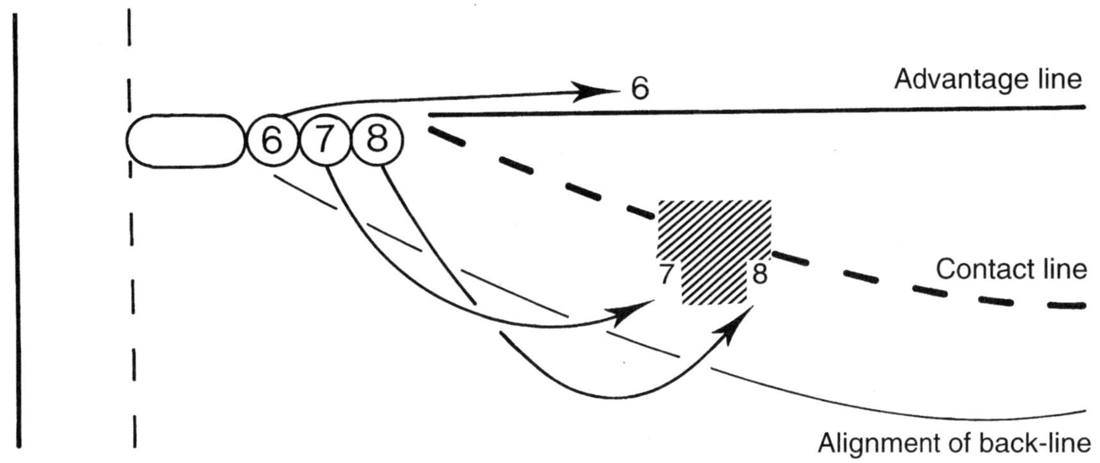

(C) WIDE

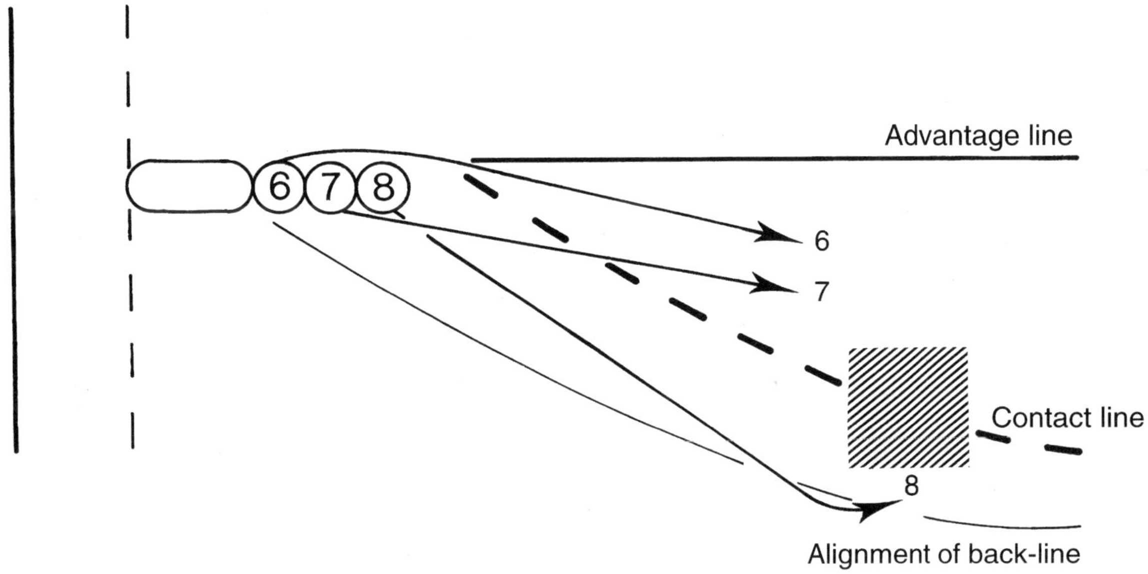

excellent example of a loose forward using the correct running angles.)
- One loose forward supports to the front in case the backs break through. From a scrum to the right it is usually the right flanker.
☐ Kicks:
- All the loose forwards break forward in the direction of the kick or to the edge of the 10 m offside circle. Remember the offside laws (see chapter 3).

Support
☐ You should know where according to the triangle-principle in general play to support:
- On either side of a narrow triangle: The ball-carrier is in front and the first two supporters are on either side behind him.
- From deep: Run with your chest towards the goal-line. The target is a gap within 1 m to the left or right of the ball-carrier. Get the ball up to a metre behind or diagonally behind the ball-carrier.
- At speed: The supporter who comes fastest takes the ball.

Problems and solutions

The loose forwards do not get into the game

☐ The tight forwards are struggling:
- They are always on the retreat in the scrums and get away slowly.
- They are drawn into the line-outs and find it difficult to get clean possession.
☐ The loose forwards play as individuals without a pattern in attack or defence; they do not complement one another.
☐ The loose forwards have specific shortcomings:
- Physically, as individuals, they are too weak or slow and/or in combination, they are too slow, short and weak. Technically they are also weak, especially as far as dispossessing opponents is concerned (e.g., they do not keep their eyes on the ball or they do not communicate with one another; see Tips).
☐ The loose forwards are mostly in front of their backs when the backs make contact. This is the result of poor communication with their halves.
☐ The backs do not bring the loose forwards into the game.
- They do not keep the ball available. The "friend in need" of the inside centre on the right is the right flanker and the "friend in need" of the inside centre on the left is the left flanker. (When the centres do not deliberately retain the ball and/or make it available, the loose forwards cannot get into the game.)
- They do not try to stay on their feet.
- They allow mauls and rucks to develop. The loose forwards then have to work much harder to gain possession.
- The closest back does not play the ball immediately but waits for the loose forwards to do so. The best loose forward is the closest player, irrespective of his position!

How can the other players help the loose forwards?

Key players

Ball-carrier
☐ He retains possession for your team by:
- passing the ball in time; and
- making sure his team-mate can take the ball from him if he cannot pass.
☐ He is not afraid of contact.
☐ He tries to stay on his feet as long as possible.
☐ He always turns in such a way that the ball is on his team-mates' side.
☐ By straightening in the upper body coming up with the ball at the last moment, his team-mate can take it from him more easily.
☐ He does not panic when he feels, or is, isolated.

First two supporters
☐ They determine, together with the ball-carrier, whether momentum stays on the ball (see chapter 5).
☐ They move onto the ball to get into a supporting position quickly; they do not wait for the ball!

Tips

When you have possession
☐ The fewer of your team-mates who go for the ball when the opponents block it, the faster and more easily you retain possession.
☐ When the opponent tries to smother the ball, rip the ball up, or down, and pass by using your wrists.
☐ When an opponent has a firm hold on the ball, immediately talk to your first supporter, who:
- goes for the ball and digs it out with shoulder and arm, or gets both arms round it from below and rips it or twists it out (he must see the ball if he wants to take it away quickly) and passes to the second supporter, who drives forward.
☐ When the first supporter cannot get the ball out immediately:
- the second and third supporters go for the opponent's wrists or thumbs, break his grip on the ball and push with their shoulders; the first supporter then passes the ball to the fourth supporter, who drives forward.
☐ As a last alternative, all the forwards go into scrum formation with the first supporter acting as hooker. The players up front stay on their feet and, with the ball in possession, drives through the opponents.

When the opponents have possession

☐ When you can see the ball, go for it and take it off the opponent.

☐ When the ball is protected:
- try to turn the ball-carrier so that the ball is on your side, your first team-mate then goes for the ball and your next two team-mates isolate the ball-carrier;
- tackle the ball-carrier so that he goes to ground - once down, he has to release the ball - and your first team-mate then drives over the ball.

☐ When a maul is formed around the opposing ball-carrier:
- go in from behind directly opposite the ball;
- bind; and
- together with your team-mates, push the maul back.

When do you drive with the ball and when do you form a ruck or maul?

General

☐ Your objectives are:
- to take the ball as quickly as possible through the weak spot(s) in the defence; and
- to keep speed on the ball.

☐ The ball-carrier usually has three choices:
- The first choice is to drive. As long as he can move forward with the ball, he does so. Before the ball is blocked, he passes to a team-mate, who comes in fast from behind.
- While he is still moving forward, he places the ball on the ground and his team-mates go over it fast in ruck formation. The aim is that the ruck will draw the opponents in; then, using a quick pass to a forward, he begins another drive. Alternatively, the ball is fed to the back-line who usually execute a blind side movement.
- If he is stopped, he retains possession and he becomes the first player in a maul. If your mauling technique is good, it is a safer way of retaining possession, although the ball usually reaches the back-line more slowly.

To summarise

☐ If the ball is in front of the forwards, the choice sequence is:
- a drive; or
- a ruck or
- maul.

☐ If the ball is behind the forwards, the choice is:
- if there is enough time, play to the sides; or
- if there is not enough time, get control by means of a maul.

The above is explained in detail in the chapter on decision-making.

9. Problems and solutions: the back-line

It's as difficult as we make it

Passing
Most players know how to pass. The problem, however, is:
☐ When?
- Rather too soon than too late.
☐ What direction?
- Towards your team's speed.
- Away from cover defence.
- To the outside (with an ordinary or skip pass).
- To the inside (with a scissors pass, back pass or back-flip).
☐ What length? (in broken play).
- Short when you are among a lot of players.
- Long across the width of the field when you have breached the first line of defence.

Tips
☐ Keep the passes short (a long pass tends to force the receiver diagonally across the field), except where it is necessary to do otherwise in the case of a tactical manoeuvre.
☐ Pass the ball slightly in front of the receiver:
- Between shoulder and hip-height. Every ball passed at or behind the receiver's body means a loss of 3 m to 5 m for the wing as well as the loss of a potential try. When the ball is too far in front of the receiver, on the other hand, you limit the possibilities of what he can do with it.
☐ A quick pass is preferable to a hard pass; it gives the receiver time to sum up the situation ahead of him.
- Keep the torpedo pass for skipping; use the softer, lob-type passes for rainy weather.

Forwards remember:
- Keep your passes shorter; lean slightly forward with your upper body and turn your shoulder slightly to the side the pass is going; a slight pushing action is usually involved.

Ball receiver:
☐ The receiver's approach to handling should be to attack the ball (move onto the ball)!
- This makes it easier to run straight and corner the opponent in your attacking channel.
☐ Keep your elbows bent and shoulders turned slightly to the passer; catch the ball opposite the shoulder on the side the ball is coming from (in practice, your left hand will be just in front of your right shoulder if the ball comes from the right).

Observing
Observing enables you to beat your opponent even before you have the ball.

To improve a player's vision on the field of play must be one of the coach's main targets. In rugby this does not happen naturally as it does in soccer and hockey. In soccer and hockey you can pass the ball in any direction. The players are forced to scan the field for the open spaces. Rugby players are not allowed to pass forward and are more inclined to look sideways, to where they are passing.
☐ Before you have the ball, ask yourself the following questions:
- Where are you on the field?
- From which set piece are you playing (a scrum, line-out, etc)?
- Where is your opponent? Is he on your inside? The chances of beating him on his outside are good (with a move or dummy scissors with your outside player, who gives you a big outside gap). Is he on your outside? The chances of beating him on his inside are good (take a short pass from your inside player at the last moment or do scissors with your inside player, who comes across very diagonally).
☐ When you have the ball, you must keep an eye on what is happening in front of you so that you can quickly react to the defenders, e.g., with a dummy pass when your immediate opponent moves up too fast and too wide in defence (if a player does not see a gap, he will not take it!).

Alignment
☐ The normal (or pre-planned) position:
- Starting off from the correct position is a prerequisite for a successful movement (the movement determines the position; it requires self-discipline!).
- Mislead the opponents by standing in a different position before the time (take up the correct position only after the ball is in play, e.g., after it has been put into the scrum).
- *Remember:* The faster the players' hand speed, the shallower they can stand.
- Stand close together. The closer together the backs are, the easier it is to run into positions where they can support each other.
- Apply the following basic guideline: Back but not deep. (However, don't forget back-line play is about variation.)
☐ The unplanned movement:
- This occurs mostly during second-phase play or counter-attacks.

- Keep in mind simple guidelines like run off the ball according to the triangle principle and that obvious diagonal running is followed by straight running and short passes to the outside or inside (move onto the ball!).

Running

□ Direction:
- Run with your chest towards the opponents' goal-line.
- Straighten up before you have the ball (drift before the pass comes so that you can run straight into the ball again and through the gap; softer passes make this easier).

□ Run off the ball:
- If you cannot see the number on the back of the ball-carrier you are not in the correct position to receive the ball - otherwise there is always a risk of a forward pass (you can accelerate into the ball instead of slowing down so as not to be in front of the ball-carrier).
- After you have passed, take up position again immediately to support the ball-carrier on his inside (the ball-carrier can easily change the direction of play with an inside pass).

□ When you approach the opponent fast, he tends to come up in defence more slowly and vice versa. Bear this in mind when you attack the advantage line.

Variation

□ The opponents must be kept guessing about the length of the pass and the type of pass (e.g., is it going to be an ordinary or a skip pass?).

□ Vary the following:
- Passes: The direction and type (ordinary pass, skip, scissor or back pass, back-flip, etc).
- Starting positions: Along the length (stand deep and take the ball shallow); across the width (move closer or further across the width before the pass); blind and open side (stand open side and take the ball blind side); etc.
- Running: Speed play (deliberate, obviously slowing down the pace before you accelerate quickly; direction (sidestep and swerve); a combination of the two (a sidestep by the inside centre before he accelerates to take a short pass from the fly-half).
- Kicks: For territory (into open spaces); to exert pressure (up and unders); to regain possession (chip kicks or grubbers).
- Tactical manoeuvres: Wide to the outside; to centre field; close to set play; blind side.

Advantages of aligning flat in attack

□ Your opponent approaches you faster (thus he is committed to the tackle. He cannot shift on the defence to cover your team-mate on thc outside).

□ Your opponent approaches you in a straighter line (it is also easier for the attacker to run straight: the flatter the pass, the straighter the run).

□ You can catch and pass faster (this is particularly important for the pass from fly-half to inside centre).

□ When you cut their line of defence out of this shallow position, the opponents' second and third lines of defence are severely stretched.

The different passes

Ordinary pass

Tips

GENERAL (ELEMENTARY) METHOD

□ First use your eyes, then your hands!

□ Your forearms should play the key role when you are passing.

□ Go for the ball with:
- a stop hand (your left hand when the ball comes from the right; see p. 48); and
- a control hand (your right hand when the ball comes from the right).

□ Drop your forearms slightly when passing:
- The speed stays on the ball.
- You do not have to pull the ball back before passing - use your forearms (the ultimate aim should be to keep the pass on the same level).

□ Keep your elbows just above hip-height against your body at the top of your pants:
- to facilitate and speed up the pass.

□ Advantages:
- It is a simple and rhythmical movement.
- It is ideal in wet weather.

□ Disadvantages:
- The ball cannot be passed a long distance.

TORPEDO PASS USING YOUR WRISTS

□ First use your eyes, then your hands!

□ The same catching action as explained above is recommended.

□ There is a big difference in the passing action:
- There is a wrist action with both hands in the direction of the pass.
- The top hand puts spin on the ball (with a rolling movement from the little finger to the thumb).

□ Advantages:
- It is excellent for long passes (skips).
- It is easier to control in windy conditions.

□ Disadvantages:
- Difficult to execute with slippery hands in wet weather.
- You easily pass too hard and force the receiver/catcher to run across the field.

Skip pass

Objectives

□ To beat the opponent with the speed of the ball across the width - not the depth - of the field. In a planned skip, starting positions are important.

SKIP PASSES

FLY-HALF TO FULL-BACK

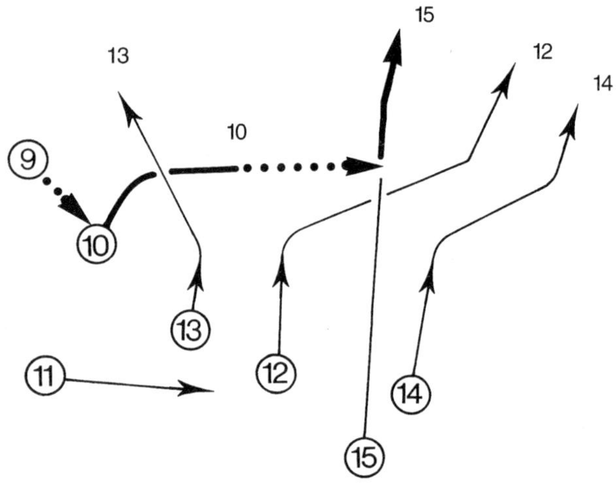

☐ To get the ball past the point of pressure when the player on your outside would, with a normal pass, get the man and the ball at the same time.

Requirements
☐ Don't skip pass when the opponents are far away because they will have enough time to drift across to the receiver.
☐ Don't skip pass in depth for the same reason as above.

Examples
☐ When the fly-half runs with the ball from a scrum, he skips his inside centre because, by running, he uses up space and puts his inside centre under pressure.
☐ When the fly-half is stationary and the inside centre runs with the ball, the outside centre is skipped. Here it is the inside centre who uses up space and the outside centre who is under pressure.
☐ The same principles apply to back-lineplay from the line-out. Exceptions are, however, possible for tactical reasons, e.g.:
- The fly-half can remain stationary and skip his inside centre when he wants to get the ball quickly to the outside backs. He probably has more players there than the opponents (his full-back and blind-side wing).

Long or short pass

General
☐ The wrong decisions result in the following:
- interceptions;
- forward momentum being stopped; and
- potential tries being lost.

Tips

SHORT PASS
☐ In broken play, when the players of the two teams are

SHORT PASSING

FLY-HALF TO INSIDE CENTRE

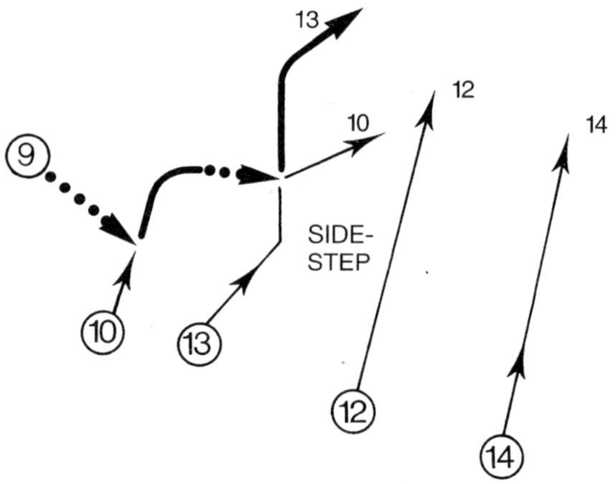

intermingled, preferably a short pass in depth, to a player who is coming fast from behind.
☐ In wet weather, a pass to a player who is running straight.
☐ When the opponents' defence is focused on the outside field, beat them on the inside.
☐ To join your forwards more easily.
☐ When forwards start to drive with the ball.

SHORT PASSING

FLY-HALF TO FULL-BACK

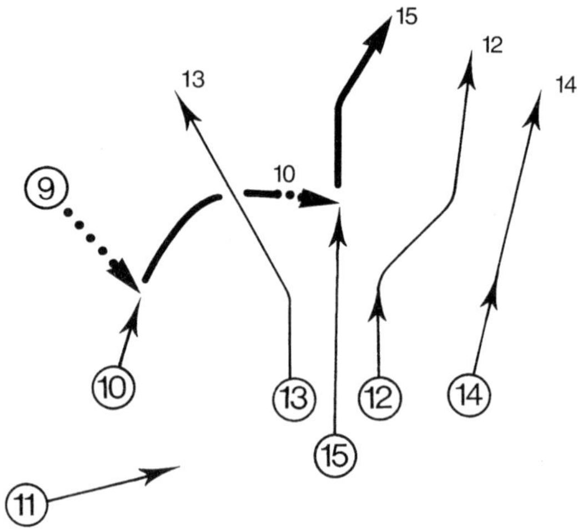

LONG PASS
☐ When the defence close to the set play (scrum, line-out, ruck, maul) is strong.
☐ After one of the backs has broken through at the tackle-line:
- get the ball to where your team can move it fastest (this is usually the wing); or
- get the ball away from cover or cross-defence.

□ Examples: When the fly-half breaks the line, the ball quickly goes as far as the second-last player, who eliminates the last defender. (If the full-back is in front of him, he first draws the full-back and then passes to the outside; if the full-back is not in front of him, he passes to the outside immediately.)

Scissors pass

General

□ When the opposing back-line lies very flat and/or comes up quickly on defence; or
- against a shift-defensive pattern; and
- in general, when the opponents come up quickly on defence.

□ The ball-carrier:
- moves diagonally across the field;
- keeps his eye on the receiver; and
- passes as late as possible, preferably when his opponent is already in the process of tackling him and therefore can no longer stop the receiver.

SCISSORS PASS

FLY-HALF TO INSIDE CENTRE

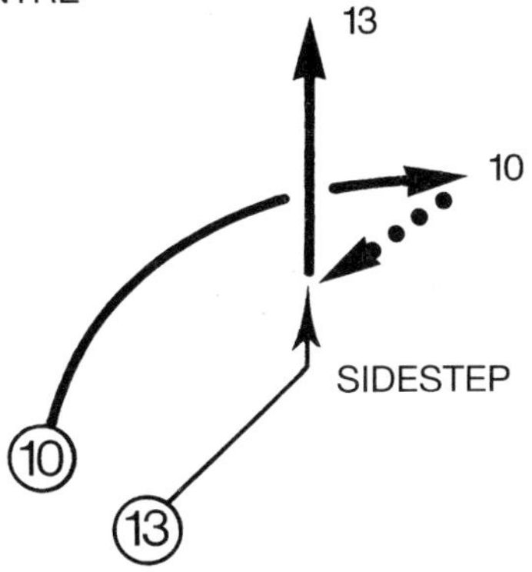

□ The receiver:
- stands slightly deeper (the opponent does not easily see this from the front but he does if you stand wide);
- moves diagonally across the field with the ball-carrier and in this way misleads his direct opponent;
- straightens with a sidestep (with his chest to the goal-line), i.e., he speeds up;
- times it in such a way that he gets the ball slightly deep and can still react to something unexpected;
- goes straight through the gap because this is the shortest route and the gap is open for only a split second; and
- moves slightly to the outside as soon as he is through the gap, away from the cover defence, which makes it easier for the rest of the back-line to link up again.

Common mistakes

□ The ball-carrier:
- runs too straight and does not open the gap or eliminate his opponent;
- passes too soon and forces the receiver to run to the inside (the movement usually ends at the scrum, etc., where it began); or
- passes to the wrong side and the receiver momentarily loses sight of the ball: to pass in this way the ball-carrier has to turn his upper body, completely exposing his ribs to a tackle.
- executes the move too deep behind the advantage line enabling the opponents to see what is coming. If the ball carrier is tackled his loose forwards are at a disadvantage.

□ The receiver:
- stands too wide and flat and has to run diagonally to the inside;
- moves off too soon and has to run diagonally to the inside;
- runs straight from the start; thus the opponents can detect what is coming and prepare themselves for it;
- does not concentrate on the ball; or
- does not move out after he is through the gap.

Back pass (or inside pass)

INSIDE PASSING

CENTRE TO FULL-BACK

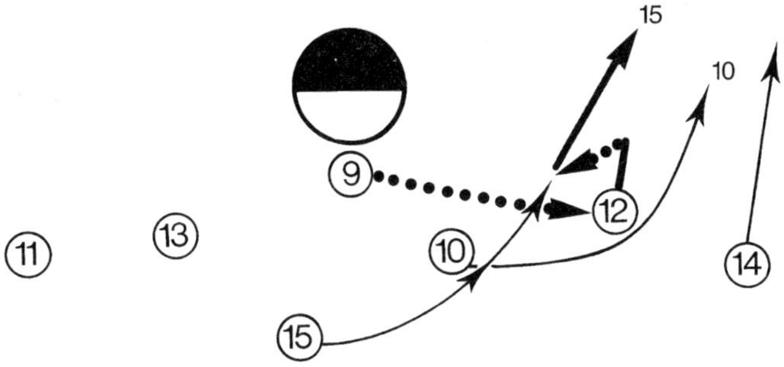

INSIDE CENTRE TO BLIND-SIDE WING

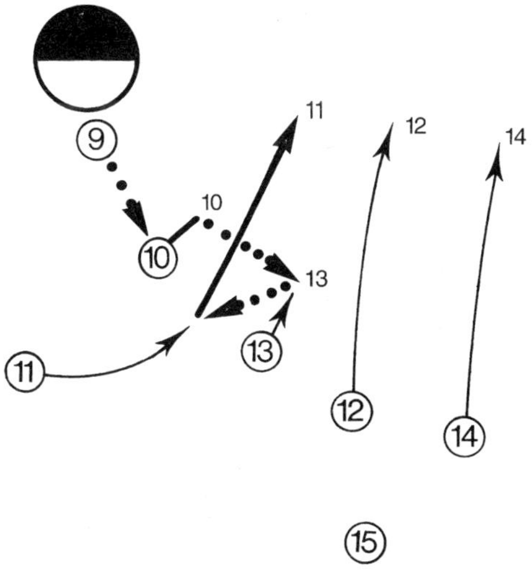

SCISSORS PASS

FLY-HALF TO OUTER-CENTRE

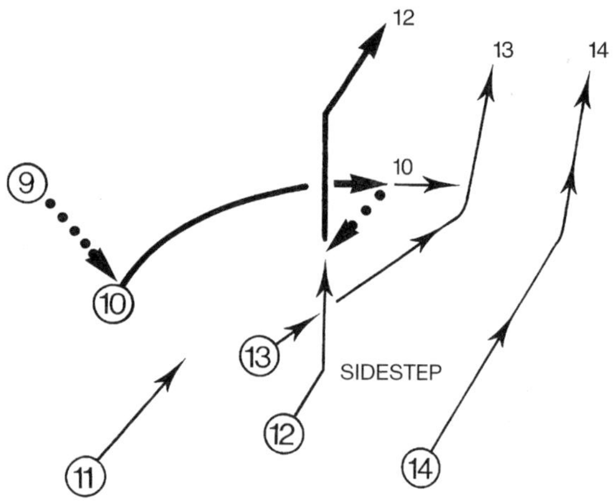

Objectives

☐ To keep the ball in play and prevent yourself from crossing the touch-line with the ball.

☐ To keep speed on the ball and prevent the opponents from isolating you with the ball so that a ruck/maul eventually develops.

☐ To beat the cover or cross-defence, usually on the inside.

WHEN TO USE INSIDE OR SWITCH PASS

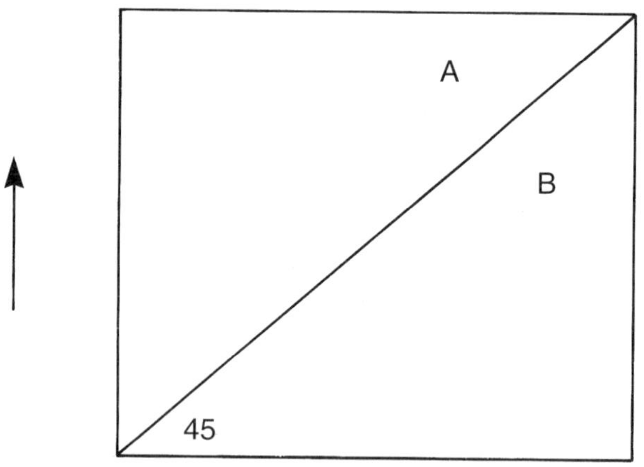

As long as the ball-carrier is running in *triangle A,* he can give an inside pass

When he is in *triangle B* he must use the switch pass due to his angle of running

Prerequisites

☐ Support on the inside:
- from deep; and
- with speed according to the triangle principle.

☐ Do not run more diagonally than 45°. In the case of the ordinary back pass it becomes increasingly difficult the more diagonally you move away from the direction you want to pass to. At some point, you will only be able to use a one-handed pass.

The role of the halves in the team

Their main tasks are:

☐ to make sure that the team:
- plays forward (every time a movement ends, the halves must look to see whether the team has moved closer to the opponents' goal-line); and
- scores;

☐ to keep the opposing forwards guessing; they therefore have to decide where the team can play most effectively:
- open side; or
- blind side:

☐ should the team make use of:
- backs;
- loose forwards; or
- kicks.

Remember: The backs and forwards should play in such a way that they keep one another in the game!

The above-mentioned decisions are determined by:

☐ Scrum dominance:
- Now you can depend on a great deal of help from the loose forwards (use your loose forwards to run at their backs from the scrum, leaving your back-line free to round off the attack).
- The opponents' loose forwards gradually fade away as the match develops (the opposing cover defence slowly weakens).
- Be ready for counter-attacks from tight-head possession.

☐ Line-out dominance:
- Play to the touch-line because you regain possession.
- Because the opponents' loose forwards know their team is being beaten in the line-outs, they deliberately remain outside. Throw in to the back of the line-out to draw them in. Attack wide with the back-line after a dummy move back to the forwards, e.g., a dummy scissor between the fly-half and inside centre with a skip to the outside or full-back in the back-line (take the defending loose forward out of the game).

☐ Tight-loose dominance:
- Deliberately create second-phase play.
- Be prepared to use possession lost by the opposition (turn-overs).
- Because the opponents' loose forwards are drawn in, weak spots develop in their defence immediately next to the tight-loose. The halves can break! Hit the weak spots with tactical play, e.g., with a loose forward who specially stays out of the tight-loose for that purpose.

☐ Weaknesses in the opponents' team:
- General (set play) (see pp. 53-54); and
- as individuals. Here the issue is any weaknesses in the players themselves. These are usually pointed out before

the match. Be on the lookout, however, for opportunities that may arise during the match as a result of injuries!

☐ Alignment:

Remember: Keep an eye on the opponents' wings and full-back (especially when it is a scrum).

- Open-side wing deep: The weak spot is wide on the open side.
- Open-side wing shallow: Attack centre field with cutting movements, put an extra man in the back-line (the full-back, blind-side wing or loose forward) or combine a dummy movement with an extra man.
- Blind-side wing shallow: Kick to the weak spot behind the scrum in the box (scrum-half: a chip kick behind the blind-side wing; fly-half runs to the open side and changes direction with a kick back into the box behind the blind-side wing).
- Blind-side wing deep: The weak spot on the blind side close to the scrum creates an opportunity for shallow play to the blind side (e.g., the scrum-half to the blind-side wing, the eighth-man to the scrum-half, the scrum-half to the loose-head flank, who has broken up and gets the ball to the right of the scrum - the right blind side).

Remember: When the blind-side wing is uncertain, it not only creates possibilities for attack but also influences the positional play of both the full-back and the open-side wing.

☐ Sudden changes from tight play:

☐ Scrum:

- Wheeling: In general, play in the same direction as the wheel. Play against the wheel is, however, possible. When the eighth-man flicks the ball to the scrum-half (2 m to 3 m back).

☐ Line-out:

- If the throw-in does not reach the predetermined point, make tactical adjustments immediately. When the line-out moves out of the line-out offside lines, be first to play according to the requirements of the maul.

☐ Tight-loose:

- The determining factor is the speed at which the ball comes back from the forwards. Play first quickly in the same direction as the previous movement. The fly-half must, however, look where gaps may develop. If the ball

DEFENCE: WEAKNESS IN ALIGNMENT

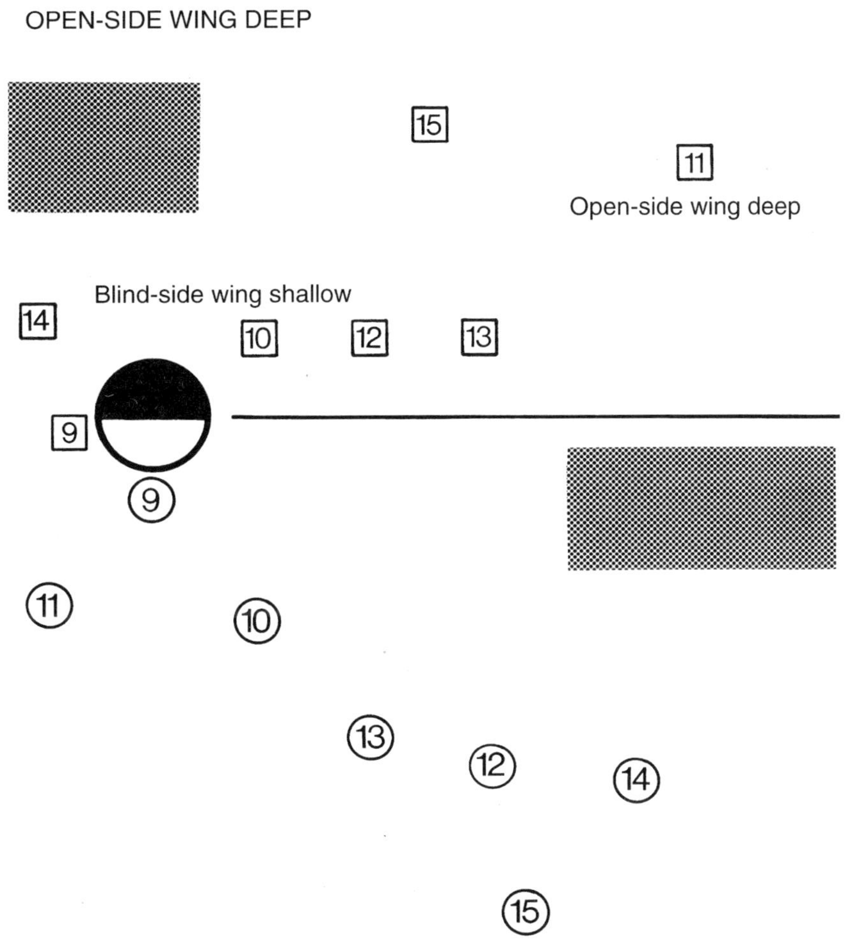

N.B. The fly-half always checks where the opposition's wings and full-back are before he decides on tactical moves

DEFENCE: WEAKNESS IN ALIGNMENT

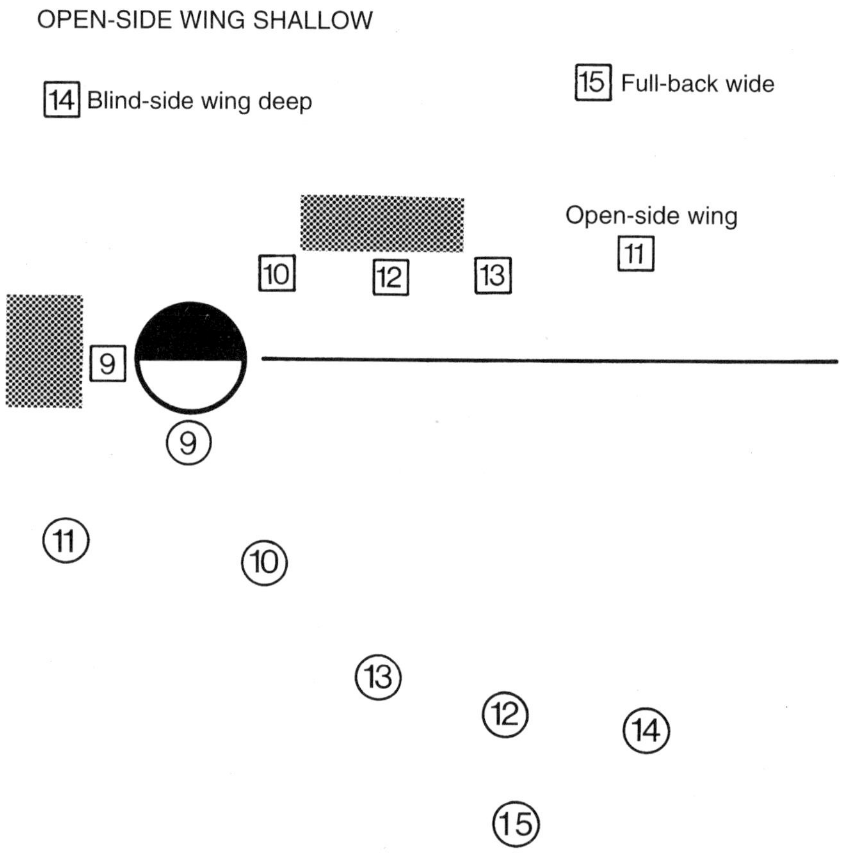

N.B. The fly-half always checks where the opposition's wings and full-back are before he decides on tactical moves

emerges slowly a change of direction is possible.

☐ Your task can be greatly facilitated by:
- the full-back, who has a good view of the game; and
- the players, who keep their eye on their direct opponents for individual weaknesses and errors in positioning.

Remember: When there are no weaknesses in the opponents' positioning, the high up-and-under remains the best way to create uncertainty.

The halves stay under pressure

Possible causes

Scrum possession

☐ The scrum is under pressure and/or the ball stays in the scrum too long.
- Play the fast ball (channel 1) and teach the hooker to strike the ball into the eighth-man's or scrum-half's hands (this is much easier when the eighth-man goes down between the left flanker and left lock).

☐ The eighth-man is inexperienced.
- He does not know how to control the ball and keeps it for an unnecessarily long time. He should push the ball with his left foot to the right side of the scrum to protect his scrum-half and he should go down between the loose-head flank and lock. Although this weakens the scrum, the scrum-half is better protected.
- He does not know what to do when the scrum moves back on the tight-head side. He should flick the ball with one hand back to the scrum-half, who should stand 2 m to 3 m away.

☐ The scrum-half gets into position too slowly for a standing pass.
- Get your feet in position!
- Make sure your front foot points to the fly-half; this determines the direction of the pass. In addition, your hands can now also move the shortest possible route to execute the pass.
- Give a long stride when you want to pass the ball quickly (except in the case of a wrist pass).

- Firstly keep your eyes on the ball in order to get it under immediate control.
- Look at a specific target to ensure a more accurate pass.
- Keep your chin down so that the ball does not travel too high or with a curve.
- In windy conditions use your wrists in a torpedo pass to obtain distance and accuracy.

☐ The fly-half does not create space for himself.
- He starts moving to the open side before the scrum-half even touches the ball and he starts running too soon. He should wait until the ball is travelling through the air, or move in the same direction as the ball, or remain stationary.
- He starts his move up to the blind side too late and too diagonally: thus the pressure is simply transferred to the next back. He should first move to the sideline and then shoot forward instead of trying to get into position diagonally across the field.
- He does not adjust his starting position according to the scrum-half's changed situation (e.g., after a wheeling scrum).

LINE-OUT POSSESSION

☐ The scrum-half's alignment is incorrect next to the jumper.
- If the ball now lands between him and the touch-line in collecting the ball, he first has to move away from the direction to which he wants to pass.
- He should therefore stand opposite the first prop and move with the throw-in so that the ball is always between him and the eighth-man.

☐ The scrum-half is comfortable passing only to one side.
- On his "uncomfortable" side, he first has to turn before he passes.

☐ Compared with the fly-half, the scrum-half is, in most cases, unprotected at the line-out.
- Rather than take the pressure himself, he should pass. The fly-half can usually do more with the ball. The fact that the scrum-half is under pressure does not mean the back-line is under pressure!

☐ The fly-half does not adjust his position to the place in the line-out where the ball is thrown.
- He should take the ball thrown to No. 4 and deeper in the line-out at least 5 m infield of the 15 m line. Here he has room to run. A ball won at the front of the line-out forces him to drift with the pass or even catch and pass it while remaining stationary. (Pressure from the loose forward at the back of the line-out.)

☐ The fly-half should remember that, from a line-out, the inside centre is the least under pressure.
- The fact that he as fly-half is under pressure does not mean the entire back-line is under pressure!

POSSESSION FROM THE RUCK OR MAUL

Most pressure occurs in the following cases:

☐ The halves play in the wrong direction.
- In the second phase after a scrum, ruck or maul: Play in the same direction as the previous movement of the scrum. If you played to the right of the scrum and retained quick possession, you immediately play to the right again from the next ruck - away from the cover defence!
- Second phase after a line-out gives you a choice: Play back blind side or further to the open side, very close to the ruck or maul or deep and wide with an extra man.

☐ The halves misjudge the type of the possession.
- Quick possession from second phase after a scrum, ruck or maul: Play fast and shallow in the same direction.
- Quick possession from second phase after a line-out: Play open side shallow (if you play back fast, the forwards are still in your way).
- Slower possession from second phase after a line-out: Play blind side.

IN WHICH DIRECTION TO PLAY

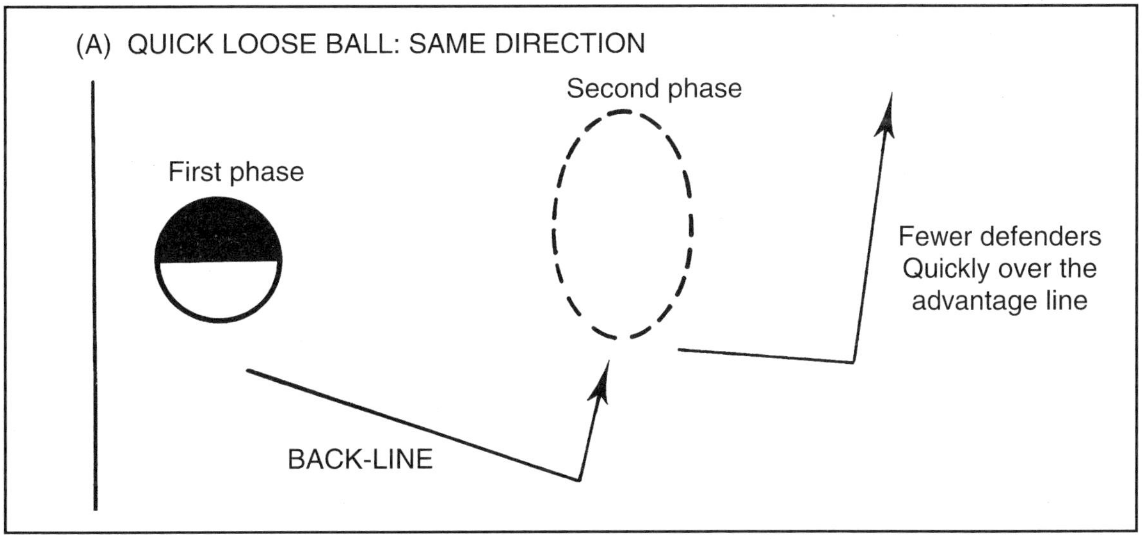

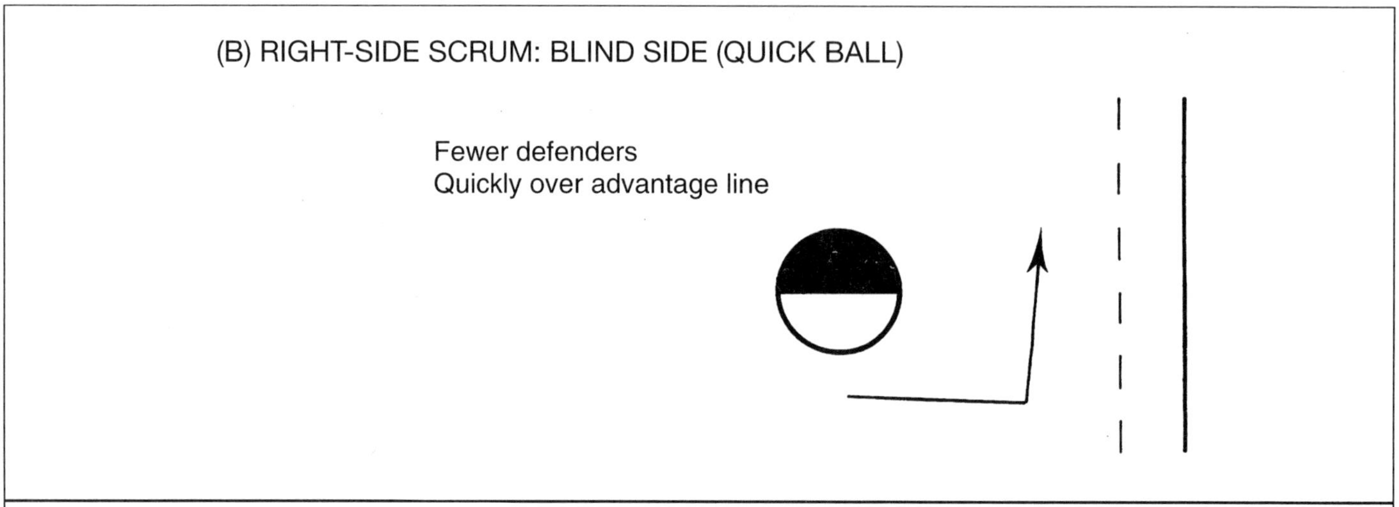

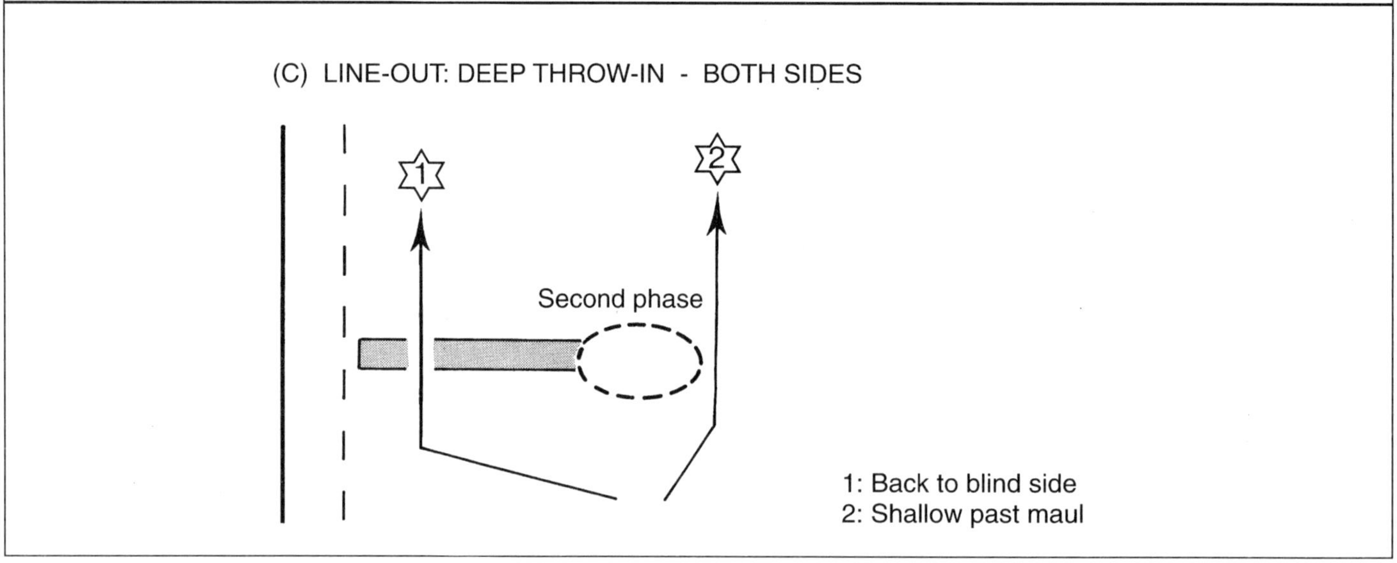

- Very slow possession from second phase after a line-out: Play as though you have scrum possession or deliberately set up a ruck or maul close to the forwards to first suck in the defenders before renewing the attack.

Remember: Halves often put themselves under pressure; they are mostly under less pressure than they imagine. Get the ball past yourself to the point where there is the least pressure. The inside centre is under the most pressure when the ball is won from a scrum and under the least pressure when it is won from a line-out.

The backs run across field

General

☐ Most players are not even aware that they run across field. A player who looks up when he runs with the ball will immediately see if he is running diagonally across the field.

☐ The correct starting position helps a player run straight. When the back (the fly-half or centres) stands in such a way that his stomach faces the scrum-half and his furthest foot is in front and points to the scrum-half, it is difficult for him to run diagonally across the field.

☐ A long, hard pass usually forces the receiver to run diagonally.

☐ If a player runs diagonally on the inside, the mistake is magnified to the outside if one of the outside players does not correct it. When a fly-half runs very diagonally, the inside centre either drops out of the back-line, or comes straight up for a short pass outside the fly-half or drops out of the back-line and comes straight up so that he can support deep on the inside of the fly-half. The same applies when an inside or outside centre runs diagonally. Straightening means running straight before you get the ball! The problem of running diagonally starts 99 per cent of the time with the fly-half and inside centre.

Solutions

Scrum possession

FLY-HALF'S STARTING POSITION

☐ The worst place the fly-half can stand is behind the scrum. From here he is forced to run diagonally. In this case he should rather remain stationary when he receives and passes the ball.

☐ If you are 5 m to 6 m from the side of the scrum and quite shallow (4 m to 5 m behind the eighth-man's feet):
- Remain stationary.
- Drift in the same direction as the scrum-half's pass when you receive the ball. (Pass to the inside centre and keep running until you are behind the outside centre.)
- Take the Wallaby pass made famous by Mark Ella and Michael Lynagh.
☐ If you are 5 m to 6 m from the side of the scrum and 8 m to 10 m deep:
- Run into the pass in the normal way and then pass.
- Remember the position of your body (stomach and feet!) so that you run as straight as possible.

INSIDE CENTRE
☐ He should know beforehand whether the fly-half is going to:
- remain stationary; or
- run, and in which direction.
☐ He then determines exactly where he is going to receive the ball. For this he gets a target beforehand towards which he can run as straight as possible. In practice, he generally runs diagonally for about a metre.
Remember: When the inside centre runs straight, the attacking full-back comes into his own!

Line-out possession

FLY-HALF'S STARTING POSITION
☐ Possession at the front of the line-out (think about the pressure exerted by loose forwards) force him to:
- run diagonally; or
- remain stationary and pass; or
- run in the same direction as the pass to save space and to cover or support behind the outside centre like Barry John and Phil Bennett of Wales so often did.
☐ Possession from the middle of the line-out and deeper should, provided he is in the right starting position (stomach and feet!), cause him to run relatively straight.

INSIDE CENTRE
☐ As in the case of the scrum, he should know exactly what the fly-half is going to do. He then makes sure he runs in such a way that he straightens up before he receives the ball.

Ruck or maul

OPEN SIDE
Bear the basic laws for scrum possession in mind.

BLIND SIDE (THIS ALSO APPLIES FROM THE SCRUM)
☐ The scrum-half's pass should be as flat as possible and the fly-half:
- crosses the advantage line fast; and
- beats the opponents' loose forwards more easily.
☐ The fly-half first moves sideways towards touch and then accelerates straight into the pass. He straightens before he receives the ball. A common error is for the fly-half to get the ball while still behind a set play, causing him to run diagonally. He then tries to straighten with a swing pass (hip-sink pass). This enables the defenders to shift out towards the outside.

The ball does not reach the wings

Factors to bear in mind

The ball usually reaches the left wing more easily
Most players are right-handed and pass more easily to the left.

The contact lines of set play (the scrum, line-out, maul and ruck)
☐ This line will vary according to the set pieces and will determine the space the backs have in front of them.
☐ Where is the contact line to be found?
- In the scrum and in slow possession from the ruck and maul it is very much on your side of the advantage line.
- In the line-out, the contact line is considerably closer to the advantage line. The back-lines are 20 m apart - in practice they are closer! (It depends on where the ball is thrown into the line-out. The deeper the ball is thrown, the closer the contact line is to the advantage line.)
- Blind side of the scrum: the contact line is even closer to the advantage line.
- In the case of quick possession from the ruck and maul, if you play in the same direction as you were before making contact, it is virtually at the advantage line.

Mark out the contact lines on the field so that the players can see where the ball should reach the wing.

The backs' alignment/starting position
☐ The better the handling skills, the shallower the players can align (thus the easier for the forwards to link up with the backs).
☐ Scrum-half:
- Can he pass to either side equally fast or only to one side? In respect of his "wrong" hand, he first has to turn before he passes.
☐ Fly-half:
- When he takes up a flat position, does he run forward in the usual way before he passes (instead of remaining stationary and passing or running in the same direction as the scrum-half's pass), i.e., is he using up all the space himself instead of protecting the space available to his fellow backs?
- When he wants to run forward himself, does he create space by standing deeper?
- A more difficult but effective option for him is the Wallaby pass (he moves two to three steps forward before he receives the ball, draws the opponent and passes the ball the moment he receives it.)

CONTACT LINES: SCRUM

1. OPEN SIDE: The further from the scrum, the further the contact line is from the advantage line

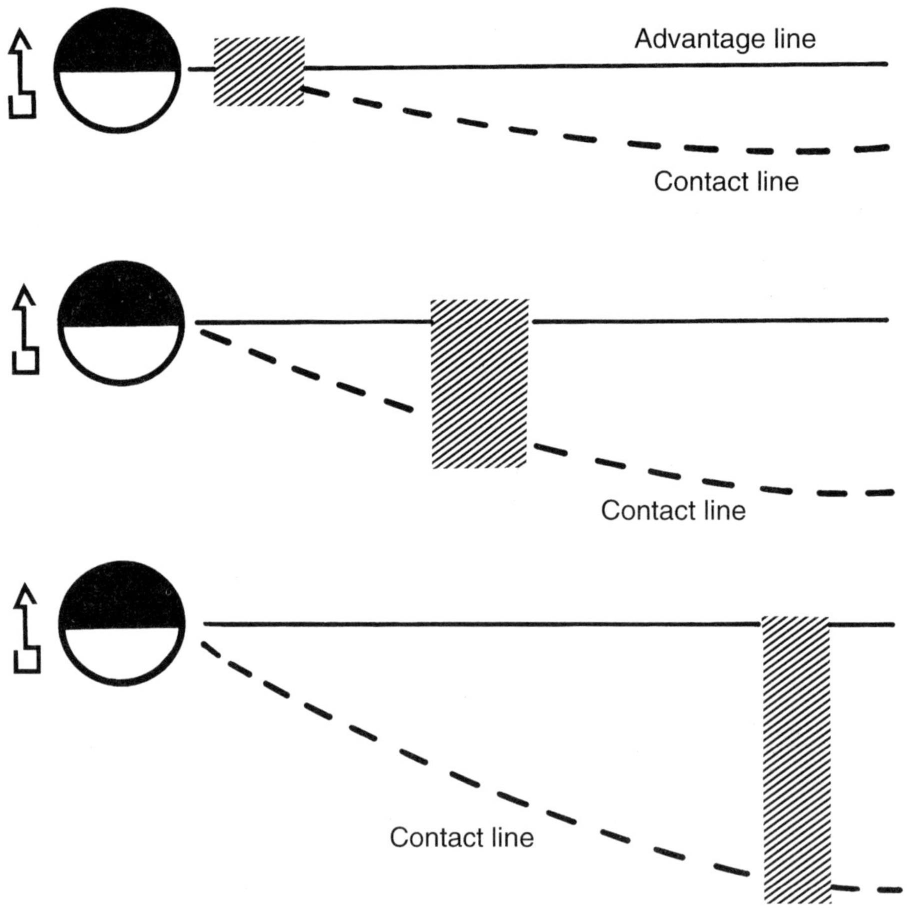

2. BLIND SIDE: Here the contact line is close to the advantage line – especially on the right

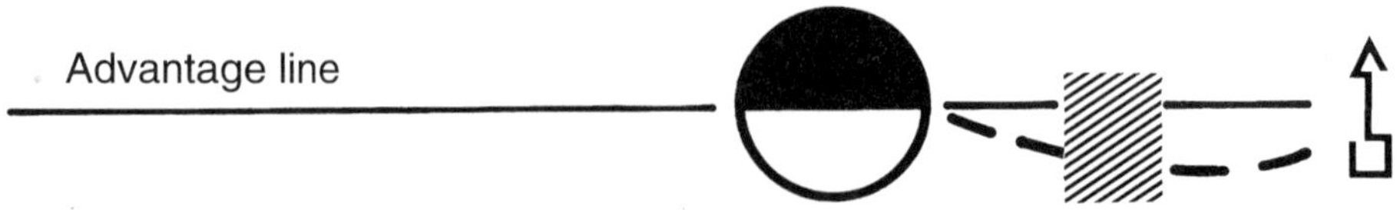

☐ Inside centre, outside centre or wing:
- Does he take up his position in such a way that his inside players can give him a deep pass?

When do the backs start running?

☐ Generally:
- Every back should concentrate only on the team-mate from whom he is to receive the ball (not on the scrum-half).
- The take-off is determined by the distance the backs are from the contact line, i.e., how much space they have in front of them. The further the contact line on their side of the advantage line, the later they take off.

□ From the scrum, the delayed take off:
- The fly-half sets off only when the ball is already coming towards him.
- The inside centre starts running a moment after the fly-half.
- The outside centre sets off a moment after the inside centre.
- The wing starts running a moment after the outside centre.
□ From the other set plays, take off is faster and depends on the contact line.

Where do the players pass the ball to?
□ Every back passes the ball just in front of the receiver.
- A common mistake is to pass too shallow (usually a soft lob pass) when the receiver is standing deep.

What if the ball is delayed somewhere in the line?
□ Only slightly:
- Because of a bad pass: Follow this immediately with a skip to neutralise the delay.
□ Considerably:
- When the eighth-man first has to pick up the ball: Again, introduce a skip pass to compensate for the delay.
- When a player has to slow down almost completely to get the ball under control: Do not pass the ball - rather push it through with a grubber to the outside backs, or with an up-and-under placed behind the opponents' back-line (i.e., convert the error on your side into pressure on the opponents) or deliberately creates second phase.

Easy ways of getting the ball to the wing
□ The fly-half remains stationary when he catches and passes the ball.
□ The inside centre passes to the wing with a skip.
□ The players play to the left (because passing to the left is slicker for right-handed players, which is what most players are).

The players' attempts at launching counter-attacks fail

The counter-attack depends on attitude, handling, support, time and space, individual skills and the right decisions about where to attack.

Attitude
Believe every ball you gain from the opposition is a potential try. Every player should also have confidence in his abilities and those of his team-mates and not hesitate after he has started a counter-attack.

Handling
The expression "a handling mistake is a gift try for the opponents" applies to both teams. The speed at which the ball is handled is also often decisive.

Support of the ball
□ Deep: Someone must ensure that the ball is moved forward at speed. This creates space - and gaps - and the opportunity to switch direction, especially if the defence isn't disciplined.

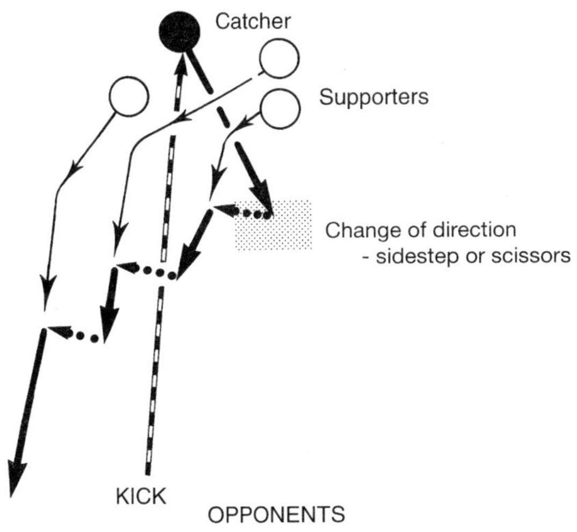

□ Across the width of the field: To beat the defence - when there is no pressure across the width of the field - with the speed of the ball. The first two passes are usually long and flat, thereafter the ball is moved forward at speed.

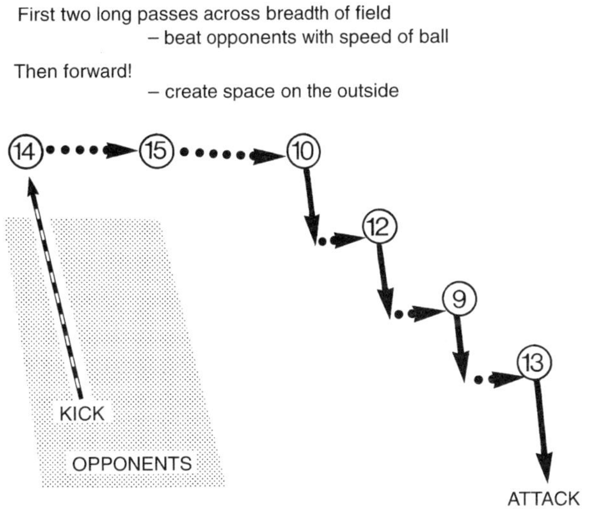

Time and space
□ Time is necessary so that:
- the player can begin a counter-attack. The time needed varies according to the situation of the player, his team-mates and the opponents. Provided the support is there,

the split second that is necessary to pass a ball is sufficient;
- the other players can drop back to run off the ball and help with the counter-attack. The easiest counter-attack to stop is the one where the ball-carrier has to run forward appreciably before he can link with a team-mate.
☐ Space is sometimes necessary so that:
- the player who begins a counter-attack can decide where to attack or keep the opponents busy or mislead them until he has sufficient support.

Individual skills
The sidestep, the dummy pass and speed create more opportunities for a counter-attack by the full-back and wings. (The 1973 match between the All Blacks and the Barbarians illustrates this excellently.)

The right decisions about where to attack
A counter-attack can fail simply because the first player makes the wrong decision or the supporters do not run themselves into position in time.

Tips on making the right decision
☐ Ball against the touch-line (see p. 30):
- No pressure in centre field: Attack across the width.
- Pressure in centre field: Dummy attack to midfield followed by switch back toward touch-line, otherwise immediately attacks to the blind side. The try that won the Wallabies the 1991 World Cup was started off by Tim Horan in this way.
- Pressure across the width of the field: Only players with exceptional individual skills like a sidestep and dummy pass can begin a counter-attack.
☐ Ball in centre field:
- On which side is the most pressure? Play to the other side. First make a dummy move towards the pressure point and then play away to the other side.
- On which side is the most support? Play to that side.
- Everything equal? Let your backs attack their forwards (it is usually easier to run at forwards than at backs).
☐ Facilitate the choice:
- Recreate the different situations in practices and drill the entire team in how to handle them.

Hints on counter-attacks

When the opponents kick
☐ The catcher usually knows where he is on the field but his team-mates can help him by shouting, e.g.:
- You have time!
- Play safe!
- Time, centre field open!
- Time, centre field pressure!
- Time, go forward!

From tackles (see p. 29)
☐ If there are quite a lot of defenders in front of you:
- Get the ball under control.
- The first player picks or flicks up the ball for the second player. If you pick up the ball and try to run yourself, you slow the game down and give the defenders time to get to the ball.
- The second player comes from deep and runs past the player with the ball within 1 m to his left or right through the gap.
- If you get the ball behind the last defender and there are no more defenders at the back:
- The first player kicks the ball through so that all the defenders have to turn around.
- The other players, who follow up fast, play on.

From knock-ons (see p. 29)
☐ The first player gets the ball under control.
- If he is still among the other players, he does the same as in the case of a tackle.
- If he is behind the defenders, he immediately tries to move towards the goal-line as fast as possible and/or plays the ball away from the cover defence.
- An easy option when a centre or full-back, coming into the line, drops the ball, is to immediately attack to the blind side.

Interceptions
☐ Here the key factor is the direction in which the player who intercepts is running.
☐ There is a vast difference between intercepting a pass running towards your own goal-line and running towards the opposition's goal-line.
☐ If you are running towards your own goal-line:
- You will immediately find yourself under pressure.
- Pass the ball away from pressure across the width of the field and mount a counter attack close to the other touch-line. The try is usually scored against the opposite touch-line from where you've intercepted the ball.
☐ If you are running toward the opponents' goal-line:
- Shoot away on the shortest route to the goal-line. If the opposition catches up with you and you do not have support, kick the ball towards the goal-line.
- If you are headed off or hauled in on your side of half-way and you have support close by, pass the ball in time and stay close!
☐ If you are headed off in the opponents' half and you do not have support close by, kick the ball towards the goal area for yourself. If you do have support close by, keep the ball alive at all costs.
Remember: Most counter-attacks originate with the full-back and wings and are then taken further by the rest of the team.

10. Tactical manoeuvres

We can do anything we want if we stick to it long enough

Approach

☐ This is an essential and challenging part of the game.
☐ It can change the course of a match.
☐ Tactical manoeuvres are not gimmicks!
☐ To be effective
- they should be aimed at specific weak points which may vary according to the opponents;
- try to get your forwards running onto their back-line players.

☐ Every player must understand the concept of the contact/tackle-line:
- It is on the attackers' side of the advantage line.
- It is far behind the advantage line when you play wide.
- It is closer to the advantage line when you play shallow or blind side.
- The further back it is, the more difficulty the forwards have getting into the game (except if they know where the point of contact is going to be).

☐ There is a specific spot on the field for every movement from where it succeeds more easily. Practise it there:
- first only with the players who take direct part in the movement:
- then with the team members who have to support if something goes wrong;
- first without opponents;
- then only with those opponents who must be outmanoeuvred during the movement; and
- finally against the full team.

☐ The movement must be simplified as much as possible for every player:
- Teach each individual player to concentrate only on his part of the movement, e.g., only on the team-mate from whom he receives the ball instead of the whole movement (this sharpens his timing).

☐ The sequence in which a movement is usually executed is:
- first the surprise movement; and
- then the dummy movement.

☐ If something goes wrong after a movement has been called but before it is executed:
- the movement is dropped; and
- the individual players immediately make adjustments.

☐ Every tactical manoeuvre must be covered because a player can make a mistake; a team is most vulnerable when it attacks.

Weak spots in defence

General

All teams have specific weak spots in their defence due to the nature of the game and due to the physical abilities and skills of the players. We are looking at the weaknesses from the point of view of the attacking team.

Scrum

☐ It is easier to attack the right side of a scrum because:
- there are fewer defenders; the scrum-half stands on the left side with his opponent;
- the attackers can cross the advantage line and bring their forwards into the game more easily; it is difficult for the left flank to defend there (he is often too late to see what the scrum-half is going to do; since he has to push in the scrum, he is not in a good position to stop the scrum-half behind his forwards); and
- it is important that the ball comes through the scrum fast.

☐ There are more opportunities for attack from a centre scrum because:
- there is quite a lot of space;
- you have support since you are playing close to your forwards;
- you can play to the left and right (this has the same advantages as mentioned above); and
- you can use changes in direction (e.g., the eighth-man passes to the right to the scrum-half, who passes to the centre left of the scrum, or the scrum-half passes to the right to the fly-half, who passes to the left to the full-back).

☐ In the case of a scrum close to the touch line:
- the weak spot is wide provided the open side wing stands deeper than his centres.

☐ In the case of a wheeling scrum:
- the weak spot is within a metre of the eighth-man in the direction the scrum is wheeling.

Line-out

The place where the ball is thrown in chiefly determines where the weak spot will be:

☐ In the front of the line-out: The defenders at the front of the line-out do not have much room to manoeuvre, except the hooker. (Can he stop a heavy forward(s) peeling off at full-speed?) It is easy to support at that point, because your supporters are close by and usually know about the attack beforehand.

INSIDE PASSES MIDFIELD: SCRUM ON THE RIGHT

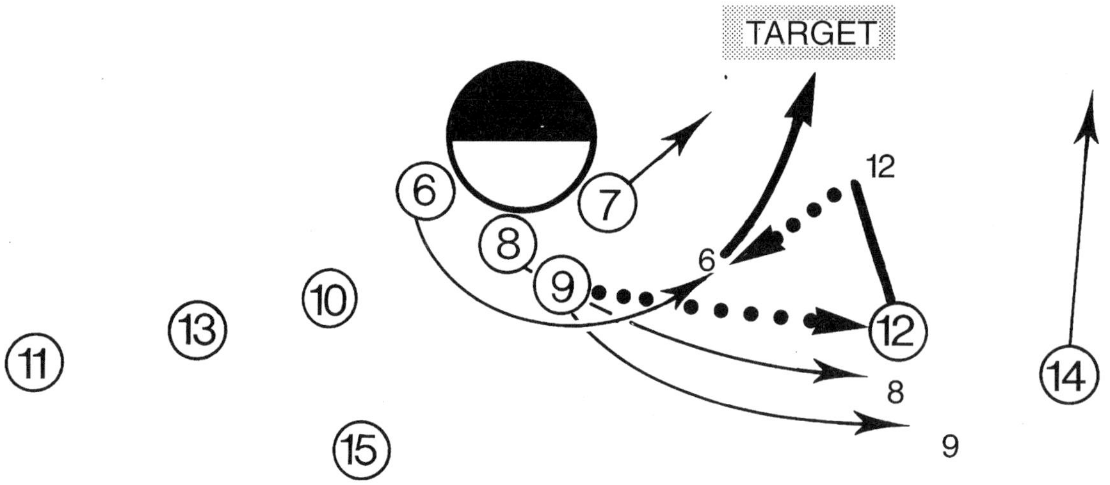

EXTRA SUPPORT TO THE RIGHT

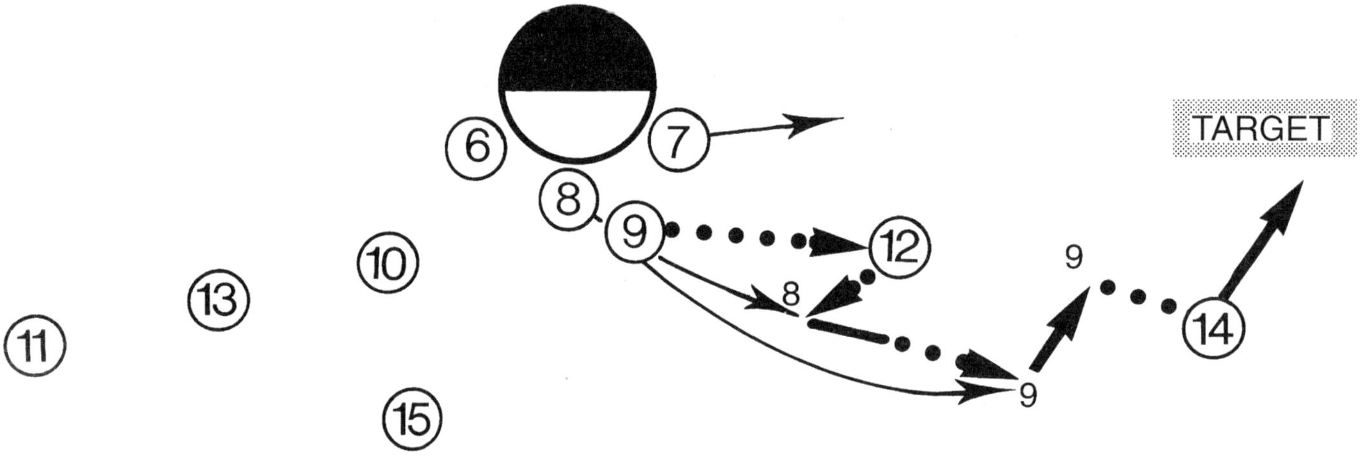

☐ In the middle of the line-out: Here the weak spot is directly opposite the catcher in the case of a push drive. The defence is spread out across the width of the line-out and cannot resist a sudden, concentrated push in the middle. (The same can be done near the goal-line at the front of the line-out.)

☐ At the back of the line-out: The weak point is within 3 m to 5 m immediately behind the line-out. The defenders at the back go for the ball and those at the front often go back too slowly.

☐ Behind over the top of the line-out: In this case the weak spot is within a metre to the left or the right of the ball catcher. The defending backs tend to stand a few metres apart when they go up in defence while the defending forwards are beaten by the speed of the throw-in.

Ruck or maul

☐ The direction in which to play is determined by:

- whether the contact is close to the scrum, e.g., against the fly-half or the number eight standing out, or out wide against a centre/wing;
- the speed at which the ball is available at the second phase;
- the opponents' pattern of defence, e.g., whether they keep forwards out on the fringes or whether every forward is committed to the ruck/maul.

☐ When a back is tackled in a line movement after a scrum:

- If the scrum is infield and contact is close to the scrum, there are options on both sides of the ensuing ruck/maul.
- If the scrum is close to touch and contact is at centre, immediately play shallow in the same direction as the previous attack (i.e., away from cover defence) or within a metre of the tackled player (the defenders are usually 3 m to 5 m apart) by using forwards as runners.

☐ When a back is tackled in a line movement near the back of a line-out:

- if possession is slow, play back to the touch-line from where the ball was thrown in (only the hooker is left to defend; the backs are either on the open side or too deep) or if possession is quick, away from the forwards by either using backs to attack out wide, or forwards as runners to attack close to the tackled player.
☐ When a ruck or maul develops after a tackle:
- in midfield the weak point is within a metre, i.e., close to the tackled player
- wide out, immediately play shallow in the same direction as the previous attack.
☐ When the forwards are the cause of a ruck or maul in a line-out (watch whether the opposing forwards stand out!):
- after a drive in the middle of the line-out, the weak spot is within 2 m to 3 m on either side of the ruck or maul, with open side as first choice; and
- after a peel off at the back of the line-out, the weak spot is either within 2 m to 3 m open side of the ruck or maul or back towards the touch-line from where the ball was thrown in.

Driving
A weak point can develop during an open drive (i.e., when the players run with the ball) within a metre on either side of the ball-carrier provided support comes from deep and comes fast.
☐ Keep the pattern of defence in mind!

After a kick-off or drop-out
☐ Whether the opposing forwards stay out on the fringes will determine the type of attack to be used.
☐ In a normal kick-off or drop-out, the weak spot is within 2 m to 3 m of the open side or blind side for a player coming from the opposite side. (In this way he surprises his opponents.)
☐ Further away from the touch-line, the weak spot is either within 2 m to 3 m on the open side or 5 m to 8 m on the blind side for the scrum-half and blind-side wing or hooker.
☐ Still further from the touch-line, the weak spot is between the fly-half and his forwards. The forward who catches the ball runs diagonally away from the opponents' forwards and passes the ball to his eighth-man, who runs straight to the goal posts (principle of running angles).

From kicks
☐ Along the length of the field and near the touch-line, the weak spot is:
- on the opposite touch-line provided there is uneven pressure across the width of the field; or
- right in front of you if the opponents move to centre field expecting a counter-attack across the width of the field.
☐ Along the length of the field and in the centre, the weak spot is:
- to the side from where the least opponents are coming or where you have the most support.
☐ Along the length of the field and diagonally across, the weak spot is right in front of you.

☐ From up-and-unders closer to touch, immediately to the blind side.

Skip moves

From the scrum
☐ An effective skip travels across the width of the field and not in depth.
☐ A skip is in fact a pass past a pressure point.
☐ A skip to the left is easier because most players are right-handed.
☐ Skip to a player who cuts the line, to any side but particularly to the right. The opponents' scrum-half cannot help with defence there.
☐ Skip to play round the outside, particularly to the right. The opponents' scrum-half cannot help with defence.
☐ Vary!

From the fly-half

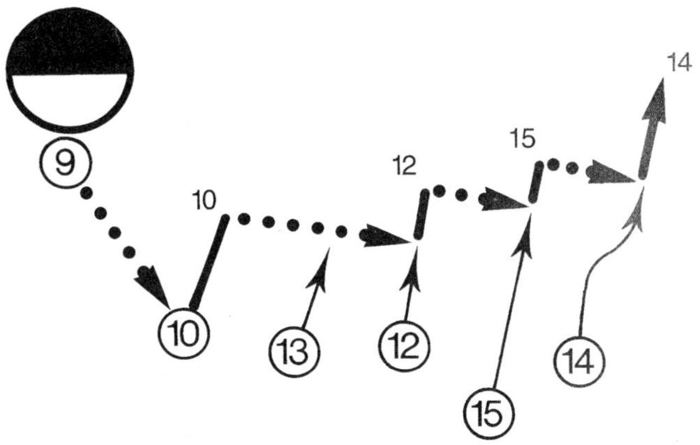

☐ The fly-half stands deep, runs with the ball, draws his opponent and keeps the opponents' inside centre guessing.
☐ A skip past the inside centre (the pressure point). The ball virtually goes through the inside centre's hands (the straighter the inside centre runs, the greater the gap for the outside player who has to cut the line).
☐ A skip across the width (not depth):
- to the full-back (who comes in between the centre and wing);
- to the wing (the full-back comes in outside the wing); and
- past both centres to the full-back (who comes into the line outside the outside centre).

From the inside centre
☐ The fly-half:
- stands relatively shallow and close to the scrum;
- remains stationary while he receives and passes the ball or moves one metre into the ball and passes; and
- passes deep to the inside centre.

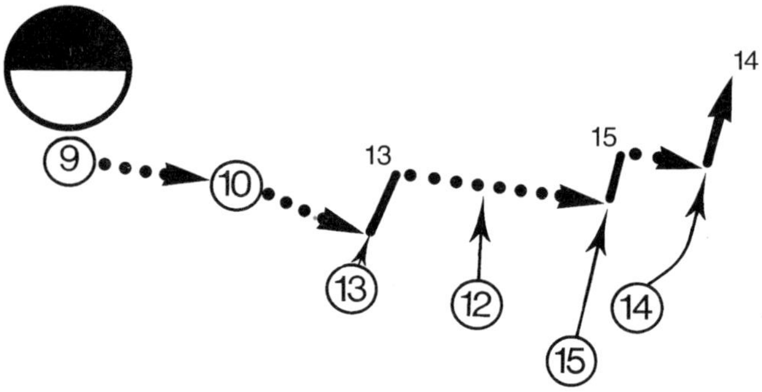

□ The inside centre:
- stands deep;
- receives the ball deep and runs as straight as possible and, at the most, 1 m and 2 m diagonally;
- runs with the ball for at least 5 m, draws his opponent and keeps the opponents' outside centre guessing;
- skips the outside centre - the ball virtually travels through the outside centre's hands (the straighter the outside centre runs, the greater the gap for the player on his outside who has to cut the line)
- or passes to the full-back, who comes in between the outside centre and the wing (the full-back cuts the line);
- skips the outside centre and the full-back and passes to the wing (who stays on the outside); or
- skips the outside centre and the wing and passes to the full-back (who comes in on the outside).

Example of the outside centre being skipped and playing himself

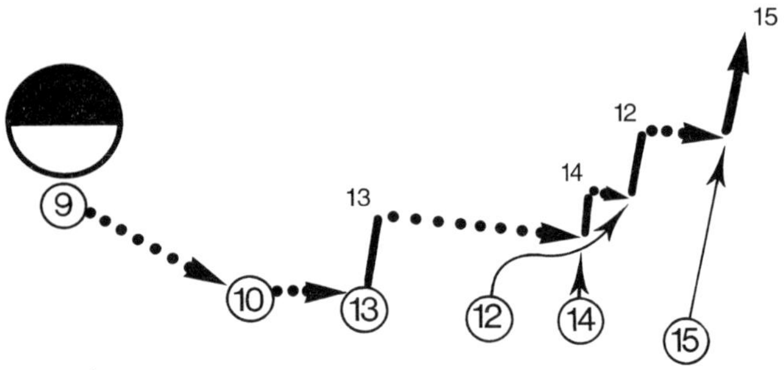

□ Starting position:
- The fly-half and two centres stand deep and virtually next to one another.
□ The fly-half:
- passes almost without running to the inside centre; and
- immediately moves across behind the outside centre.
□ The inside centre:
- first runs with the ball, draws his opponent and keeps the opponents' outside centre guessing; and
- skips his outside centre and passes to the wing; or
- passes straight to the wing, who moves to the inside for the pass and passes on his outside to the outside centre, who in the meantime has come round.
- The full-back shoots up right on the outside, where he takes the pass from the outside centre.

Tips

The same principles can be applied from a centre scrum:
□ The fly-half skips the centre and passes to the wing.
□ The centre who is skipped joins on the outside.
□ The full-back now supports on the inside of the centre (because there is less room to manoeuvre between the scrum and sideline).
□ An effective way to stop the defence from the inside, is to use the skip and run around (the receiver cuts to the inside to stop the defence whilst the skipped player takes the pass on the outside).

Two skips in one movement

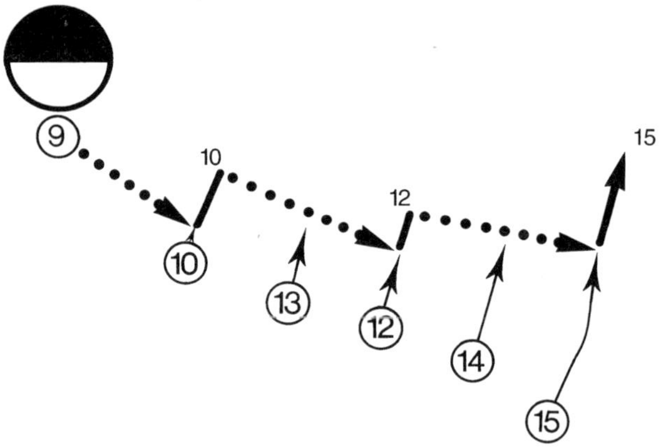

Starting positions
□ The fly-half takes up position very deep and gets the ball deep (if he stands shallow, he is not allowed to run with the ball).
□ The rest of the back-line stand more or less next to one another (back but not in a staircase alignment).
□ The fly-half:
- gets the ball deep;
- runs with it and draws his direct opponent and his opponents' inside centre; and
- skips the inside centre in such a way that the ball virtually passes through the inside centre's hands (it is important that the inside centre runs straight).
□ The outside centre:
- runs with the ball as long as he can and draws his opponent and the next player on his outside; and
- skips the wing or full-back and passes to the full-back or wing right on the outside. Timing is, because of the danger of interception, very important!
Remember: This movement is for crossing the tackle-line on the outside. The least risk is to the left. It is most effective in the opponents' half.

From the line-out

Remember: Keep in mind the principles of the skip!
□ The position in the line-out where the ball is won (2, 4, 6) determines where the best position is to skip from, e.g., 2-skip from 10; 4/6-skip from inside centre.
□ Most teams tend to skip from the fly-half regardless of the position from which the ball has been won. When

skips are used from possession won at 4 and 6/7, the opponents are still too far away. Thus the defence simply moves across the field and prevents the man-over-situation.

☐ When the inside centre skip passes, he ties up the defenders (the loose forwards, fly-half and inside centre) and creates gaps in the outside field more easily.

☐ A popular move to stop the cover-defence is passing from the fly-half to the inside centre who returns the pass to the fly-half running behind him. The fly-half then skip passes the outside centre to the full-back and wing running wide.

Tactical manoeuvres can consist of a combination of changes in respect of position, the direction in which the players run, the types of passes, etc. The major objective is always to attack the weak spots or create confusion in order to create weakness in the defence.

SKIP AND CUT COMBINATION
SEE HOW COMPLICATED A TACTICAL MOVE CAN BE. THE WALLABIES USED THIS MOVE TO SCORE A BRILLIANT TRY AGAINST THE BRITISH BARBARIANS

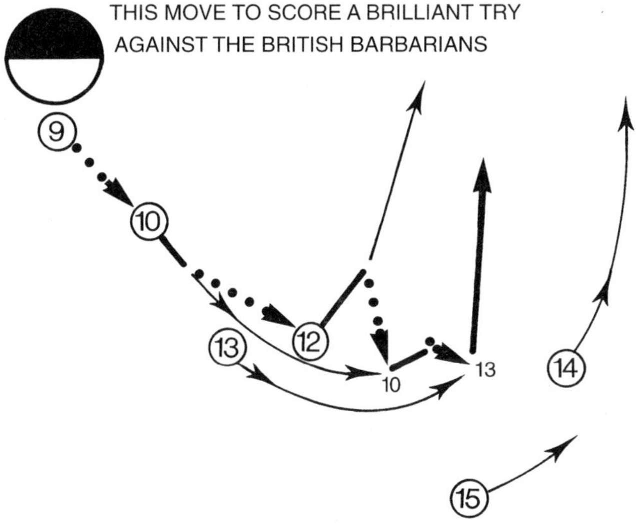

11. Defensive patterns

The harder you work the harder it is to surrender

General

Every player must know how he, as an individual, can defend most effectively.

When the American Eagles toured South Africa in the mid-seventies, I first heard their coach use the expression: "If you tackle an opponent, hit him on his numbers!"

This prompted me to take a closer look at the art of tackling and I was convinced that we'd eventually be forced to examine the way we teach our youngsters to tackle.

Famous tacklers in Springbok rugby like Jimmy White, Ryk van Schoor, Butch Lochner, Mannetjies Roux and Joggie Jansen had one thing in common: The *point of contact* where their shoulders crashed into an opponent was just above the waist. The waist is nearly on the same height as the numbers on the Americans' jerseys, so there has to be some truth in the Eagles coach's remark.

Let's have a closer look at the point of impact. Generally youngsters are taught to go in low and tackle an opponent around the knees or even around the ankles. To me it is absurd to tell somebody, in whom you want to instill confidence, to tackle where he has the biggest chance of getting hurt. To go for the knees means he has to tackle a hard target that is on the move, laterally and vertically. This promises one thing: some time or other the kid's face will strike the opponent's knees or boots. The mid-rib area, on the other hand, is a much more stable and softer target.

Of lesser importance than the injury factor, but still crucial for the right approach and attitude is that the *youngster won't learn that tackling is about tackling the ball.* After all, rugby is about possession.

Does this mean the tackler should only aim for the mid-rib area? Not at all; there are times when it is safe and effective to tackle low. To know when, coach and player should use their common sense and respect the laws of physics. In layman's terms it means that the speed and the direction in which ball-carrier and tackler are moving must be kept in mind when tackling.

In practice it comes down to the following:

☐ *If the ball-carrier is stationary - or moving slowly - the tackler can hit him at full speed* in the mid-rib with little risk of being injured himself. This is what happens when a full-back catching the up-and-under, is floored by one of the charging centres. Some of the most breathtaking tackles in American gridiron happen in exactly the same way.

☐ *If both ball-carrier and tackler are moving at speed towards each other,* someone, inevitably, will be injured. Most likely it will be the tackler's shoulder or neck area.

☐ *If the ball-carrier is charging towards the heavier tackler,* the latter can tackle him from the front as long as the main force goes in an *upwards* direction. By doing this, the tackler skilfully uses his advantage in weight to redirect the two colliding forces. The All Black loose forwards Zinzan Brooke and Michael Jones are especially fond of tackling backs who cut back to the forwards in this way.

☐ *If the tackler is confronted by a much heavier ball-carrier coming at speed* the safest and most effective action might be to apply the Judo-principle and use the speed of the attacker to bring him to ground. Although the purists might not like this approach, as the ball-carrier won't be tackled backwards, the smaller/lighter tackler will at least stop the movement. With a little bit of luck, the ball-carrier may even lose the ball forward in the tackle.

☐ *When a back cuts through at speed with only a stationary full-back waiting,* the latter will deliberately give him space to run to the one side before exploding into him from the side. The famous Welsh and British Lions' full-back JPR Williams, was renowned for this. The success of this type of tackling depends on strong legs and shoulders and the way the tackler can launch himself, hitting the ball-carrier slightly from behind in the hollow of the knee.

To the tackler. Next time you tackle, remember the game is about possession. Use the tackle fit for the situation and avoid injury. It is no use being a hero for one tackle only to be sidelined for weeks or even crippled for life!

Tips

☐ Keep the opponent on your outside:
- In this way you run the radius of a circle while he runs the circumference. You have the shorter distance and need less speed, making it difficult for him to beat you on the inside.

☐ You tackle the ball, so the target is above the player's hips:
- It is a softer target and results in fewer injuries.
- It is a more fixed target than, for example, his legs, and therefore cannot be used to mislead you as easily.
- His arms are involved in such a tackle and he cannot pass the ball easily.

The one-on-one situation

☐ The speed and the direction in which the ball-carrier is running determine the type of tackle.

- You can only take him head-on and hit him backwards when you have the advantage of speed and weight (if you try to take him head-on when he is approaching you at speed, you are surely in for a shoulder injury). Try to hit him upwards, forcing him off his power base, i.e., his legs.

☐ When the ball-carrier has the advantage of speed, use his speed (the judo-principle) and pull him to the ground so that the ball is on your side.

- If he tries to beat you on the outside, or you are covering across field and the tackle is made from slightly behind, go for the back of his knees (small injury risk).
- Sometimes, when both attacker and tackler are more or less stationary, it is best to just block the ball and keep the ball-carrier on his feet in order either to prevent quick release or get possession.

☐ Hit the ball-carrier hard so that he loses control of the ball. This is possible when you are a good defender and have an advantage of weight and strength. The ball can then be played immediately.

☐ Turn the ball-carrier around when the opponent is heavy and strong on his feet so that the ball is on your side:

- In this way you isolate the ball from the opposing supporters.
- You start a maul in which you can either win the ball or kill it.

☐ Tackle the opponent low and get him down on the ground immediately (when a small scrum-half wants to stop the forward momentum of a big forward). Your first players then drive over the ball and start a ruck, where it is easier to defend.

The one-on-two situation

This can create a great deal of uncertainty, especially in the case of an inexperienced defender. The golden rule is that only one attacker should get past, preferably not the outside one!

Options

☐ When the attackers run diagonally across the field:

- the defender stays with the inside player and shadows him in such a way that he starts running even more diagonally and, when he passes, the defender tackles the second attacker. This is easy because the second attacker has to run much further than the defender.

☐ When the attackers run parallel to touch and the ball-carrier is heading straight for the defender:

- the number of defenders on the inside and the distance to the defender's goal-line determine what the defender should do.

☐ When the defender has team-mates on the inside:

- he closes off the outside to prevent the attacker from beating him there. To do this he blocks the outside attacker (without the ball if necessary) so that his closest team-mate to the ball-carrier can tackle from the inside. The fact that he blocks the outside player usually makes the ball-carrier hesitate and the inside defender can then reach him more easily.

☐ The distance from the defender's goal-line:

- When there is only one defender relatively far from his goal-line (e.g., outside the 10 m line as in the case of an interception), he tries to stay between, and slightly in front of, the two attackers as long as possible. He does this to slow them down in the hope that the distance to the goal-line will be enough to give other defenders the chance to come to his aid. (Think of David Campese's break against the Barbarians in 1984.)
- When there is only one defender close to his goal-line with no help, he must put the ball-carrier under the greatest possible pressure so that he does not have time to make a decision. He can do so by suddenly and quickly moving 4 m to 5 m forward towards the ball-carrier to upset his timing. The rule is still that only one attacker - if any - should get past.

The team should have a specific defensive pattern

☐ Defence starts with the battle for possession - when you have the ball, you do not have to defend!

☐ The first line of defence is one on one; the main objective here is to tackle the ball-carrier behind the advantage line.

☐ Players basically defend in channels or zones, i.e., when an attacker moves out of a defender's channel, the defender into whose channel he goes tackles him.

☐ The cover defence defends immediately behind the first line when it is broken; the defenders must still try to contain an opponent behind the advantage line.

☐ Cross-defence takes place when players defend from considerably further away after the first two lines of defence have been broken.

☐ Every player must be fully committed to the defensive pattern and know exactly what his task is. To do this, he must first understand it. You do not, for example, follow an opponent who is executing a scissor movement; you stick to your defensive channel, not to the opponent who is running out of it. In this way, you prevent a gap from opening up.

☐ Every player must know exactly what his task is. It should, where possible, be straightforward and should preferably involve only one opponent.

☐ The team should have more than one option available. This depends on the opponents' pattern of play, their individual players and where on the field play is taking place. The back-line, for example, defends to the inside or outside (by way of shift or drift defence) and the loose forwards in a line-out all defend forward or across the field.

☐ Someone, preferably the fly-half, must tell the first-line defenders every time which pattern they are to use from each facet of play.

□ The defenders must move as a unit on command. This eliminates uncertainty, inspires confidence and prevents gaps from opening up.

Scrum

Scrum on the left

Remember: Here you can use your scrum-half against the opponents' back-line.

First option - [Man on]

The scrum-half goes for his opponent and the rest of the back-line tackle one on one.

DEFENCE: LEFT SCRUM

(A) TO THE INSIDE

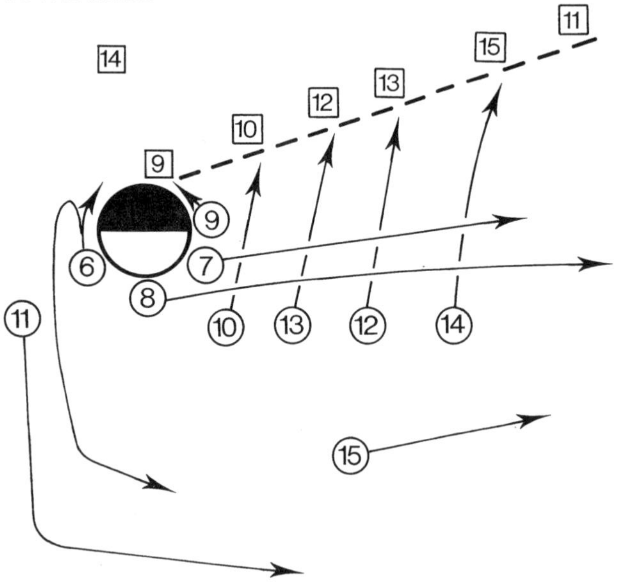

FIRST LINE (ONE ON ONE)

□ The scrum-half goes for his opposite number and puts him under pressure. If the scrum-half does not get him, he goes for the fly-half or moves across behind his fly-half and inside centre, who in the meantime have moved up. After the opponent has passed the ball, every back closes the possible gap on the inside of his team-mate.

SECOND LINE (COVER DEFENCE)

□ The right flanker breaks forward diagonally and first closes the gap on the inside of his fly-half. He then moves across behind his backs and closes all the inside gaps. If a back breaks through, play moves towards the right flanker.

□ The eighth-man moves in behind his fly-half and inside centre right across the field for chip kicks or in case a back cuts through. (Never overrun the ball!) In this way it is difficult to get beaten with a back-flip or scissors pass.

THIRD LINE (CROSS-DEFENCE)

□ The left flanker first makes sure play does not go in his direction. If the ball goes to ground in front of him, he moves forward. The same applies if he is close to the opponents' goal-line. If the opponents do not play towards him, he moves back deep; if they change direction, they will bring the ball back towards him.

□ The left winger first goes back deep for possible kicks in the box (never turn your back on the ball when you drop back) and then, after the fly-half has passed, he follows right across the field.

□ The tight forwards: The two on the right side of the scrum take the shortest route to the ball while the three on the left move slightly deeper in order to come in behind the ball.

ADVANTAGES AND DISADVANTAGES OF THIS DEFENSIVE PATTERN

□ Effective:

- In very wet and muddy conditions.
- In a strong cross-wind against the direction of the passes.
- Against a scrum-half who is struggling and is not on top of his game.
- Against an inexperienced number eight who is struggling to control the ball at the base of the scrum.

□ Vulnerable against:

- an extra attacker in the back-line.
- skip passes.
- a combination of the previous two.

Second option - [Shift]

The scrum-half marks the fly-half and the rest of the backs each move on one position.

(B) TO THE OUTSIDE

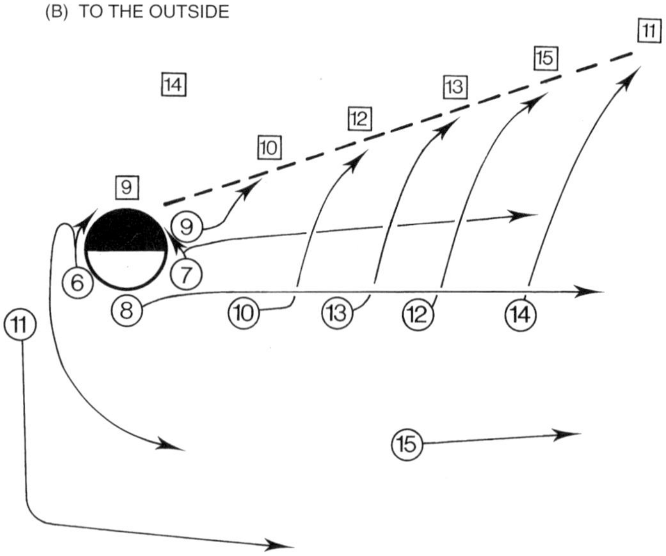

FIRST LINE (ONE ON ONE)

□ The scrum-half stays on the inside of the ball and exerts pressure as far as possible. While the ball is still in the scrum, he - as well as the rest of the backs - moves 2 m to

3 m across to the right. (He'll quickly notice how far the referee will allow him.) From there they come up on the inside of their respective opponents.

□ After an opponent has passed, every back closes the possible gap on the inside of his team-mate. The backs should not cross, i.e., deviate from their formation, no matter what the opponents do.

SECOND LINE (COVER DEFENCE)

□ The right-side flanker first marks for the opposing scrum-half and then moves 3 m to 5 m across the field. He closes all inside gaps. If a back breaks through, play moves towards the right-side flanker.

□ The left flanker's task remains the same.

□ The eighth-man's task remains the same.

THIRD LINE (CROSS-DEFENCE)

□ The same applies as in the first option against extra attackers in the back-line and skip passes.

ADVANTAGES AND DISADVANTAGES OF THIS DEFENSIVE PATTERN

□ Effective:

- Against extra attackers in the back-line, skip passes and a combination of the above.
- With a fast scrum-half.
- Against a slow or nervous fly-half.

□ Vulnerable:

- Against an eighth-man who plays well with his scrum-half (because he makes your scrum-half and right flanker hesitate).
- Against a team that wheels a scrum to its left (because often defence is weak precisely in the direction towards which the scrum wheels).

Scrum on the right

Remember: Here your scrum-half cannot defend on the open side.

DEFENCE: RIGHT SCRUM

(A) TO THE INSIDE (STAND TO THE INSIDE OF AN OPPONENT)

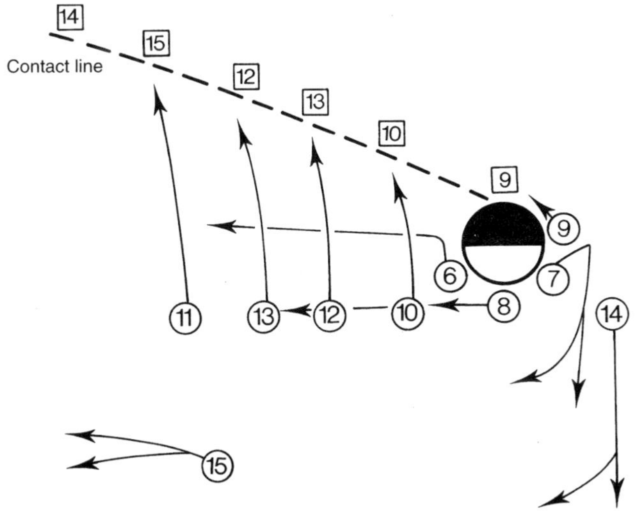

First option - [Man on]

The back-line defends one on one from the inside.

FIRST LINE (ONE ON ONE)

□ The scrum-half puts pressure on his opponent. When the opposite fly-half stands very deep, he can pressurise him too.

□ If the number eight plays the ball, he tackles him from behind.

□ When he cannot get close to his opponent, he drops back deep, moves round behind the scrum and goes on the cross-defence.

□ The left flanker tackles the first opponent who comes round the scrum. When the scrum-half passes the ball, he goes off forward and diagonally slightly behind and on the inside of his fly-half to prevent an inside break.

□ Every back, from the fly-half on goes up on the inside of his opponent. After the opponent has passed the ball, every back closes the possible gap on the inside of his team-mate. The backs should not cross or hesitate, no matter what the opponents do.

SECOND LINE (COVER DEFENCE)

□ The eighth-man first closes the inside gap between the fly-half and the scrum (in case the left-side flanker does not move up) and then moves across the field for chip kicks behind the fly-half and inside centre. (Do not over-run the ball.)

THIRD LINE (CROSS-DEFENCE)

□ The right winger first goes back deep for possible kicks into the box (never turn your back on the ball when you drop back). Only after the opponents' fly-half has passed does the right winger move across the field.

□ The right flanker first makes sure the halves do not change the direction of play to his side before he moves back deep behind his scrum if he expects the fly-half to kick to his corner. If not, he moves right across the field. When a scrum is deep in the opponents' half he can move forward to the fly-half.

□ The scrum-half drops back deep behind his scrum if he cannot get close to the ball, except when the attacking fly-half plays so deep that the scrum-half can reach him. (Be careful not to expose the blind side the way the Scottish scrum-half did when Joost van der Westhuizen scored in the match SA vs Scotland in 1994.)

□ The tight forwards: The three on the left side take the shortest route to the ball while the two on the right side do the same, but a slightly deeper running angle.

ADVANTAGES AND DISADVANTAGES OF THIS DEFENSIVE PATTERN

□ Effective:

- Because it is a simple pattern.
- Because it closes inside gaps.
- Because it is well suited to wet and windy weather.

☐ Vulnerable:
- Because the attackers can, with an extra man in the line, either confuse the defenders or get through on the outside.

Second option - [Shift]
The fly-half goes for the inside centre and the other backs each move on one position.

(B) TO THE OUTSIDE (STAND TO THE OUTSIDE OF AN OPPONENT)

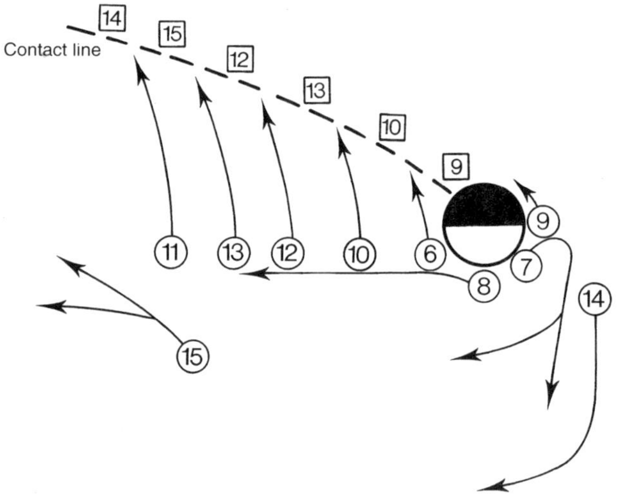

FIRST LINE
☐ The scrum-half does the same as in the first option.
☐ The fly-half initially stands on the inside of his opponent, first moves 3 m to 5 m across when the opponent concentrates on the ball and then goes for the inside centre.
☐ The rest of the backs: Each back from the fly-half on, while the ball is in the scrum, first moves 2 m to 3 m to the left and then shoots up on the inside of his opponent. After the opponent has passed the ball, every back closes the possible gap on the inside of his team-mate. Backs should not cross, no matter what the opponents do.
☐ The left-side flanker is a key player in this pattern. He first goes for the opponents' fly-half and then moves across the field to close the inside gaps. It is preferable to let the opponents' fly-half beat him on the inside rather than the outside. Despite being a calculated risk, the scrum-half should nevertheless be ignored in this defensive pattern.
☐ The eighth-man first covers behind his left flanker, before moving across and closing the inside gaps. Look out for chip kicks.
☐ The rest of the pack follow the first option.

ADVANTAGES AND DISADVANTAGES OF THIS DEFENSIVE PATTERN
☐ Effective:
- Against an extra man in the back-line (an attacking full-back and/or blind-side winger).
☐ Vulnerable:
- Because defence is weak on the open side close to the scrum (everything hinges on your left-side flanker);
- Because it is difficult to apply when the fly-half gives a long pass to the inside centre (your fly-half has to move out very wide but does not do so because he does not want his opponent to beat him on his inside).
- If the opponents' eighth-man and scrum-half play close to the scrum.
- Because inexperienced players can easily panic on defence.

Midfield scrum
Remember: The halves must defend on different sides.

DEFENCE: MIDFIELD SCRUM

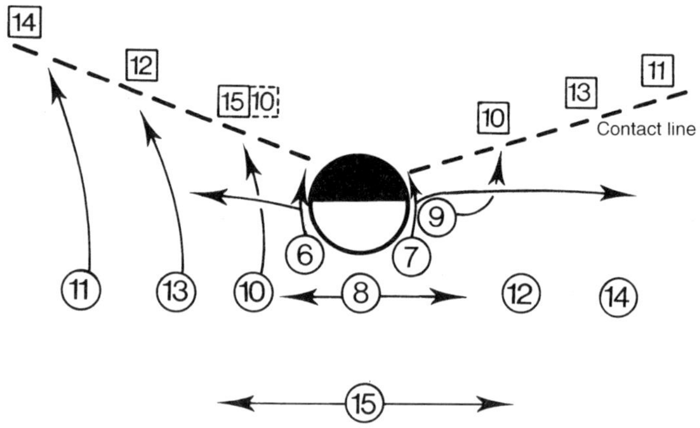

Starting positions
☐ The scrum-half defends on the right hand side against the opponents' fly-half or full-back.
☐ The fly-half defends on the left hand side against the opponents' fly-half or full-back.
☐ The centres defend shallow, one on each side.
☐ The wingers defend slightly deeper, one on each side.
☐ The full-back defends against the opponents' fly-half.

The opponents play to your left

FIRST LINE
☐ The scrum-half puts the greatest possible pressure on his opponent. If the opposing fly-half stands deep, he puts him under pressure too. Don't forget to tackle the number eight if he plays the ball.
☐ The left flanker breaks to the front and tackles the first opponent who tries to break around the scrum, e.g., when:
- the scrum-half either runs with the ball or plays to his eighth-man or left flanker, who comes round;
- the eighth-man plays either to the scrum-half or to the left side flanker, who drives; or
- if the fly-half passes the ball quickly, he moves right across the field and closes all inside gaps. Play will move towards him. The flanker should remember if he continues going forward, the back-line will beat him with the speed of the ball and he will not get to the ball again.
☐ The fly-half:
- goes up on the inside of his opposing fly-half if the latter plays in that direction himself;

- stays in his defensive channel in case his opponent does a dummy run-around and the inside centre passes inside to the full-back;
- tries to tackle behind the opposing forwards; and
- closes the inside gap where his centre is.

☐ The left centre moves up with the fly-half.

☐ The left wing moves up on the inside of his opponent (the radius of the circle versus the diameter principle). He should not hesitate if his opponent closes up for the swerve because then he cannot beat him round the outside.

SECOND LINE (COVER DEFENCE)

☐ The eighth-man:
- first falls back a metre, looks, moves quickly to the left (in this case) and closes all inside gaps (he should not overrun the ball).

☐ The right centre:
- as soon as he is sure the opponents play to his team's left, quickly moves over to the other side (not too shallow).

THIRD LINE (CROSS-DEFENCE)

☐ The right-side flanker:
- first makes sure the movement does not go to his side; and
- then goes deep behind his scrum; deep in the opponents' half or, if the opponents play very deep, to the front.

☐ The right wing:
- first moves back a little deeper in case the opponents' halves kick in his direction; and
- then moves across the field.

☐ The tight forwards: The first three closest to the ball take the shortest route towards it and the last two move towards it more deeply.

The opponents play to your right

FIRST LINE

☐ The scrum-half has two options:
- he puts pressure on his opponent (e.g., deep in their half); or
- he goes for the fly-half or full-back (i.e., the player who gets the ball from the scrum-half) when he expects him to play wide on his side. He initially stands close to his opponent while the ball is in the scrum and then moves 2 m to 3 m across the field before he goes up at full tilt on defence, otherwise the opponent beats him on the outside.

Remember: Vary! The opponents' scrum-half should always feel under pressure.

☐ The right-side flanker:
- advances when the scrum-half goes for the fly-half or full-back (his target is the first player who tries to break through on his side close to the scrum); or
- moves diagonally when the scrum-half goes for his opponent (he closes the gap between the scrum and right centre).

☐ The right centre: The same applies to the left centre in an attack to the left side.

☐ The right winger: The same applies to the left winger in an attack to the left side.

SECOND LINE (COVER DEFENCE)

☐ The eighth-man first observes while still in the scrum by just lifting his head and then going at full speed to the right (in this case). He then does exactly the same as in the case of an attack to the left side. (Do not overrun the ball!)

☐ The fly-half, as soon as he is sure the opposition are playing to his team's right side, quickly moves over to the other side and defends as shallow as possible.

☐ The left centre: The same applies to the fly-half except he moves deeper.

THIRD LINE (CROSS-DEFENCE)

☐ The left flanker:
- first makes sure the movement does not go to his side; and
- then moves deep behind his scrum;
- deep in the opponents' half or, if they play very deep, he can break forwards.

☐ The left wing: The same applies to the right winger in an attack to the left side.

☐ The tight forwards: The first two closest to the ball play towards it and the last three play deeper.

Full-back

He is, first and foremost, a defender, and secondly an attacker. His defence is inextricably linked with the duties of his two wings. The easiest way to cover the unavoidable open spaces on the field from the scrum is by misleading the opponents:

☐ Deliberately leave open space for the opposing fly-half to kick into.

☐ While the opposing fly-half is concentrating on his scrum-half and the ball, the full-back moves to the "open" space. The fly-half will still kick to the space that was open!

Big blind side to your left

☐ Do the opponents have fast backs with great handling skills?
- If so, you've got to organise your defence in such a way that if a gap is left it must be close to the forwards. If the gap is left out wide they'll beat you with sheer speed.

☐ What is the weather like?
- If it is muddy, or you're playing in a strong wind, you might gamble on intackling and leaving the gap out wide hoping they won't be able to get the ball wide.

Alignment and responsibilities

☐ The fly-half takes up a position to the left of the scrum:
- His main responsibility is the second-last player on the outside, whether it is the full-back coming into the line or the right wing (if the full-back joins the line on the outside).

DEFENCE: BIG BLIND SIDE TO YOUR LEFT

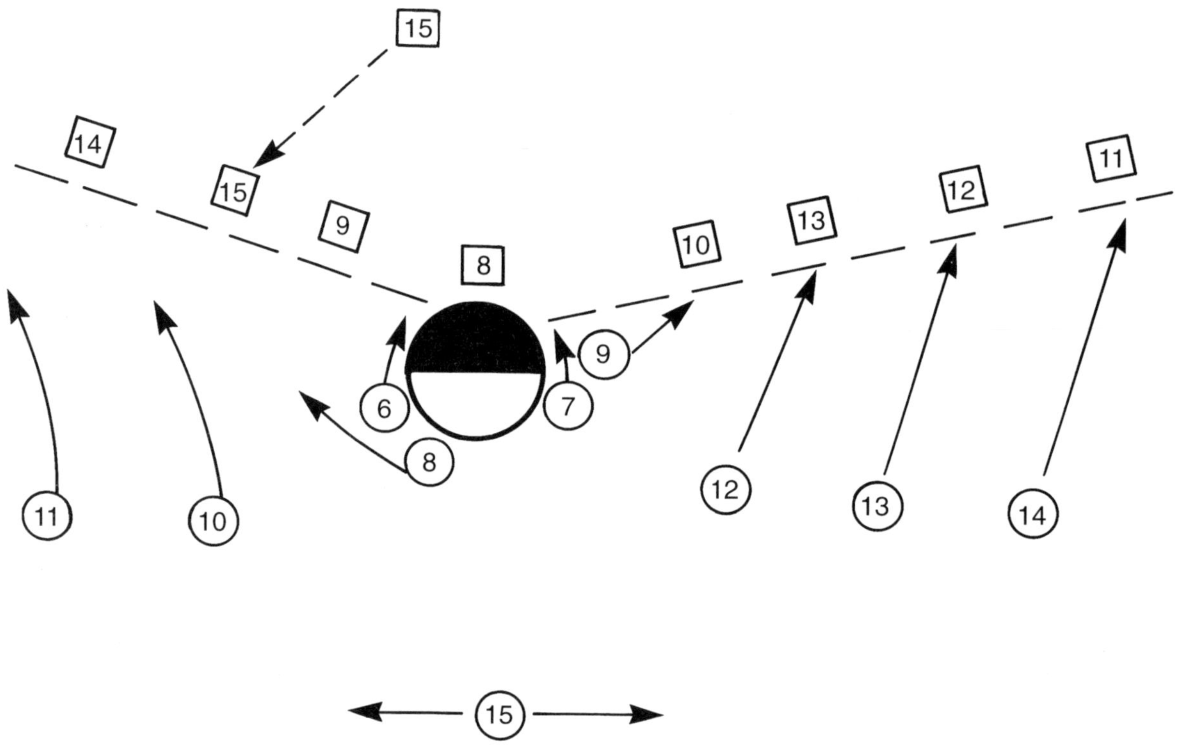

- If the scrum-half runs at him, taking a pass from the number eight, he stays with his man and leaves the scrum-half to his number eight.

☐ The left wing:
- He stays with the last player on the outside.

☐ The number eight:
- He must cover the gap between the fly-half and the scrum.
- The running scrum-half is his responsibility.

☐ The left flanker:
- He covers their number eight.

☐ Your scrum-half:
- He defends on the right against the opposition's fly-half or, depending on whether the scrum wheels, pressurises their number eight.

☐ The right-side flanker:
- He covers any play on the right between the scrum and the fly-half.

Line-out

Key factors

☐ Which position in the line-out is the ball thrown to?
- From the front up to the middle, the loose forwards can help in defence. The backs move on one position or a variation can be used (the eighth-man to the inside centre).
- To the back of the line-out, the loose forwards are drawn in and the backs mark their direct opposition.

☐ Where on the field is the line-out?
- Normally the opponents throw deeper into the line-out as they get closer to your goal-line. (Watch out for a ball on the first jumper close to your goal-line!)

First option

FIRST LINE

Give the opponents the worst possible possession.

☐ The jumpers go for the ball (they anticipate beforehand where it is going to be thrown in) by looking to see:
- whether his opponent gives an indication he is ready to jump;
- how the opposing supporters are standing - tense or relaxed; and
- where the thrower is looking.

☐ The jumpers can prevent two-handed catches:
- If your opponent beats you to the ball in front of you, get a hand over his shoulder in between his arms; or
- if he beats you to the ball behind you, swing your inside arm back.

☐ The supporters:
- immediately move towards the ball;
- take the ball away or block it; or
- push the catcher back towards his goal-line, i.e., away from his support.

☐ The hooker:
- defends at the front of the line-out by putting pressure on the scrum-half;
- stands in such a way that he cannot be bound and prevents blind side breaks;

- when the ball is taken cleanly, stays on the blind side (he goes in only when he can win or block the ball);
- when the ball is knocked on or bounces about, goes up on defence; or
- when the ball is passed away quickly, goes back deep behind the line-out for cross-defence. (These are difficult decisions until the opponents' pattern of play becomes clear.)

☐ The eighth-man (at the back of the line-out) goes for:
- the fly-half while his own fly-half goes for the inside centre (usually deep in the opponents' half); or
- the inside centre while his fly-half covers behind the back-line (when he is sure the opponents are attacking wide).

☐ The rest of the back-line adjusts to what the eighth-man and fly-half do.

DEFENCE: LINE-OUT

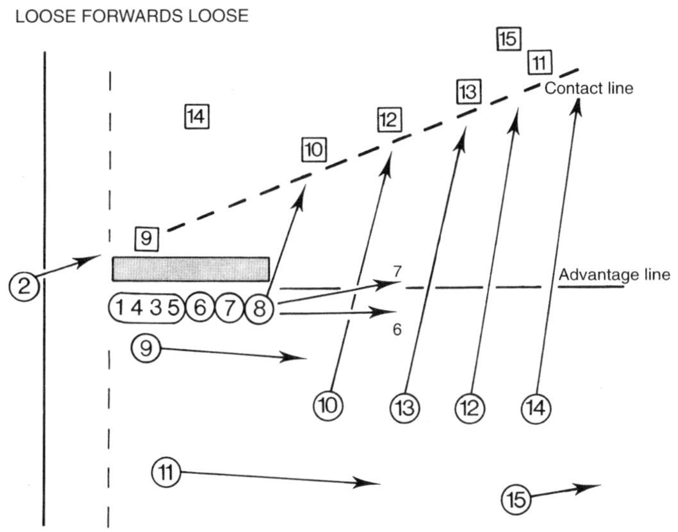

DEEP THROW-IN

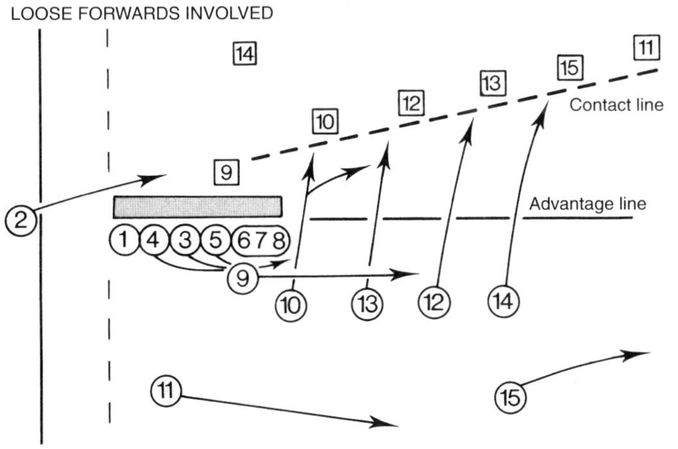

SECOND LINE (COVER DEFENCE)

☐ The second-last loose forward (usually No. 7):
- first makes sure the scrum-half does not break; and
- then goes up diagonally across the field just in front of the advantage line (not too far forward because then he does not get to the ball), staying on the inside of the ball-carrier to stop all inside breaks. (If he chooses the right line, the ball-carrier will ultimately reach him.)

☐ If the third loose forward (the one supporting the second jumper in the line-out):
- gets away quickly, he runs along the advantage line (this is the easiest way of getting back into the game); or
- gets away slowly, he runs deeper behind the advantage line (otherwise he is completely out of the game).

☐ The scrum-half moves up across behind the back-line to:
- clear all chip kicks over the fly-half; and
- stay on the inside of the ball-carrier.

THIRD LINE (CROSS-DEFENCE)

☐ The blind-side winger:
- first stays in position until the fly-half kicks or the inside centre passes (he must guard against a kick back to his touch-line); and
- then moves across the field, staying on the inside of the ball-carrier.

☐ The tight forwards take the shortest route to the ball. This will be shallower when the opponents run with the ball a lot and deeper when the opponents kick a lot.

Full-back

He guards against kicks and tackles the ball-carrier in case he gets through. The fly-half helps him when the eighth-man goes for the inside centre.

Peeling off

In front of the line-out

☐ Where is the line-out?
- The opponents will not easily peel off round the front if they are further than 30 m to 40 m from your goal-line. The closer to your goal-line, the greater this possibility. It is a good policy to say out loud: "They are going to peel off round the front!" (The opponents often change their minds.)

☐ Does it look as if the ball is going to be thrown to the front, e.g., 10 m from your goal-line? The hooker must:
- watch closely whether the front jumper and his two supporters are preparing themselves for a shallow throw-in. If so, he must stand slightly deeper so that the opposing hooker cannot tie him into the line-out;
- stay out of the line-out so that he can defend up front (he tackles the player peeling off so that he does not cross the advantage line).

☐ The tight forwards and the tight flanker:
- immediately move towards the ball;

- are the first players who must stop their immediate opponents; and
- try to force the attackers out over the touch-line.

☐ The two loose forwards at the back move out of the line-out towards their goal-line. This is often the shortest route to stop the attackers. They are now also in the right place in case the attackers switch direction and play infield.

At the back of the line-out

☐ Where is the line-out?
- The opponents seldom peel off in their own half. The closer to your goal-line, the greater this possibility.

☐ Does it look as if the ball is going to be thrown in deep? Anticipate by looking at:
- the hooker's throw-in action (whether he pulls back more for a deep throw-in);
- the position of the feet of the first jumper and the two props (are they standing in such a way that they can quickly get away to the back?), their eyes (are they concentrating on the ball or not?) and who in the line-out is tense.
- the jumpers at the back of the line-out, who may be more concerned with whether they have enough space to be able to jump.

COUNTER-STRATEGIES

☐ General:
- Call out loud: "They are going to peel off round the back."

☐ The jumpers:
- They either try to get the ball or to spoil the possession for the opponents.
- The first four players in the line-out (1, 4, 3 & 5), as soon as the ball passes over their heads, move as quickly as possible to the back of the line-out. (They must stop their opponents before they can head for the defending back-line.)

☐ The tight flanker bursts through the line-out towards the player peeling off when the ball is tapped back or deflected.

☐ The second-last player (the jumper) either tries to get the ball or makes sure the opponents do not control it.

☐ The last player (the eighth-man):
- does not go for the ball; in this way his opponent cannot block him or bind him into the line-out (unless of course the ball is thrown right at him);
- stands slightly away from the advantage line before the throw-in;
- forgets about the ball and quickly takes up a position a metre deeper in midfield;
- keeps his eyes on the player peeling off; and
- tackles him behind the advantage line.

☐ When the other forwards arrive and:
- the opponent has been tackled, they go over the ball by means of a ruck;
- the opponent is on his feet in a maul, they join the maul from behind or slightly from the side. (This makes things difficult for the opposing supporters.)

☐ The inside backs (especially a strong inside centre):
- If the forwards are caught unawares, the inside backs should not hesitate to stop the player peeling off as close as possible to the advantage line. A loose forward immediately takes up the back's position in the back-line.

Short line-out

☐ Do you know the laws? This is essential for effective defence. (See chapter 3 on the laws of the game.)

☐ How many opponents are in the line-out? The pack leader must immediately call out: "Two/three/four/five-man line-out."

☐ Which players in your team stay in the line-out as jumpers?
- Two-man: Usually the two locks or a lock and a loose forward (he is a good choice particularly if he has the ability to jump high and do line-out work at the back of the line-out).
- Three-man: Two locks and a tall loose forward.
- Four/five-man: Add a loose forward every time, with your biggest prop as the fifth player.

☐ Who from your team is the scrum-half? A loose forward who:
- is strong in defence; and
- has good ball control in case you win the ball.

☐ The hooker stays out and he makes sure no-one breaks around the front of the short line-out.

☐ Beat the opposing jumpers for the ball by standing man against man. Do not allow yourself to be misled by opponents moving around in the line-out. Concentrate on the ball!

☐ In case the jumpers break through the line-out, your acting scrum-half or loose forward tackles any opponent who breaks through in the middle. If that doesn't happen, help at the back or the front of the line-out (in your own 22 - be careful at the front; always be ready in case the last player in the line-out moves back for the ball).

☐ Another alternative in the two-man line-out is for your loose forward acting as scrum-half, to stand close to the 15 m line and the line of throw-in. He covers any deep throw-in, while the other two players in the line-out each covers the space in front of him. Thus no one can be misled by opponents moving around in the line-out.

☐ Behind the line-out: The remaining forwards stay close to your fly-half and move up on defence as soon as the line-out is over (make sure everybody knows the situations which cause the line-out to be over).

☐ The maul or ruck that can develop after a deep throw-in behind and over the top of the line-out:
- The vulnerable places are the blind side and 2 to 3 m close to the tight-loose.
- In the case of a two-man line-out, a specific forward and the scrum-half cover the sides (the hooker defends blind side and the scrum-half open side).

Maul or scrum

Key factors

☐ The following players are usually trapped:
- The loose forwards: One or two, often all three.
- The backs: Mostly centres and wings.

☐ The tight forwards usually get to the tight-loose last:

☐ Defence is vulnerable:
- within 2 m to 3 m on the sides of the tight-loose;
- when the maul is moving forward and the forwards go in to stop the momentum, blind side (because no-one is guarding there) and open side out wide (especially when a back is trapped in the tight-loose);
- when the tight-loose is static, blind side and wide on the open side;
- against any cutting movements (cover defence is weaker or there is none at all because the loose forwards are trapped).

☐ Specific players must therefore be given specific tasks. Example:
- The hooker always defends on the blind side. It is a simple task that he should never forget, no matter how tired he becomes. He enters the ruck/maul only if he can win or smother the ball. His defence on the blind side is forward (if he waits for the attacker, he will be beaten).
- The scrum-half defends on the open side.
- The number of players who defend on either side of the tight-loose can vary but there must be at least two. This is not where the tight forwards should defend; their weight and strength are needed in the tight-loose (except when the ball-carrier goes to ground).

☐ The available - fewer in number - backs (two possibilities):
- Every back goes up as fast as possible and tries to prevent the ball from reaching the open side wide (that is where there is a weak spot!) The weakness of this system of intackling is that, if the opponents get the first three passes away or skip passes, they beat you on the outside.
- The backs move up more slowly but in line and shift outward while the opponents are passing the ball (they must prevent gaps on the outside). A weakness is that gaps develop on the inside and that players become lazy to move up quickly. This defensive pattern usually works well with experienced backs.

☐ The second line of defenders:
- The backs on the blind side.
- The first players to get away from the ruck/maul.

Remember: If your team is experienced, the last forwards take up the line of defence as soon as they see their backs are trapped in the tight-loose.

Counter-attack

From kicks

A kick straight down the touch-line

☐ Here a clear distinction must be drawn between the players who are:
- inside a 10 m circle of the catcher;
- outside the 10 m circle but still in front of the kicker; and
- behind the kicker.

☐ The players who are inside the 10 m circle must first get out of it before they are allowed to play.

☐ Those outside the 10 m circle but still in front of the kicker (usually the forwards!) are not allowed to move forward:
- before they are placed on-side by the kicker or a team-mate behind the kicker; or
- before the catcher has knocked the ball on, passed it, kicked it or run with it for 5 m.

☐ Play as soon as the law allows!

☐ The backs move up in a line across the field (rather go up slower and stay in line than move up fast individually and create gaps).

☐ When one player is far ahead of his team-mates, he must take shorter steps on approaching the catcher to ensure balance and facilitate a possible change in direction.

LOOSE FORWARDS: APPLYING PRESSURE WHEN THE HALF-BACKS KICK

(A) SCRUM POSSESSION – KICK TO NEAREST TOUCH-LINE

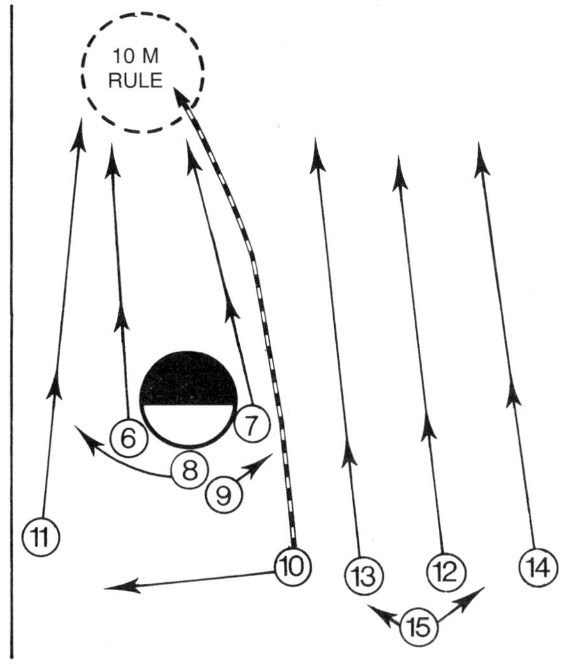

□ When two players move in towards the catcher, one goes to his left and the other just to the right of him. He cannot beat you on the outside because you each have only one side to change direction to.

□ The last player, i.e., the one furthest from the catcher, moves across the field right opposite the ball. He is the last line of defence.

(A) LINE-OUT POSSESSION – KICK TO NEAREST TOUCH-LINE

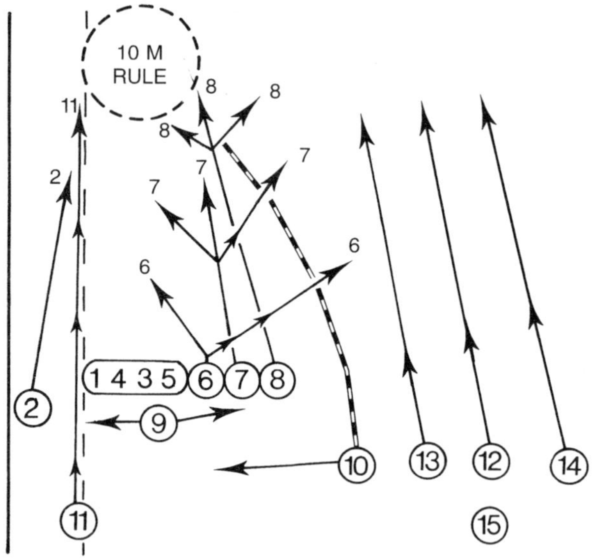

A long kick diagonally across the field

Remember: The defending team must respect the offside law!

□ The back-line adheres to the same principles.

□ The forwards immediately look to see:

- whether the counter-attack is straight ahead. The closest forwards move in behind their backs. The forwards further off stay in midfield in case the opponents take the ball quickly and then attack across the width;
- whether the ball is being passed quickly across the width.

(B) SCRUM POSSESSION - KICK DIAGONALLY ACROSS THE FIELD

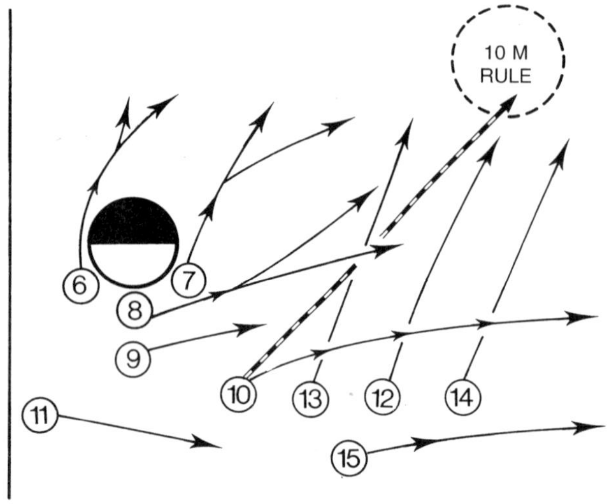

The forwards move up and immediately put pressure on the attacking back-line to force them to make mistakes behind their forwards.

This creates opportunities for your own counter-attacks.

Remember: Someone must immediately take the initiative and call: "Counter-attack!" The players then instinctively do what they have been practising.

General hint on defence against extra man in attacking back-line:

Some defensive patterns are based on each back going for his direct opponent and the full-back and blind-side wing tackling the extra man in the back-line. They usually have the arrangement that the blind-side wing covers any cutting movement up till the inside centre and the full-back covers cutting movements wider out. When the extra man, for example, goes into the line on the inside, i.e., between the fly-half and the forwards, the blind-side wing tackles him while the rest of the defenders block their opponents to the outside.

(B) LINE-OUT POSSESSION - KICK DIAGONALLY ACROSS THE FIELD

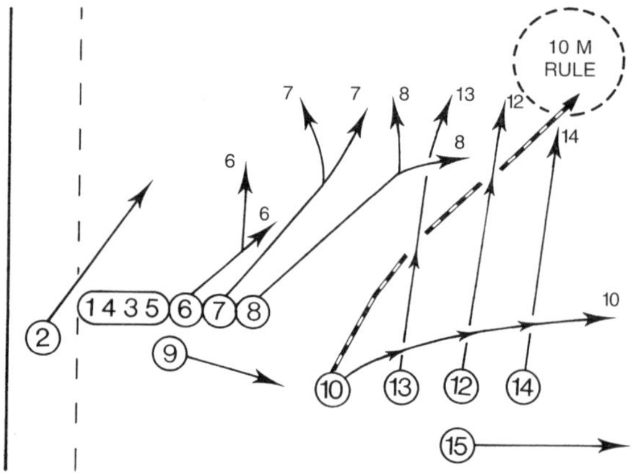

12. Influence of weather/ playing conditions

Never fight the conditions; use them

Rain

General

☐ The game is somewhat slower because:
- the players handle more slowly and make more mistakes;
- it is more difficult to win a lot of ground because the players move more slowly and kicks do not travel as far;
- the stronger (in the legs) rather than faster player comes to the fore.

☐ An adjusted handling technique is required:
- The eyes (concentration) become even more important.
- Both hands are kept behind the ball.
- The ball is passed more softly (a torpedo pass will land on the ground!).
- A pass does not travel as far.
- The stop hand becomes more important.

☐ It is more difficult for the ball-carrier to change direction. The most effective player is the one who runs straight. (You slip when you suddenly change direction by, for example, sidestepping. Because it is wet, you cannot build up enough speed to beat the opponent on the outside as in the case of a swerve.) The direction of attack is therefore changed with a pass, e.g., a short or scissors pass.

☐ A different scrum technique is required:
- The forwards should go down fairly close to the opponents otherwise the front row will cave in.
- The forwards position their feet more underneath their bodies to prevent themselves from slipping and to maintain the force of the forward push.
- Strength in the scrum is neutralised to a certain extent by wet weather because the players cannot get a firm footing.

☐ Line-out play changes drastically:
- The players stand as close as possible to each other to prevent a breakthrough (in very wet conditions, it is often best to allow the ball to go to the opponents and then simply to break through).
- The throw-in is softer; it is more a pushing than a throwing action.
- Most balls are thrown in to the front half of the line-out. Be ready to throw in deeper when the ball has dried out.
- The supporter (sweeper): More balls ricochets out of the catcher's hands. The sweeper therefore comes in from a deeper angle so that if the ball ricochets towards him he can move forward with the ball instead of diagonally or across.
- Except for the catcher and two players on either side of him, the rest of the players immediately move towards the ball; they drive round the front of the line-out or drive on the front lock.
- It is an ideal opportunity to play with the forwards. Drive on the second lock (keep out a forward to drive again from this second phase).

☐ The emphasis falls on rucks rather than mauls because wet conditions favour rucks. It is more difficult for the ball-carrier to stay on his feet and the basis for a maul is therefore weak. The ruck holds less risk:
- The ball does not roll or hop around on a wet field.
- The forwards therefore have a static target over which they can drive as a unit.
- It is easier for the ball-carrier to put the ball down on the ground than to pass it to a team-mate.
- The rest of the forwards then bind and simply drive and over the ball.
- A wet ball is more difficult to pick up.
- There is less risk attached to driving over the ball than trying to pick it up.

☐ Driving forward play comes to the fore:
- Less risk is attached to a forward taking the ball from his team-mate than the ball being passed.
- The forwards are closer together (they can concentrate their strength more).
- The players quickly learn to run off the ball deep.

☐ Because the backs are not as quick on their feet on a wet, heavy field, their play is usually aimed at crossing the advantage line and allowing their forwards to join:
- Blind side with the backs, joined by the loose forwards.
- Blind side with the loose forwards, joined by the backs.
- Field side with cuts through the backs, joined by the loose forwards.
- Kicks: In the box (behind the scrum, line-out or tight-loose - slow possession from the loose); high up-and-unders (for the centres or wingers and loose forwards); short grubber kicks (for the centres or wingers and loose forwards because it is more difficult for the opponents to control than a short kick and easier for the kicker's team-mate to exert pressure).

☐ Strategy for back-line play in respect of attack: It is important to play with the forwards:
- Starting positions are aimed at straight running; run diagonally to mislead the opponents.
- Vary the distances between the inside backs constantly.
- It is difficult to defend in wet weather
+ if your opponent suddenly plays wide, e.g., a long pass

between the fly-half and inside centre or between the two centres (this prepares the way for short passes),
+ against short passes (a short pass to the inside centre, who initially stands wide; a short pass to the extra man - the full-back or wingers - in the back-line) or
+ a change in direction (with a scissor, back pass, etc).
☐ Defence: Of primary importance is to close the inside gaps (the defender cannot stop on a slippery surface):
- It prevents the attacker from easily joining his loose forwards and forces the attacking loose forwards diagonally across the field.
- It makes changing direction more difficult.
- The cover defender must always keep the ball between himself and the touch-line towards which is being played (he should never overrun the ball!).
☐ The ball on the ground:
- that is kicked towards you and tends to skid from the grass more than it tends to bounce: pick it up with both hands (keep your elbows together!);
- that is kicked behind you towards your goal-line: slide onto the ball with the upper part of your body between the ball and the opponent, get the ball under control with your arm closest to your goal-line and immediately get up with the ball; and
- that is kicked out in front of you towards the opposition goal-line: in your half - kick forward as hard as possible; close to the opponents' 22 or goal area - dribble forward and try to retain control with short kicks.

Remember:
☐ Even in wet weather the ball is dry in the beginning.
☐ There is a big difference between:
- playing conditions on a grass field that is wet: here the ball can be handled and carried;
- playing conditions on a wet, muddy field where handling is extremely difficult; here a lot of kicking takes place and the opponents' errors are exploited.
☐ During night matches the dew on the grass often makes the ball slippery. This is particularly the case with the synthetic balls that are used nowadays.

Wind

Key factors
☐ How strong is the wind?
☐ In which direction does the wind blow over the field?
☐ Is there a possibility that the wind direction might change?

How strong is the wind?
Wind has a great psychological effect on players who are not used to playing in it. This can be largely eliminated as soon as they realise that:
- the wind is, in most cases, to the disadvantage or advantage of both teams (a strong wind does, of course, hamper the team that plays 15-man rugby more than the one that plays 10-man rugby);
- in normal windy conditions (stormy weather excluded) effective rugby can still be played with slight adjustments as long as you know how to play in the wind.

The direction of the wind determines to a large extent the pattern of play.

Wind blowing straight down field (playing with the wind at your back)

ADVANTAGES
☐ You can immediately corner the opponents in their half and put them under pressure.
☐ A good place-kicker can score points from a longer distance away while his opponent's kicking range against strong wind is drastically shortened.
☐ You can build up a lead that exhausted opponents will not be able to catch up with after the half-time change around.
☐ Wind can die down during a match or even change direction in the second half.

DISADVANTAGES
☐ You cannot immediately utilise the advantage of the wind because the players are tense at the beginning of the match and make unnecessary mistakes.
☐ Players begin to panic when their team, playing with the wind, does not score the expected number of points. This leads to more mistakes.
☐ A small difference in the score at half-time is demoralising for your team but, of course, encouraging for the opponents.

General strategy
☐ Retain ball possession within 40 m of the opponents' goal-line.
☐ The tight forwards must carry out their basic tasks! (Hard-working loose forwards are a great asset.):
- Scrums and drives exhaust the opponents.
- Line-out play is important. There are usually more line-outs.

(*Remember:* It is difficult and unwise to throw the ball to the back of the line-out.)
☐ Play from the set facets (the scrum, line-out and tight-loose) with the backs (the halves, full-back, winger and loose forwards) in such a way that the least handling mistakes are made. Examples:
- Play blind side.
- Play open side with cuts and/or dummies.
- From the scrum: The scrum-half with the eighth-man or flankers together with backs, who play shallow.
- From the line-out: A peel off to the front and at the back and a push drive followed by a rolling maul.

☐ Put maximum pressure on the opponents' back-line:
- Play as shallow as possible.
- Play to the touch-line where the fly-half is forced to kick with his weakest foot.

Kicking

□ From your 22: Kick to the touch-line to gain ground.

□ Outside your 22: Kick the ball deep down the field rather than out on the full. If you kick out directly, your opponents have a line-out throw-in opposite the place you kicked from.

□ Between the two 10 m lines: Kick high up-and-unders in such a way that your own players can catch the opponents in possession. The stronger the wind, the more difficult this is. (The wind takes the ball away from your team towards the defenders or even across the goal-line.) Beware of giving away possession. (Do not kick the ball into touch simply because you do not know what to do with it!)

□ From your own 10 m line: Use chip/grubber kicks (the stronger the wind, the less effective this is) and long rolling kicks to the corners.

□ In the opponents' half: Short grubber kicks are very effective! (The wind has little effect on the ball, you put great pressure on the defender and you can regain possession more easily.)

Handling

□ The backs stand closer together because long passes lead to mistakes.

□ The player who passes the ball:
- aims more at the receiver's body because the wind pushes the ball forward away from the receiver; and
- passes slightly faster because the slower the ball travels, the greater the wind's effect.

□ The player who receives the ball:
- "fetches" it with his hands because the wind tends to affect the ball's flight most over the last couple of centimetres before he catches it; and
- concentrates on the ball until it is in his hands.

Playing into the wind

General strategy

□ Ball possession is of the greatest importance. If you lose the ball, the opponents drive you back to your goal-line with a single kick.

□ The tight forwards make sure the opponents get the worst possible possession. The real contest in the line-outs is in front. Loose balls must be prevented.

□ Play so that your loose forwards can get into the game:
- Play blind side.
- Use cuts to the open side.

□ The forwards must support close together and deep.

□ The backs' cover and cross-defence is important.

Kicking

Remember: Kicks meant for the touch-line must be out.

□ From your 22: Kick straight into touch.

□ Outside your 22:
- kick in your half, blind side with rolling kicks to the touch-line; and
- kick open side with rolling diagonally across the field (so that the full-back has to play under pressure against the touch-line if the ball is not out).

□ In the opponents' half:
- kick blind side with rolling kicks to the touch-line and chip kicks over the top of the first defender for repossession;
- open side kick grubbers for your team-mates (too short rather than too far) and chips over the top of the back-line (this is in the attackers' favour because the wind holds the ball back).

□ In their 22: Kick only if a try can be scored!

Handling

□ It is easier against the wind because the wind blows the ball towards the catcher (therefore pass slightly ahead of your team-mate).

□ If your ball retention is good, keep possession against wind rather than kick the ball.

When the wind blows across the field

□ This influences the backs more than is realised:
- They get most line-out possession from the touch-line where the wind is blowing to. Their passes are therefore against the wind. Passes between the halves are inclined to come through unevenly.
- They can use only long passes in the direction of the wind because the ball travels further.
- Against the wind they have to use either ordinary, cut or scissor passes.
- When they kick for the touch-line against the wind and do not get the ball out, the opponents can take the initiative with counter-attacks.

□ This influences the forwards:
- When the throw-in into the line-out is against the wind, everyone knows the ball cannot be thrown in deeper than the middle of the line-out.
- Only with the wind can all the jumpers be used (i.e., are there possibilities for variation).

Sun

The sun's influence on the game depends on:

□ The direction in which the field lies:
- On a field lying east-west, the influence is much greater because the players have to look straight into the sun for one entire half either early in the morning or late in the afternoon.

□ The time of play:
- The lie of the field determines the extent to which the sun bothers the players either early in the morning or late in the afternoon.
- At noon, when the sun is at its highest, up-and-unders are a problem for the catcher.

A good coach will always make sure beforehand how his players can best exploit the effect of "sun in the eyes" on the opponents.

Floodlights

With the increase in night matches under floodlights, the coach must take account of:

☐ the quality of the lights because, the weaker the lights:
- the more it is to the advantage of the team that plays "high kick and charge" rugby;
- the more difficult it is for the referee to pick up mistakes in the tight-loose.

☐ players with poorer vision (i.e., those who need spectacles off the field) will have significantly more problems seeing clearly and are therefore prone to making many more errors.

☐ due to the dew on the grass, the ball tends to be more slippery.

13. Short-cut tips for the coach

Wise men don't learn from their own mistakes, but from somebody else's

What should I keep in mind when dealing with inexperienced players?

The inexperienced player's problem is:
- ☐ to read the situation on the field
- ☐ which facet of loose play to implement
- ☐ where to play to from a specific situation
- ☐ technique
- ☐ communication

How will I spot the quality player?

The top player:
- ☐ can read the game
- ☐ always seems to have time on his hands
- ☐ positions himself in time
- ☐ knows the weak spots to attack
- ☐ knows at which pace to take the ball
- ☐ anticipates the "needs" of fellow players out wide
- ☐ never quits supporting the ball

Tense players

Question
Some of my players are extremely tense before a match. Does this influence their ability to perform and, if so, what can I do about it?

Answer
☐ Tension before a match is a normal phenomenon and essential for achievement. Too much tension, however, drains the player and lowers his performance level. The cause of this is fear of failure. The inexperienced player worries too much about the final result, i.e., winning, instead of concentrating on what he should be doing. He should tell himself: "I'm firstly going to do my best as far as my basics are concerned and then, if possible, I'll help my team-mates. If the opponents still win, it's because they're better players." Set an attainable objective for each player so that, irrespective of the result, he will feel at the end of the day that something was achieved and not all was lost.
☐ A player's psychological preparation is as important to success as his physical preparation. Get your players to visualise for a few minutes every day:
- how they are going to carry out their basics;
- the field and the spectators;
- how they are going to play against their opponents under various weather conditions; and
- what pain, accompanied with exhaustion, feels like.

☐ When their concentration lapses, they make mistakes:
- Teach your players to break up a match into shorter units and play a unit at a time. For example, concentrate on what you are going to do when you get the ball from the scrum; when it is over, relax until the next facet of play. (This approach should be taught during match practices.) At the end of a match they should be exhausted mentally from pure concentration.

☐ Get indicators that show how tired the opponents are. Everyone becomes tired - including opponents! Who reaches the next facet of play first? At which point in the match can you dominate your opponent psychologically?:
- On first contact? Seldom with the experienced opponent; it is possible, however, if he is inexperienced.
- Play a low-risk game during the first 15-20 minutes (this does not mean the team is not going to attack; what it does mean is that only low-risk movements are going to be used).

Backs that give away points

Question
In their 22 m area my backs often make mistakes from which the opponents score. How can I prevent this?

Answer
☐ Within 20 to 25 m of your goal-line:
- make sure not to be caught with the ball, i.e., either pass or kick to touch; and
- use the grubber kick only if you have a comfortable lead or are far behind in points. In the latter case it is a last-ditch attempt to get points.

A team that doesn't score

Question
My team plays close to the opponents' goal-line but simply does not score. Why not?

Answer
☐ Continue concentrating on your basics; do not become over-enthusiastic.
☐ Retain possession, even if you have to run back! Kick only in the case of a "foot pass" for a try.

☐ When you do not know where to run in broken play in the opponent's half run towards the goal posts.
☐ In case of an attempt at a push-over try from a 5 m scrum:
- If the first attempt fails, try again but start with the concentrated push only after the ball has been brought under control in the scrum (the opponents' loose forwards will probably break up more quickly to defend outside the scrum and your scrum will therefore have the advantage).
☐ All the players should believe that if they stick to basics, they will score eventually.
Remember: You have repeatedly practised all the movements. Confidence!

The desire to win leads to bad decisions and unnecessary mistakes, especially near their opponents' goal-line

Question
What can I do to correct this?

Answer
Break up the "winning idea" into smaller parts for each player. Every time a loose-head prop goes down quickly in a scrum and puts the opposing tight-head prop under pressure, for example, he "wins"; every time an opponent is tackled behind the advantage line, the defender "wins". The cumulative result of all these "winning facets" usually leads a team to victory.

My players often choose the wrong options on attack

Question
What are the weaknesses to look out for in any defence?

Answer
Weak spots in defence
☐ due to the laws
☐ the tackle-situation
☐ after driving
- by an individual
- from ruck-situation
☐ dynamic rucking
☐ static second phase

Weak spots - the laws and tackle
☐ laws in general
- ex. quick possession from scrum play to the right
☐ present-day laws
- 3-4 forwards on the sides waiting
- weak spot often in the middle
☐ tackle
- within 2 to 3 m from tackled player when close to set piece
- blind side when at centre or further out

Weak spots - second phase - dynamic
☐ after the first drive
- gaps close to the ball
☐ after second time driving
- gaps close on right running angle
- gap where referee is standing

Weak spots - second phase - static
☐ first concentrate in the middle
- draw in forwards standing out
☐ then create gaps out wide
- dummy pass
- combinations: extra player, pass and running angle

My players don't know when to pass in depth, or lay the ball back, or to place the ball

Question
What should I advise them?

Answer
In-depth passing
☐ just before being isolated
☐ time to turn
☐ support in depth can be seen
☐ in mini-maul
☐ to speed up play

Laying the ball back - ball-carrier
☐ when going forward aggressively
☐ just before being isolated
☐ when facing the opposing goal-line
☐ can see (sense) own support but not pass
☐ just before being forced into touch
☐ to keep speed on the ball

Placing the ball - the ball-carrier
☐ technique determined by closeness of opposition
☐ pushing it back with most of the opponents on their side of the ball
☐ keep it close to the body when in midst of several players

What should the supporters do when the ball is laid back or placed?

Answer
Laying the ball back - supporters
☐ those who can't pick up the ball
- go over the ball and clean up the opponents close to the ball
☐ those who can pick up the ball
- drive through the middle or play wide into space

Placing the ball - first supporter(s)

☐ Decision: Ball or opponent?
☐ first opponent few metres clear
- pick up and drive or pick up and pass
☐ first opponent onto the ball
- take him away and leave the ball to next supporters

Placing the ball - second supporter(s)

☐ Ball already up from the deck
- drive onto ball into gap close to ball-carrier
☐ Ball still on the ground
- opponents close by: take them away
- no opponents close by: play the ball

Placing the ball - last supporters

☐ close by
- clear up or
- drive on
☐ further away
- position opposite weak spots in defence

What are the options for attack when the ball is ripped from a fellow player?

Answer

Ripping - first evaluate possession

☐ quick ball or
☐ slower after mini-maul or maul or
☐ after first driving

Rip - quickly and to the blind

☐ usually from backs
☐ ripper on feet
☐ to forwards or backs running into space
☐ same direction

Rip - slower and to the blind

☐ from backs or forwards
- mini-maul or maul
☐ ripper goes to ground
☐ forwards clean up
☐ play to blind side
- away from loiterers

Rip - after first driving

☐ loitering opposing forwards drawn in
☐ clear up the blind
☐ halfbacks decide on direction of play
☐ any direction possible: depends on time of release

How to "read" the opponents' back-line

Question

How can my team judge from the opponents' back-line what they are planning?

Answer

☐ Watch closely to see which backs are talking to one another. They are usually the ones who are going to be involved in a movement.
☐ When the fly-half and centres stand deep, they are going to play to the three-quarters.
☐ When the fly-half and centres align flat:
- the halves are going to play with the loose forwards;
- the fly-half is going to play blind side; or
- the halves are going to kick.
☐ When the fly-half stands shallow and the inside centre deep:
- the fly-half is going to run with the ball (is the inside centre perhaps coming for a scissor movement?); or
- the fly-half is going to stay where he is and the inside centre is going to do the running (is the inside centre perhaps going to play wide with a skip pass?)

Defence against unknown tactical back-line play

Question

What action do my players take when they see the opponents' backs planning something but do not know what?

Answer

☐ Try to "talk them out" of the movement.
☐ Go up in defence more slowly but stay in line. This throws their timing - on which most movements depend. They then execute the movement too soon and you can see what is coming.

Advice against good defenders

Question

How does my team play against a back-line that defends well?

Answer

☐ Create uncertainty in their ranks:
- Play blind side, especially in the beginning of the match.
- Stand deeper so that the opponents come towards you and then kick grubbers and short kicks behind them (they will quickly begin to move up more slowly and unevenly).
- Change your starting positions all the time and take up position as late as possible for the movement you have decided on.
- Use skip passes and extra men in the line to confuse the opposing players.
☐ Do not show when you have been bruised during a tackle!

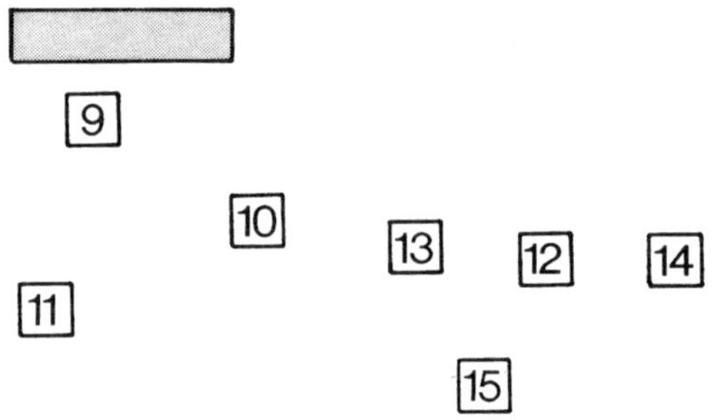

WHAT DO YOU SEE?
Centres standing shallow

DEDUCTION
Fly-half: Play shallow
Kick
Forwards play

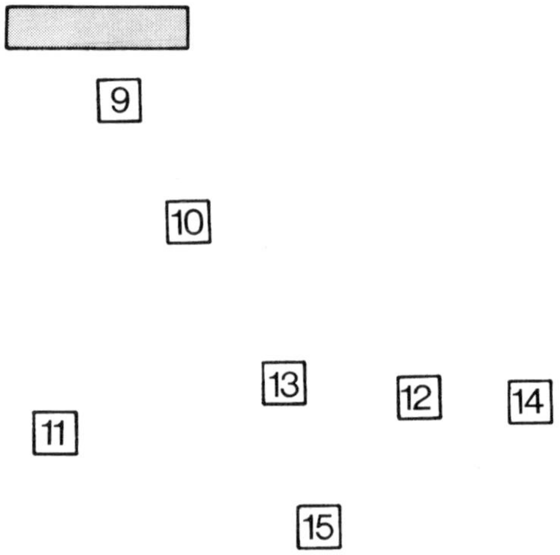

WHAT DO YOU SEE?
Inside centre is deep
Full-back is slightly behind line-out
Blind-side wing is deep

DEDUCTION
Possible change of direction by inside centre to the blind-side wing

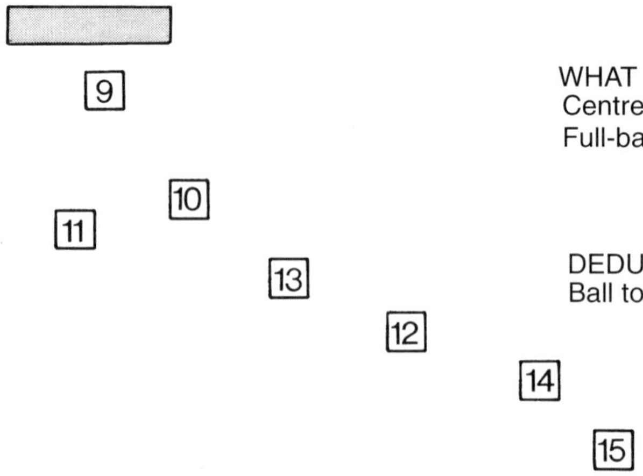

WHAT DO YOU SEE?
Centres are deep
Full-back is wide

DEDUCTION
Ball to open side

INTERPRETING OPPONENTS' FORMATION AT THE SCRUM

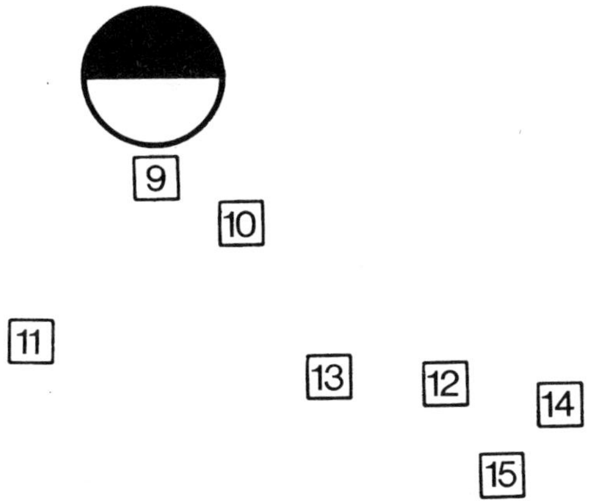

WHAT DO YOU SEE?
Fly-half (10) stands shallow
Inside centre (13) stands deep

DEDUCTION
Fly-half and inside centre are planning something

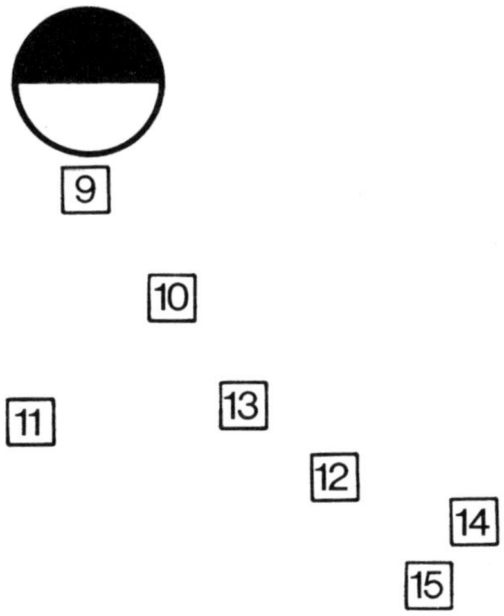

WHAT DO YOU SEE?
Fly-half and inside centre stand deep

DEDUCTION
Ball is going to open side

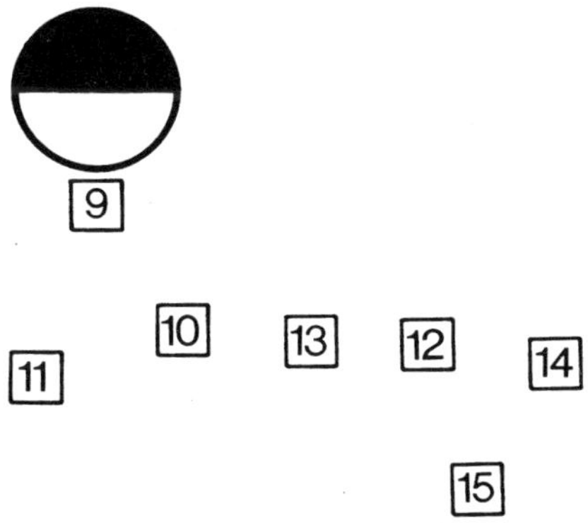

WHAT DO YOU SEE?
Entire back-line stands shallow

DEDUCTION
Half-backs and loose forwards play:
to blind side
kick

The opponents' fast winger

Question
What does my team do when the opposition has a very fast winger?

Answer
☐ Keep the game on his side of the field.
☐ When he has the ball:
- try to tackle him the moment he gets it; or
- if this is not possible, go on the defence slightly wider than usual. (Make it more difficult to beat you round the outside. Rather let him beat you on the inside. On the outside he won't be caught but, if he breaks to the inside, cross and cover defence may be able to stop him.)
☐ When you have the ball:
- stand wide and take a short pass from your centre at the last moment, thus beating your opponent on his inside (you may be slower but at least you are running straight, i.e., the shortest route); or
- use cut, scissor and/or back passes to beat him with the direction of the pass (because the movement is disguised and executed late, he has to change the direction in which he is running completely and he cannot stop you).

The kicking fly-half

Question
How does my team play against a fly-half who kicks touch-, place- and drop kicks well?

Answer
☐ Very few players kick equally well with both feet. In your half, play towards the sideline, where the kicker has to kick with his weaker foot.
☐ Good kickers like to kick. Take the initiative and force him to kick where you want him to.
☐ Deliberately cut the fly-half off from his inside centre so that he is forced to kick:
- Let your full-back and wingers create conspicuous open spaces on the field to which the fly-half can kick (they then move back into these open spaces while the ball is on its way to the fly-half; he will still kick where the open space was!).
☐ Avoid penalty kicks in your half:
- Know the laws.
- A line-out is preferable to a maul or ruck that can end in a penalty kick.

The struggling place-kicker

Question
What tips can I give my place-kickers?

Answer
☐ Place kicking is inextricably linked with:
- attitude (what is going on between the kicker's ears! - he must believe in his ability and relax); and
- technique.
☐ Teach the beginner the soccer kick.
☐ Do not interfere unnecessarily with the place-kicker.
☐ When the kicker is really struggling, keep the following aspects in mind:
- Keep your eyes on the ball.
- Concentrate but stay loose.
- Start kicking practice close to the goal posts and gradually move away without putting yourself under pressure.
- Your footing in respect of your non-kicking foot is extremely important. It should point in the direction of the goal posts. Try to place it in the same spot every time. The closer it is to the ball, the shorter distance the ball travels.
- Your chest must, at the moment of contact, face the goal posts; the ball usually travels in the direction your chest faces.
- Strike the ball with the bridge of your kicking foot. When it is turned lengthways towards the inside, you get greater distance. Listen to the sound when your foot strikes the ball.
- Your kicking foot should strike the ball just under the point of gravity. This way you get greater distance. Watch the flight of the ball through the air. When it spins fast, it means you kicked it too low.
- Kick through instead of towards the ball.
- In wet weather, the right-footed kicker should aim slightly left of his normal target because his left foot tends to slip slightly and he pushes the ball more easily to the right.
Tip: Kickers often underestimate the distance they can kick comfortably. With the goal posts as the centre, draw a semi-circle 5 m out from where the 22 and the touch-line meet. Most kickers will be surprised to see how close this line brings them to the 10 m line. If the kicker practises from the circumference of the semi-circle, he will have confidence in his kicking ability up to the 10 m line. Matches are won or lost by kicks up to 40 m!

The kickers do not reach the touch-line with their kicks

Question
Why is a reliable kicker suddenly not reaching the touch-line with a penalty and/or free kick, and thus allowing the opponents to launch a counter-attack?

Answer
☐ The kicker's chest must face the point on the touch-line where he wants the ball to go out. This prevents the ball from slicing off his foot infield. This applies particularly to a player who kicks to the left touch-line with his right foot and vice versa.

☐ In wet weather, the kicker must deliberately forfeit 5 m to 10 m of his kicking distance because a wet and muddy ball does not travel as far and his gripping foot tends to slip slightly.

Advice against heavy, strong forwards

Question
How does my team play against a team with heavy, strong forwards?

Answer
☐ Keep the game as fast as possible; heavy forwards do not like crisscrossing the field, particularly not if they have to turn back!
☐ Limit the opportunities for physical contact:
- Avoid scrums (or use channel one for a quick ball to No. 8 packing between 6 and 4) and ordinary line-outs (disrupt those that do take place as much as the rules allow).
- Keep the ball "loose" (pass the ball in time and so prevent static loose mauls or scrums from developing).
☐ Put as much pressure on the opponents' backs as possible:
- Force them into making errors behind the advantage line.
- Let them kick away possession to where your defenders are waiting.
☐ Create open spaces on the field (away from the opponents' forwards) to which their halves can kick. Organise your defence in such a way that you can move the play, before the opponents' forwards can catch up (you did, after all, arrange beforehand who was going to cover those open spaces!)
☐ Even the best pack of forwards eventually disintegrates when it constantly has to retreat.

Light forwards against a heavy pack in the scrum

Question
What should my light forwards do in a scrum against opponents who have a heavy pack of forwards?

Answer
☐ Avoid scrums. Concentrate on your handling so that scrums result from mistakes of the opponents (your team then has the put in). Play the ball as fast as possible. Avoid mauls and rucks, which can end in scrums (rather play the ball into touch from where you contest the line-outs).
☐ Go down as late as possible. Wait until the scrum-half has taken the mark.
☐ Go down as low as possible. This applies especially to the front row, which then enables the rest to do the same. It is easier to take the pressure when your joints are virtually straightened.
☐ Let the second row and eighth-man lock beforehand and bind very tight. The more stability in your pack, the less energy you waste.
☐ As soon as the front rows make contact, the ball must be put in.

The opponents wheel the scrum

Question
What can my team do when the opponents constantly wheel our scrums?

Answer
☐ First find out why they are wheeling the scrum:
- Is it because their scrum is strong and they want to force more scrums?
☐ Eliminate handling errors and restrict the number of scrums.
☐ Remain a tight unit and scrum hard when they try to wheel. It will tire them and make them change their tactic.
☐ Is it to place your back-line in an unfavourable position for attack?
- Prevent the wheel by hooking a fast ball (channel 1) into the eighth-man (who goes down between 4 and 6) or the scrum-half's hands.
- Utilise the wheel by going with it to just before 90° (when you have to scrum again). Let your No. 8 pick up the ball and helped by the other loose forwards drive on in the same direction as the wheel.

Question
What can my team do to counter opponents who deliberately wheel their scrum to the left, i.e., the tight-head side of the scrum goes back?

Answer
☐ The tight players and leftside flanker scrum hard. This prevents their eighth-man from easily picking up the ball to start a movement (his tight players are under pressure).
☐ The scrum-half pressurises their No. 8.

Counter-strategies for line-out specialists

Question
What do we do against a team with very good line-out jumpers?

Answer
☐ Avoid line-outs. Kick the ball out only when you have to. This ensures that it's your throw in most of the time.
☐ When they throw in, unsettle the jumper as much as possible:
- Get your shoulder in front of him.
- Go for his inside arm so that he loses the ball.

- Try to turn him sideways in the air so that your supporters can take the ball from him.
- Pull him, ball and all, through the line-out to your side.
- If all else fails, push him out of the line-out to his side so that his scrum-half gets bad possession.

☐ Look where on the field the line-out is and anticipate where they're going to throw. Try to exert pressure behind his forwards. Tackle the player peeling off before he reaches the advantage line.

☐ Vary your throw-ins, go for deflection and prevent the ball going to ground between the line-out and scrum-half.

Advice against good loose forwards

Question
What does my team do when the opponents have strong loose forwards?

Answer
☐ Every player in your team must see himself as a loose forward. The player closest to the ball, irrespective of his position, must immediately get the ball under control.
☐ Avoid loose balls. Concentrate on handling! Any loose balls must be behind the opponents' loose forwards.
☐ The rest of the players must work closely with your loose forwards. The latter must know where the ball is going so that they can get there faster and in greater numbers.
☐ If possible, your tight forwards must scrum hard so that the opponents break out of the scrum more slowly.
☐ Use kicks:
- Your players can go up quickly and exert pressure.
- The opponents have to drop back every time.

☐ Drill your lighter forwards in the rucking technique. They can be more effective as a unit than bigger individuals/opponents who may be good in mauls.

The loose degenerates into pile-ups

Question
When one of our players is caught with the ball, pile-ups develop and we cannot win the ball quickly. Why?

Answer
The central problem lies in what the ball-carrier and his first two supporters are doing (see the part about the tight-loose in chapter 5).

I am afraid of falling into the trap of coaching rugby like rugby league. How should I approach the matter of contact?

Answer
Contact should (be):
☐ to the advantage of the ball-carrier
- to prevent injuries
- in order to keep possession

☐ of the shortest duration possible
- to interrupt the flow or speed of the movement as little as possible

☐ where the opponent is weakest
- on his arm instead of shoulder or body

☐ disrupt the tackler's timing by
- sidestepping
- a dummy pass
- changing your angle of running

My forwards are weak in mauling. For which mistakes should I look out?

Answer
☐ forwards too loose; don't bind
☐ weak footing base
- go to ground easily

☐ ball up front
- easily blocked or taken away by opponents

☐ individual player tries to take on opposition on his own
- he is isolated and loses possession

How do I stop a side with an excellent rolling-maul technique?

Answer
☐ isolate the ball-carrier
☐ destabilise the ball-carrier
- tackle upwards so that he loses his footing

☐ break arm support of supporters closest to ball-carrier
- now it is easy to isolate him

☐ illegal ways
- depends on the referee's interpretation of the law

Options for counter-attack

From kicks across field from touch to midfield or goal
☐ opponents concentrated in one part of the field
☐ catcher has time
☐ space against the far touch-line
☐ target area
☐ supporters run themselves quickly in position opposite target area

From kicks across field from midfield to touch
☐ less space in which to manoeuvre
☐ attackers must create space through
- passing
- running angles
- change of direction

☐ target area close to touch-line

Kicks close and parallel to touch - midfield open

☐ catch ball in front of attacking forwards
☐ long pass (or two) across field to space
☐ speed forward after first/second pass
- towards weak spot
- watch for uneven pressure or weak defensive alignment

Kicks - up-and-unders - pressure on midfield

☐ immediately to the blind side or
☐ dummy attack infield
☐ switch attack to blind side

Chip/grubber kicks in midfield

☐ straight ahead through the middle or
☐ 90° against the direction of the kick to the furthest touch-line
- supporters must run them into position in advance

Loose ball from tackles

☐ close to set play
- gap within 2 to 3 m from tackle
- straight ahead

☐ midfield or out wide
- immediately to the blind side

Loose ball from knock-ons

☐ immediately to the blind side
☐ towards speed

Interceptions

☐ while running back
- long pass across field away from pressure into space, then speed forward with support

☐ while running forward
- straight ahead
- as soon as possible behind pressure
+ support move onto the ball and play or
+ kick ahead and charge

Backline giving away points under pressure

Question

My back-line makes silly errors in their own 22 from which the opponents often score. How can it be prevented?

Answer

☐ Within 20 to 25 m from his own goal-line:
- No back should be caught in possession. Either pass or kick out in time.
- Use the grubber kick only when your side is leading comfortably or seemingly has little chance to win. In the latter case it is a last ditch attempt to win.

☐ Concentrate on basics and don't get overeager.
☐ Keep possession near their goal-line. You only kick if it is a "foot pass" to score.
☐ Encourage each other and make a concerted effort to score. You do have the confidence you need because you've repeatedly practised your attacking ploys on the spot.
☐ If you don't know where to run to, go for the posts.

Question

What whould my players eat and drink before a match?

Answer

This is an area in which most coaches are, in reality, laymen and players often cling to specific traditional habits. Certain physiological facts cannot, however, be ignored:

☐ A player must eat on the day of a match. It is of the greatest importance what and when he eats and drinks.
☐ It takes time for food to be digested and converted into energy. Bear in mind that meat is digested only after about four hours and that milk slows down the digestive process.
☐ Climate - temperature and humidity - plays a large role in what should be eaten and drunk. The higher the temperature, the more liquid should be taken. Salt and salt tablets immediately before and after a match should be avoided.
☐ Coaches would do well to read Dr Tim Noakes' book *Lore of running*. He provides scientifically based information about what and when a sportsman should eat and drink.
☐ The drive to achieve makes players use all kinds of remedies (some illegal), harmful or not, towards this end. Players who make themselves guilty of this are:
- the young, inexperienced player who wants to achieve;
- the veteran who does not practise regularly any more and has trouble keeping fit; and
- the player who has just recovered from an injury and is worried that he is not fit enough yet.

☐ Players must take in liquid during a match to prevent dehydration. Depending on the temperature and the position he is playing, a player should drink about 250 ml to 300 ml of water every 20 to 25 minutes.
☐ The long-distance athlete and canoeist, etc., know the feeling of exhaustion that overcomes them after about 60 to 80 minutes of intense exercise. This is caused by, among other things, a sudden drop in blood sugar level. When this happens, the participant suddenly becomes "stupid": his good judgement deserts him and he makes mistakes. Scientists contend that a rugby match is too short and, because of the numerous interruptions, not intense enough to tire a player to such an extent. The fact remains, however, that errors in a match increase as players become more tired.

To summarise:

☐ Let the player eat what he is used to during the week. On the day of the match, he should eat at least three to four hours before the match (nowadays they prefer fish and pasta to steak and eggs!)
- The sensible intake of fluid is essential.

14. Coaching and the World Cup

The basics remain the same

My intentions have been to keep this coaching manual simple. Anyone who loves the game should be able to use it. But remember the principles in this directive apply from the introduction-to-the-game level up to teams of World Cup standard.

A closer look at the teams and the rugby that was played in the 1995 World Cup will explain what I mean.

The competition clearly showed that there isn't a set pattern for all the sides to play to

A coach must adapt the way he wants to play according to his side's physical, mental and technical abilities.

The physically shorter Japanese, with their apparent lack of line-out ability, tried to keep the ball away from the touch-line because they had no chance against the taller opposition. To compensate for this shortcoming, they speeded up the game and concentrated on second phase. With their low centre of gravity and resulting elusive running style, they were a joy to watch. Nevertheless, the hard fact remained: without line-out ability they didn't have enough possession to compete at the top.

Western Samoa and Tonga had the same problem as Japan in the line-outs. Although these two sides were brilliant - even ruthless - in defence, they just couldn't get enough possession against the top sides. Predictably they lost.

Although a team tries to force its style of play on the match, the players must have an alternative

England's failure to reach the final proved just this. Having won the Five Nation's Grand Slam with their slow, mauling style of play, they believed they could do the same on the hard grounds of South Africa. They failed especially when they couldn't dominate the line-outs as they did in the Five Nations. Their slow loose forwards were run off their feet and were badly beaten to the loose ball by quicker opponents. Realising they had to run the ball to win, they could only do it from ruck ball because they were not used to passing before contact. This gave the opponents enough time to organise their defences.

Scotland, on the contrary, after being badly beaten by the Springboks at Murrayfield in 1994, realised that they must have options other than playing from a second-phase based on ruck-ball only. They cleverly varied their second phase between rucking, mauling and driving and were always in contention for a place in the semi-finals.

Vision, or the ability to read the game, is part of any top player and team

This enables a player to adapt to the ever-changing situation on the field. It helps him take the right options on attack and defence.

The Wallabies forgot it and lost the World Cup. They stuck to an apparently pre-planned and predictable game-plan regardless of what the opponents were doing. Golden scoring opportunities on the blind side, for example, were ignored as they repeatedly tried to set up second phase on the open side. In the process they slowed the game down to the pace of their lesser skilled opponents and virtually ignored the attacking flair of their backline. Thus they played a brand of rugby totally foreign to the attacking styles of their predecessors and for which both Queensland and New South Wales - where almost the entire side are from - are renowned. For only a few minutes during the entire competition they really let go and showed what a formidable side they could have been if only they had played to their strengths.

To come out on top, a side must have quality halfbacks

The way the Wallabies struggled at scrum-half clearly showed this.

This is also where France's World Cup campaign faltered. The French halfbacks couldn't capitalise on the quality possession from their forwards. Although giving excellent service to the fly-half, the French scrum-half(s) hardly ever kicked or cut the line, thereby shifting the pressure to the fly-half and the centres. To worsen matters for the French, their fly-half shirked contact. The only way he took his side forward was by kicking - and thereby losing possession. In the same way the inexperience of the promising young New Zealand fly-half Andrew Mehrtens showed up in the final. In a game-plan heavily dependent on the formidable physical ability of Jonah Lomu, and in an attempt to get the ball to the winger quickly, Mehrtens skip-passed when the opposition was still a long way off. This enabled the South African backs to read the All Black attack in time and react accordingly.

Any side which wants to come out on top must have a reliable goalkicker

Argentina lost against England because of poor goal kicking.

When Michael Lynagh missed some important kicks at goal early in Australia's match against South Africa, the opportunity to boost his side's confidence was lost. The same happened to England. When the usually reliable Rob Andrew failed as a kicker against New Zealand his side was in trouble. Stransky's boot, on the other hand, played a major part in South Africa winning the World Cup.

If you want to compete at the top, you must be mentally tough

Italy lost a possible berth in the quarter-finals in the first few minutes of their match against the hard-tackling Samoans. Psychologically they couldn't cope with the Samoans' aggression, which totally disrupted the Italians' flowing style.

Ireland, on the other hand, got to the quarter-finals more on guts than ability.

A really top side is able to use home-ground advantage or overcome it when it's in the opponents' favour

The massive and intimidating support the Springboks had in the opening match at Newlands got to the Wallabies in such a way that even experienced players like David Campese made the most elementary mistakes in defence and attack. Some of the Australian players couldn't recover from this shock and never reached the high level of which they were capable.

An organised defensive pattern and players who are committed to applying pressure throughout the match are prerequisites for a winning side

In this regard the South African side was excellent. It wouldn't be far-fetched to say that commitment in defence and up front, together with consistent goal-kicking, won them the cup.

In order to win matches consistently players must use the ball and in order to do so their basic skills must be good

New Zealand's brand of rugby was an eye-opener and did more to promote the game world-wide than the rugby played by any other team. The pace at which they played and the space players created for each other were a joy to watch.

At the same time New Zealand showed that success breeds success. The All Blacks base their attacks on quality possession rather than position and they were able to run opponents off their feet - even from within their own 22.

Be careful that your strength doesn't become your downfall

This was shown by the English and the Wallabies, whose mauling became an end in itself. Although they were successful up front they neglected their backs and eventually restricted their attacking options.

Brilliant individual players are an asset, but only it they are skilfully used

If not, they become predictable and less efficient. Because the All Blacks tried to get the ball to Lomu at every possible opportunity, the Springboks didn't have to worry a lot about the other inside backs. Even the South African centres could tackle out wide against Lomu!

The game of rugby is about the ball in the first place, and not the opponent

Canada learned this the hard way. Obviously you must be physically tough and there is no problem if you play the game that way. But the moment your focus shifts away from the ball to the opponent, you'll lose more than you win. You also place yourself at the mercy of the referee.

Don't fight bad weather conditions; rather use them to your advantage

The French will argue that they lost a place in the final of the World Cup by a few centimetres when Benazzi was stopped short of the South African goal-line. The truth is that they lost it by trying to play a handling game in atrocious wet weather.

The Springboks, on the other hand, won it by keeping the ball in front of their forwards with shrewd kicking from the base of the set pieces.

To compete at international level a player must be extremely fit

The South Africans' fitness enabled them to play for 80 or 100 minutes, whichever were required. New Zealand, on the other hand, went into the final with both Zinzan and Robin Brooke not 100% fit on account of previous injuries. Physically the two brothers just couldn't cope with a semi-final and final played on successive weekends.

Teams should stick to the style of rugby at which their players are the most effective

Wales, with a coach strongly influenced by the English, copied the latter's style of setting up second phase from primary possession. In the process they smothered the attacking ability of the once widely feared Welsh halfbacks and the running skills of their loose forwards.

Gimmicks don't guarantee success

The French three-quarters were often in the news because of their clean-shaven heads. Instead of their own hairstyles, they should have paid more attention to the opposition's styles of play.

The quality of the referee determines, to a large extent, the quality and the type of game that will be played

Since the seventies French and Irish referees have been part of some of the best rugby matches ever played.

They might be criticised for some decisions from a purely technical point of view, but they have shown an understanding of the game that has helped create an atmosphere and a background for some wonderful play.

It is hard to understand why some referees concern themselves so rigidly with the laws when a team that obviously wants to play positively is neglected in favour of a side which is intent on disruptive tactics.

Part of the reason for New Zealand's success in speeding up the game can be put down to the excellent contribution their referees make in responding to positive play.

Future developments in rugby

The World Cup has commercialised the game in a way very few people would have expected in 1987 when it started. Where national prestige and pride, as well as big money, are at stake, countries are inevitably forced into a more professional approach to the game.

Nowadays every top rugby playing country has to start its World Cup campaign at least four years in advance. This has led to a revolution as far as spotting players and scientifically preparing them are concerned. Gone are the days of a single coach running everything. New is the management team consisting of specialists in their various fields chaired by the coach as chief executive.

The seemingly non-stop preparation for international matches has put the top players in the commercial limelight as never before. As the chief performers in the international arena, their wishes and demands can't be ignored as in the past. The demands on their time which speeded up the movement towards professionalism is a fact that many administrators of the game still have to come to terms with. This brought in a new dimension for which most are not prepared or qualified.

With the expected professional approach the type of player required at top level will change. Backs, for example, can't depend on their skill alone any more. They will have to be physically strong. Apart from team management, with the amounts of money involved, player management will have to be professionalised.

As far as the game is concerned, demands for the spectacular and the speeding up of the 15-man game inevitably resulted in a changing of the laws towards consistency and simplification and creating opportunities for more action.

With rugby competing against Rugby League and Australian Rugby Rules in a world becoming "smaller" by the day on account of developing technical ability, rugby will more and more have to compete with other sports as far as spectator-participation is concerned. Strict attention will have to be paid to spoiling tactics such as the so-called "professional foul" whereby players deliberately give away penalties to avoid tries being scored against them.

The game of rugby will have to keep up with these new developments in order not to become extinct. As long as that which gave rugby its identity doesn't change.

15. Basic approach – checklist

Every coach, some time or other, has to decide what type of approach will be the best for his club or side. The following example may help him decide on a game-plan.

Basics

☐ Observe
☐ Communicate
☐ Go forward
☐ Speed on the ball
☐ Ball-carrier's skill and decision in contact situation is crucial
☐ Primary possession is non-negotiable
☐ Driving, rucking and mauling should be directed to the opposition's back-line

Scrum

☐ Aggressive but disciplined
☐ Flank forwards determine rhythm
☐ Scrum-half determines strategy after the ball is put in the scrum
☐ Wheeling - attacking and defensive

Line-out

Own throw-in

Basics
☐ Take up the space
☐ Ball off the top
  Attack with backs
  Peel off by forwards
☐ Ball taken cleanly
  Driving maul
  Halves decide from there

Attacking options normal line-out
First jumper (2)
☐ Off the top
  To the backs
☐ Taken cleanly
  Drive on two
  Peel off in front

Second jumper (4)
☐ Off the top
  To the backs
☐ Taken cleanly
  Rolling maul through the middle
  Halves decide from there

Third jumper (6)
☐ Off the top
  To the backs - all options
  Forwards peel off
☐ Taken cleanly
  Rolling maul
  Halves decide from there
☐ Five metres behind the line-out
  No. 8 plays to either own loose forwards or inside backs

Attacking options shortened line-out
☐ Versions of 2/3/4/5 men
  Use of the loose forwards close midfield or out wide

Opponents' throw-in

Basics
☐ Take up the space
☐ Compression
☐ Player at the back of the line-out

Basics on defence
☐ Possession
☐ Cover your man regardless where he is
☐ Watch out for five metres in front and at the back

Open drive (contact after first phase)

Ball-carrier
☐ Keeping possession is his responsibility
☐ Pass before contact only when eye-contact with supporter
☐ Try and prevent being isolated
☐ When isolated, two options:
  Behind forwards: stay on feet for few seconds until support arrives
  In front of forwards: Go to ground and place ball
☐ When threatened to be isolated by *several* opponents:
  Pass in depth before contact;
  Roll ball 2 to 3 m back to oncoming supporters

Supporters

☐ First observe then decide where weak spot in defence is
☐ First priority to secure the ball/possession
☐ If ball is secured, where are the opponents?
 If close to the ball, clean up the opponents
 If not, pick up and either drive through the middle or let go the half backs

Maul

Ball-carrier

☐ Hit the weak spot in defence - an opponent's outstretched arm instead of body
☐ Sidestep, dummy pass to create weakness

First player

☐ Secure the ball, then work it to the back

Supporters

☐ Clean up over ball-carrier
☐ Tightly bound - keep ball-carrier on his feet - and stay on your feet
☐ First get the maul moving, then decide on the direction
☐ If ball goes to ground behind the forwards
 Get it off the ground, stay on your feet and reorganise

Ruck

Ball-carrier

☐ Body position of ball-carrier on his feet
☐ The way he should go to ground and place the ball

Supporters

☐ In scrum formation
 Over and past the ball
 Scrum-half decides
☐ Ruck in front of the forwards good option for quick possession

Kick-off

Own ball

☐ Variations
☐ Two past the ball, two to the ball, two directly behind the ball
☐ Options of the rest of the forwards and the backs

Opponents' kick-off

☐ Blocking
☐ Control
☐ Consolidate
☐ Options
 Rolling maul
 Peel off
 Back-line ball
 Kicking

Defence

☐ The individual
 Low-risk tackling in different circumstances
☐ Organisation
 Everyone must have confidence in the pattern
☐ Communication
 The role played by the halfbacks is vital.

Back-line play

Basics

☐ Observe and decide where the weaknesess in the defence are *before* you
 receive the ball from set pieces;
 take up position in broken play
☐ Straight running before you get the pass
☐ Play as flat/shallow as your skill level allows you to do
☐ After the first phase, if the backs can't cut the defence, the back running with the ball links with one of his own forwards who should try to penetrate, or set it up for the backs to play from
☐ If possible try and pass the ball before contact
☐ Try and stay part of the movement after you've passed the first time

On attack

☐ Observe, decide and communicate
☐ Quickly into position (alignment)
☐ Get the ball to the target you want to attack in such a way that
 all the defenders from the inside are taken out of play;
 you outnumber the defenders;
 you are able to put the player who has to cut the line in the gap
☐ When in a one against one situation, attack your opponent's weak spot by
 sidestepping or dummy passing, thus either beating him to the inside or making contact on his outstretched arm instead of his upper body;
 shifting/drifting the split second before you receive the pass in such a way that you hit the gap straight on instead of trying to run around your opponent
☐ Vary your play in such a way that while causing uncertainty among the defenders you create new weak spots to attack
☐ Play with two full-backs, the blind-side winger being one of them
☐ Don't be afraid to play. It is the only way to improve. You'll be criticised only if you are either afraid to play or selfish and want to do everything on your own

Counter-attack

Basics

☐ Where are the weak spots

☐ Basically one should attack the pressure point before switching the attack away from it

☐ If possible the backs should run onto the forwards because they will have no line of defence and should easily be beaten by the swift-moving backs

Player catching the ball

☐ Must nominate

☐ When he has time on his hands

Use it to observe and decide on the direction in which to launch the attack

The supporters

☐ Run themselves into position

☐ Part played by the full-back and wings is vital to success

Penalty/free kicks

For

☐ Everyone in position!

☐ When the opposition is slow to align

Hit the gaps and support the ball

☐ When the opposition aligns quickly:

Go for touch and play in their half;

or

Execute well-drilled attacking ploys

Against

☐ Alignment!

☐ Ten metres and cover defence

☐ Delay wherever possible

Weather conditions

☐ Use them, don't fight them

Opponents' style of play

☐ Know it and be prepared, but try to stamp your authority on game

The referee

He is always in the right; even if he isn't! Interpret him and play accordingly

Conclusion

☐ You are only as good as you are on the day, so concentrate and be positive.

16. Drills

When you enjoy, you perform

When looking for help coaches invariably ask for specific drills to help them improve their coaching. To ask for help in itself isn't wrong. However, I prefer the approach spelled out by the proverb: "Don't give me a fish, rather teach me how to fish." After all, we do not play a game called "Drills", we play Rugby. It is of the utmost importance that a coach understands that drills should be seen in the context of the game.

Although there are some basic drills which are unlikely to change, there is no one set for the entire season. The remedial effect of drills is often ignored. Drills should be specific, aimed at improving skills and correcting mistakes made during a previous match.

So what is the basic philosophy behind any set of drills?

Observation

☐ To play rugby you must be able to get a picture in your mind of what is happening around you. You must be taught to *observe the situation.*
☐ This can only be done if the player is taught to look up and scan the field of play.
☐ Thereafter you must decide how to *react to the situation.*

Relaxation

☐ Every player *has a specific area in which, when alone, he feels himself secure.* The moment somebody else enters that area - and in rugby it happens quickly - he feels threatened and under pressure. This may cause him to tense up or even panic, losing a sense of co-ordination and an ability to observe.
☐ It is the coach's task to make this area of comfort to the player as small as possible, enabling the player to react coolly under circumstances in which he normally would freeze up.

Direction of running

☐ *It is human to run away from, or try to avoid, problems or danger.*
☐ On the rugby field the danger usually is right in front of the ball-carrier. His normal response will be to get away from danger. He will do this by trying to run around his opponent, i.e., by running across field.
☐ In rugby *players must be taught to run towards the danger (opponent) and pass the ball away from it.*

Handling

☐ Because the essence of playing rugby is to carry the ball, players must be efficient in this respect.
☐ The better a player's handling ability, the more time he has to execute a movement and the more relaxed and improved his vision will be.

Support

☐ As rugby is played by fifteen players on a side, players must quickly be taught how to create opportunities for their fellow players and to support the ball. In this way the value of keeping possession will be instilled at an early age.

Anticipation

☐ Rugby can be a complicated game when players don't avoid the numerous problems which can confront them.
☐ Youngsters must be taught to think and look ahead to avoid problems either for them or for the players on their outside.
☐ The way to do it is by creating real-game situations, simulations that don't carry the risk of injuries.

Understanding the game

Players must be given *a helicopter-view of the game.* If so, they will:
☐ understand the weaknesses in any defence that are brought about by the laws of the game;
☐ realise the way the backs and forwards are interdependent on each other;
☐ evaluate possession correctly and use it to their best advantage.

The above-mentioned should be foremost in the coach's mind when planning drill sessions. Although the players might not even notice it, they will reap the benefit.

Drills should be specific

They should concentrate on the following:

☐ Warm-up:

- They should be stimulating and force the players to concentrate right from the start.

☐ Develop basic skills, e.g., handling and positioning:

- All the players should, where possible, take part in all the drills, irrespective of their positions.

☐ Serve as specific preparation for different facets of play:

- They should, slowly but surely, consolidate the theory behind facets like the kick-off, back-line play after primary and second-phase possession, and joining between forwards and backs.

☐ Be remedial, i.e., eliminate mistakes:

- They should be worked out after a match to eliminate any shortcomings that arose during a match. This requires insight and initiative from the coach.

☐ Create situations where a player is given the opportunity to make decisions:

- Repeated exposure, together with the correction of mistakes, should help a player develop in such a way that he makes the right decisions most of the time.
- Emphasis should be on observation, decision-making, positioning and execution or, put simply: look, sum up, decide, get into position - and *do*.

Where drills are concerned with consolidating new skills, this should take place in the smallest space practical because:

☐ the emphasis is not on stamina but on improving skills; and

☐ the coach must be close by to correct possible mistakes immediately so that the mistakes are not repeated.

17. Drills: examples

The players must consciously learn running skills

[For the purpose of reference, the skills are numerically numbered.]

1. Let the players run with their hands in their pockets or waistband when they are not handling. (This teaches the ball-carrier to run comfortably with the ball in his hands; handling and running do not influence one another unduly.)

2. Let the players run for about 10 m to 15 m while deliberately taking short steps. (This teaches the player balance; shorter steps usually precede the sidestep.)

3. Position players in a square and let them jog to the side opposite the one where they are standing without touching one another. (This teaches a player to observe, sidestep, speed up and vary the length of his strides.)

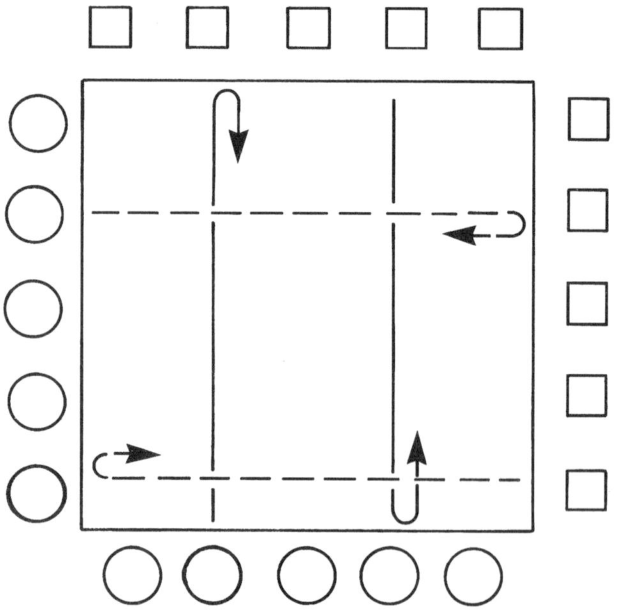

4. Divide the players into two groups. While the one group is jogging in a row, the other comes from the front and sidesteps in between those jogging in the row. (This teaches the player timing to sidestep.)

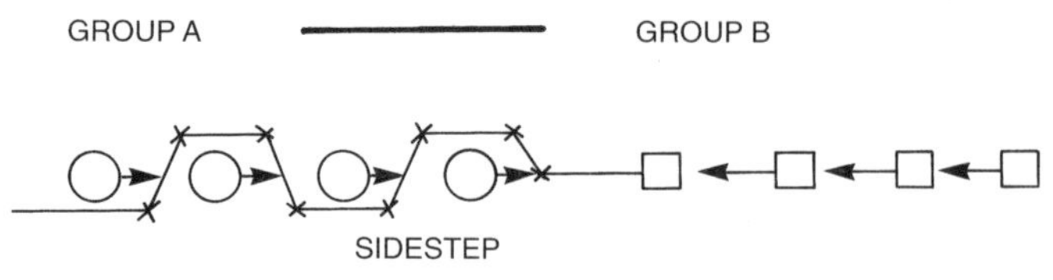

5. Divide the players into pairs. The two players stand one behind the other on the goal-line and then start jogging towards the other goal-line. On the back player's signal, both turn around, and the one who is now behind tries to touch his team-mate before they reach the goal-line. (This improves the player's reflexes and teaches him to change direction quickly and speed up.)

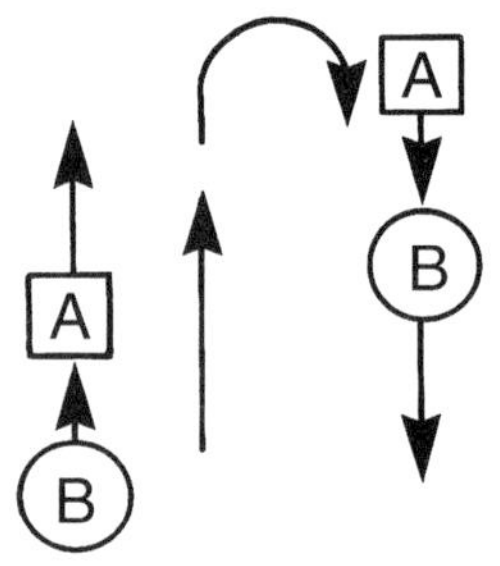

6. The forwards must learn to run in formation while driving (see p. 99, top left):
- The principle according to which forwards' support is deep, behind to the right and left, and behind the ball-carrier (in a diamond formation).
- Number the four players in the beginning so that they concentrate all the time and become used to running deep off the ball.

Few players at the beginning of practice

To teach the player to let his lower body, upper body, arms and head (eyes) function independently of one another

7. Set up a number of beacons in between which a player must jog while playing with the ball in his hands. The beacons should be positioned in such a way that they force the player to give short steps. The player must then jog around the beacons first forward and then backward. Expand the movement to include first two and then three

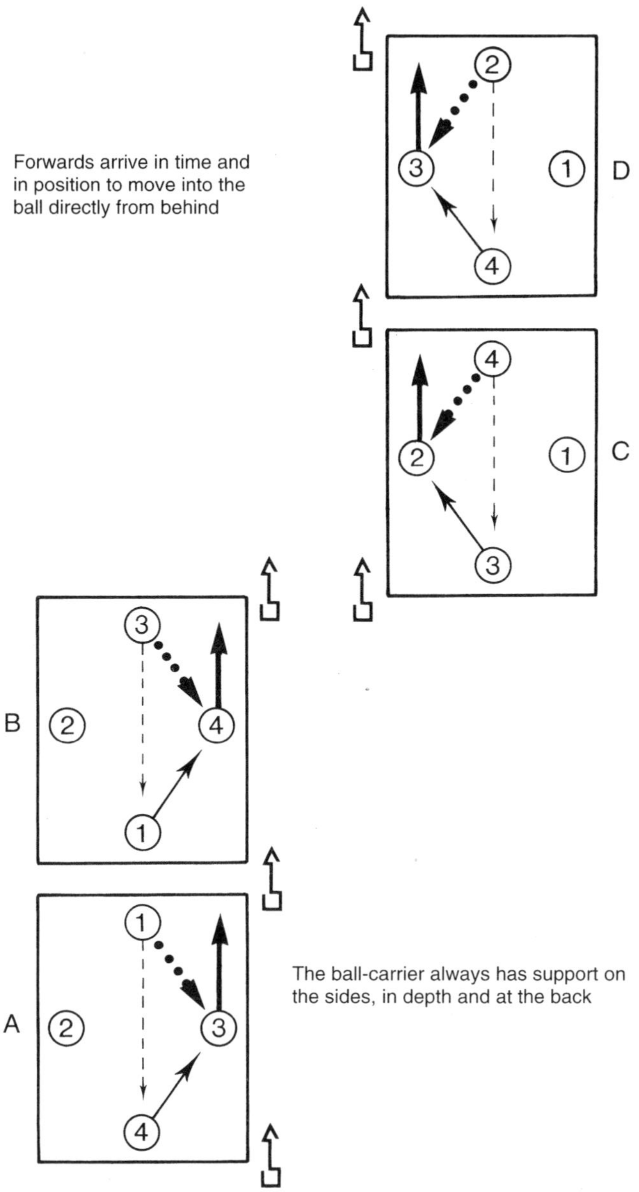

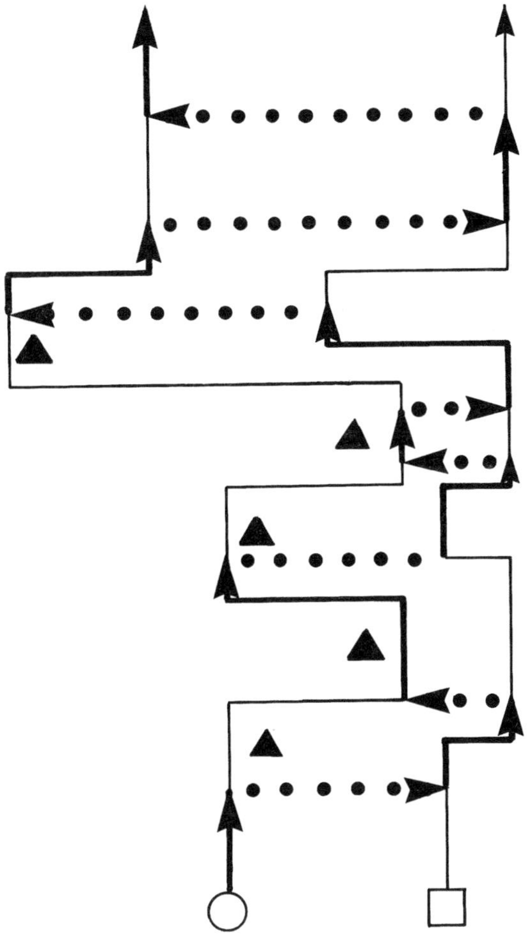

players. The middle player carries the ball and goes round the beacons; the other two do exactly the same. This teaches the player footwork, to look where he is stepping and running, and to watch the ball-carrier while running in position (see top right).

8. To give the player a feeling for the ball, he executes the following movements while running and passing to each other:
- Throws the ball from one hand to the other about 3 to 4 times.
- He works the ball round his hips from one hand to the other.
- He works the ball through his legs.

To teach the player to take the ball off an opponent in a one-on-one situation

Emphasise the correct technique because, if this can be done well and fast:
- it saves a lot of energy;
- the team obtains more ball possession; and
- the game has more flow (continuity).

The first two players determine how successful this is.

Examples

9. The players are divided into groups of three, e.g., A, B and C.

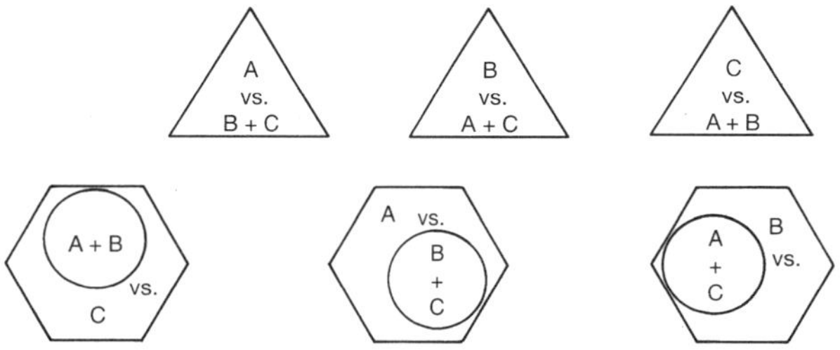

Player A is the opponent; B and C have the ball and are a team. They try to retain the ball for 60 seconds while A tries to rob it. Therefore B and then C assume the role of opponent. *N.B.:* The ball-carrier should always protect

the ball and keep it available. The receiver should go in with his shoulder to get the ball and not stand and wait for the ball-carrier to pass it to him. When the ball-carrier has his back to his team-mate, he passes the ball to his team-mate through his legs.
The defender's options are:
- When you can see the ball, dispossess the carrier.
- When you cannot see the ball, turn the ball-carrier around to your side.

10. Throwing the ball into the air. The jumper jumps and catches the ball and, as soon as he lands, the thrower tries to rip the ball.

11. Groups of four. Player A throws the ball up into the air while B, C and D quickly do jackknives or press-ups. B then jumps up, catches the ball, and throws it up into the air. All four players get a chance to throw and to catch the ball. (This combines skill with muscle stamina.)

12. Two players stand back to back and pass the ball to each other: over their heads, through their legs, with their upper body turned halfway and then turned fully. (Ball skill; suppleness.)

13. Two players handle two balls. While player A gives an ordinary pass to B, B simultaneously gives A a back-flip. (Ball skill; immediate concentration.)

14. Scrum-half pass drill. Place, for example, 10 balls in a row about 5 m apart. The scrum-half has a team-mate on either side. He moves quickly to the balls and passes balls 1 to 10 alternately to the left and to the right. After he has mastered the basic passes, the receivers vary their positions so that the scrum-half has to adapt the length of his passes every time.

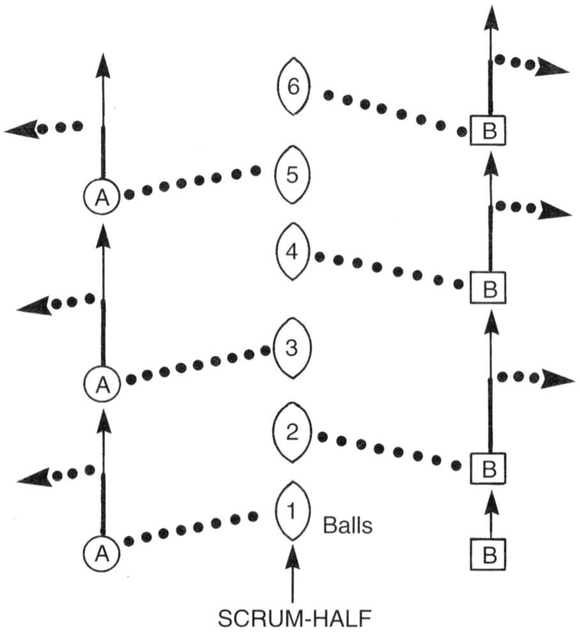

15. The players (five to six) stand in a row one behind the other. They flip the ball to one another backward over their heads and join the row at the back again, or they vary by giving one pass over their shoulder and the next through their legs. (Ball skills; suppleness.)

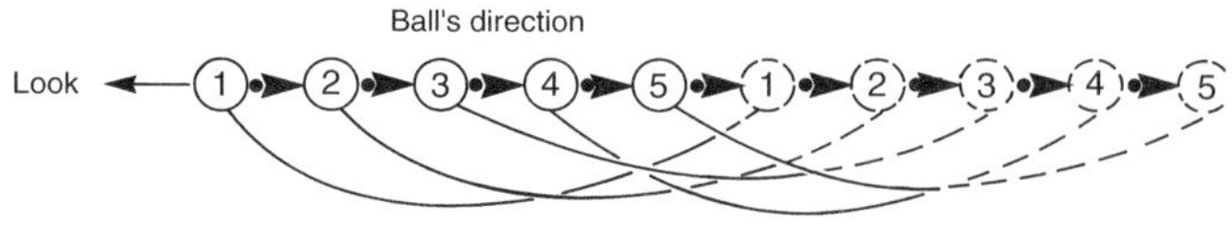

16. The players (five to six) stand side by side in a row on, for example, the 22 m line and face the goal-line. The first player gives the ball sideways to the next and joins the row again at the furthest point in the line. (Consolidates sideways passes and fast positioning.)

17. The players are divided into two groups and run in two circles - one inside the other - in opposite directions. The players in the outside circle pass balls (as many passes as possible to improve speed handling) to those in the inside circle. Vary the type of passes and their length until the ball is virtually passed from hand to hand. The same can be done in a rectangular course around two beacons. (Ball skills; timing.)

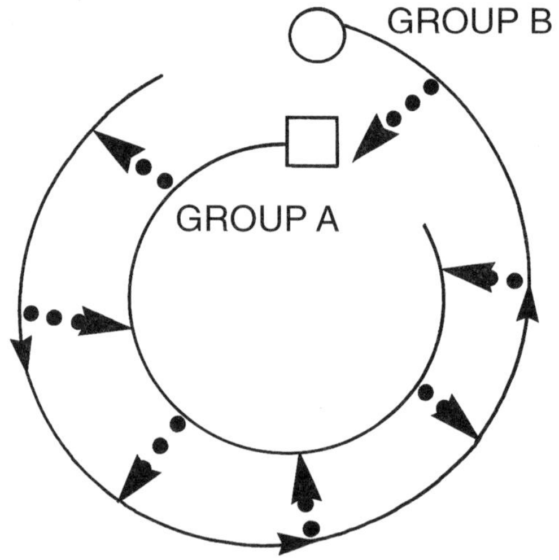

Combination of the above-mentioned skills

18. All 30 players move at random in a demarcated area of 15 m x 15 m and handle 10 to 12 balls without running into one another. They avoid contact by means of side-stepping and speed control. The coach decides on the type of pass, and uses every possible one there is. The players have to communicate and learn to make eye contact quickly before they pass the balls. Pace is important. Every ball that falls must be picked up by the passer. (Ball skills; running skills; reaction in a restricted area under pressure.)

Examples

19. Ordinary pass, gut pass, over-the-shoulder pass, back-flip, squat pass, volley ball pass, one and two-handed pass.

20. Rip the ball and pass.

21. Place the ball on the ground; the closest player picks it up and passes or flicks it up for his team-mate.

22. The ball-carrier falls to the ground and places the ball; the closest player picks it up and carries the ball further or passes.

23. The ball-carrier plays the role of the opponent.
- Is turned and the ball is ripped.
- Falls to the ground; the closest player rolls him over the ball, picks it up and plays on.

24. To learn the quick wrist pass where the passer:
- draws his opponent before he gets the ball and passes the ball the moment he receives it. (Michael Lynagh made this type of passing famous.)

A back-line faces the goal-line. Four players (1, 2, 3 and 4) do the handling and three (A, B and C) pass the balls. The four handlers stand behind one another in a row about 5 m to 8 m from the goal-line. The first handler jogs in a straight line towards the goal-line. Player A passes the ball about 2 m short of the goal-line to 1. He catches it and passes - with his chest facing the goal-line - to C virtually without going forward. He then runs, still on his side of the goal-line, in C's direction and joins the line again at the back. C passes the ball to B standing on the goal-line facing the four runners and he passes it to A. The procedure is repeated with the second handler. Two balls can be used if the handlers' skills improve. (To pass quickly without using space, the passer's foot position must be correct.)

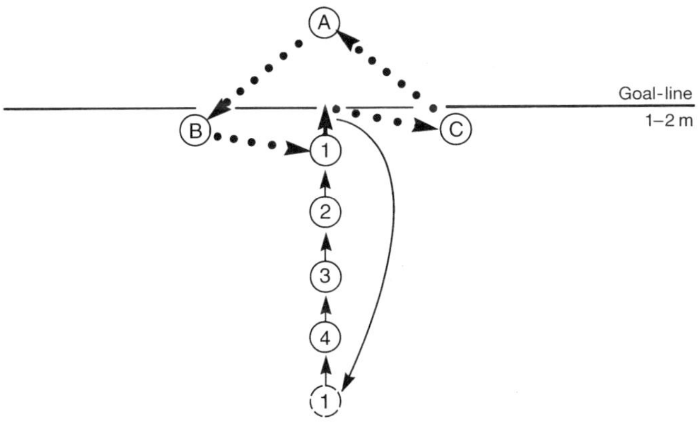

Grids

- ☐ All grids basically consist of four beacons - A, B, C and D - 10 m apart. The distance can vary depending on the exercise.
- ☐ There are up to four players per beacon.
- ☐ Every exercise lasts for 30 seconds (with 10 seconds' rest) or 60 seconds (with 15 seconds' rest).
- ☐ A quick pace and reaction are always the first priority and, only if this can be kept up, are the repetitions increased.

One ball

25. There is one player per beacon, i.e., there are four players in all. Player A passes the ball to B and runs straight to B's position. B does the same with C and C with D. D passes to A, who is now in B's original position, i.e., the passes trace the shape of a triangle.

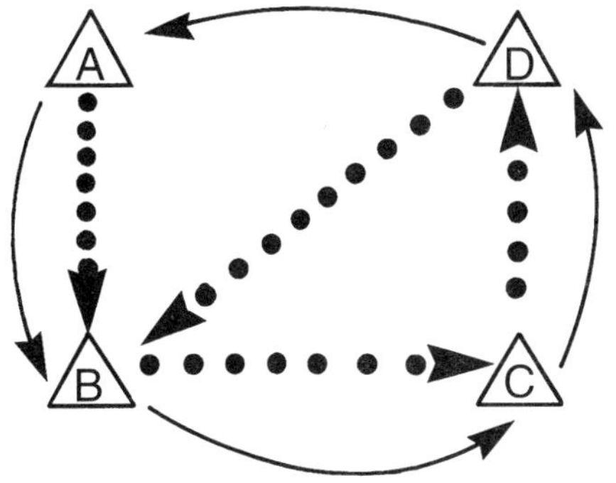

26. There is one player per beacon, i.e., there are four players in all. The ball is passed in one direction around the beacons. Player A passes to B, runs up to B's beacon and runs back again to his original position; B, C and D do the same. The faster the passes, the shorter the time each player has to get back to his original position. (Ball skills; running speed and reaction; stamina depending on the length of time.)

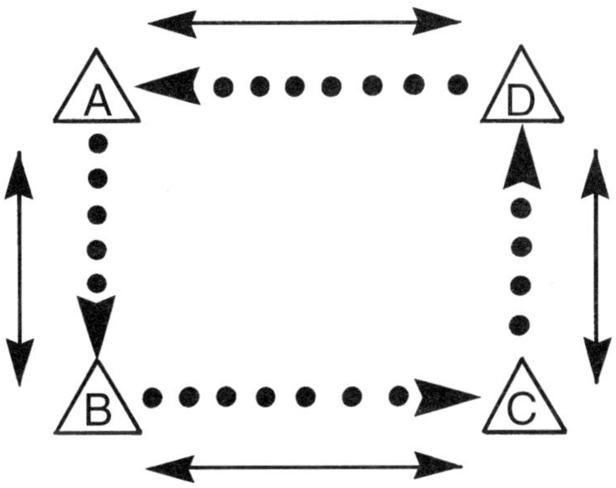

27. There is a group of four at each beacon. Player A runs and passes - close to the centre and to the right - to B, who has in the meantime moved in; B passes to C; C to D; and

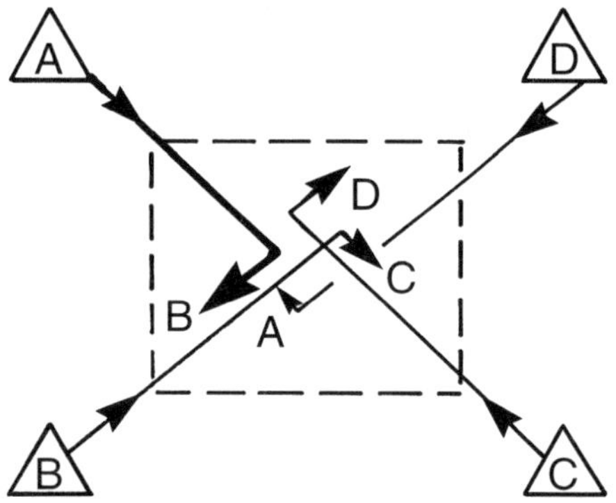

D to A. All the passes are made in the same direction and take place within 2 m of the centre. This takes a lot of concentration. (Handling skills; judging speed; joining the player from whom you are playing.)

Two balls

28. Groups A and C (with a ball) and B and D (with a ball) work together. Player A runs to the centre and passes

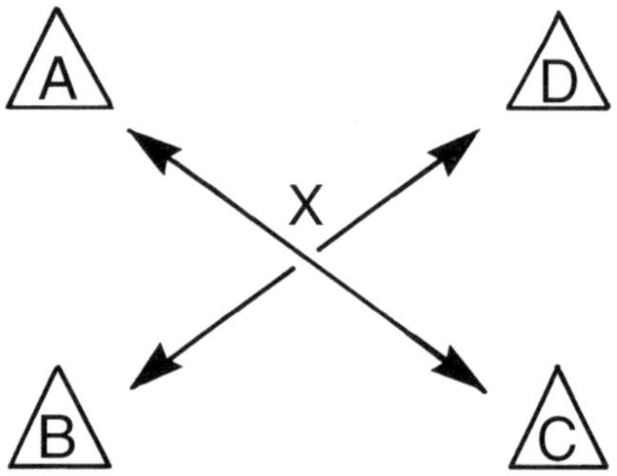

to C at X. B and D do the same. All four groups therefore work simultaneously. The coach decides on the direction of the pass and makes sure the passes are not forward! (Players learn to observe in front of them under the pressure of limited time and space before reacting.)

Variations

☐ Passes: ordinary, gut, back-flip, switch, over-the-shoulder, below-the-knee.
☐ Running rhythm: first normal; then varying strides or speed play or sidestep before passing.
☐ Other skills: like picking up the ball and placing it can also be included.

29. Player A runs to X, gives a long pass to B and runs to B's beacon; B runs to X, gives a long pass to C and runs to C's beacon; C runs to X, gives a long pass to D and runs to D's beacon; D runs to X, gives a long pass to A and runs to A's beacon, etc. Start simultaneously with a ball for A and a ball for C. (Pressure; control of running speed; summing-up a situation; handling; follow-up.)

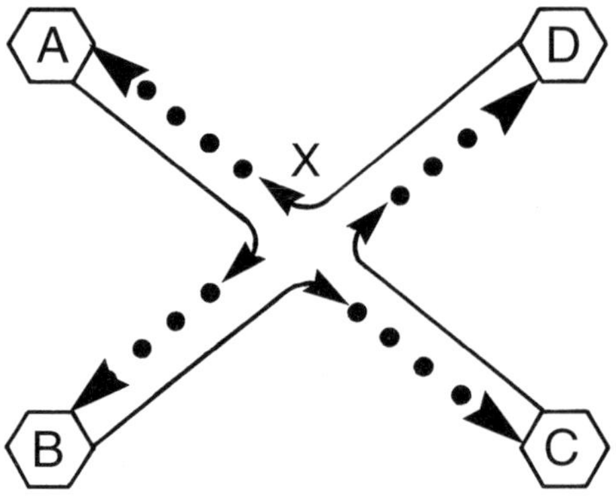

Variations

☐ A passes to B and runs to C.
☐ A passes to B and runs to D.

30. Grids. Eight players in block formation with 1, 3, 5 and 7 on the corners. Two balls for 1 and 5 respectively. At a given signal, both players pass the ball to the right,

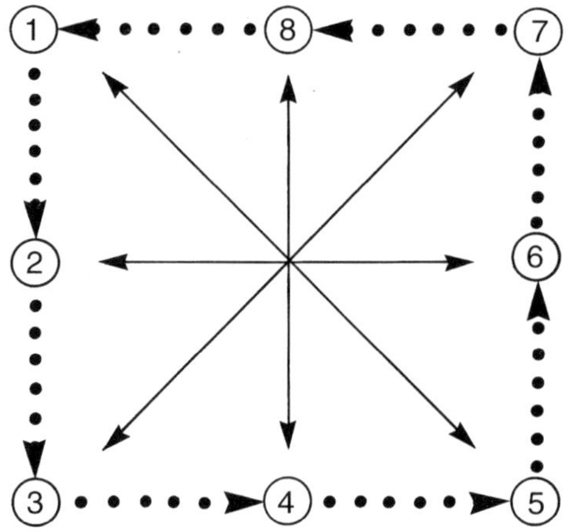

i.e., 1 to 2 and 5 to 6. As soon as 1 and 5 have passed, they quickly change positions. Players 2 and 6, 3 and 7, and 4 and 8 do the same after they have passed. In the meantime the two balls are passed as quickly as possible to the right. (Ball skills; observation; running skills; reaction; stamina.)

Section work

Grids

31. Two back lines of four to five players work round a grid of 15 m. One team's first pass starts on the ground at beacon A and the other at beacon C. Both play to the left. As soon as the ball reaches the last player, he puts it down and the attack starts again at D/B, then C/A, then B/D, until the starting points have been reached again. The aim is to teach the players to position in time so that they attack straight ahead without the ball getting inside the square between the beacons.

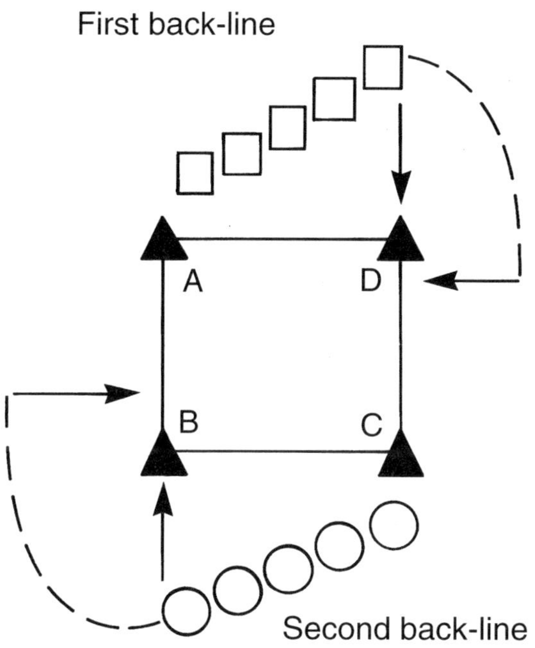

32. The same drill can be adapted slightly for the forwards. The players in the working pack begin at beacon A, drive to the middle of the grid against, for example, three to four defenders and go into a maul or ruck; they then go round beacons A and D again to the middle of the grid. The process is repeated round beacons DC, CB and BA. The forwards can even work round the beacons at the same time as the backs. (You do have to keep your head though!)

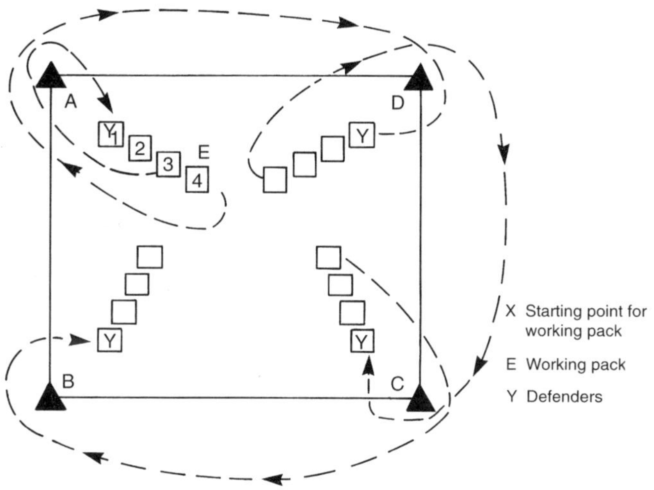

33. Grids. Teaches ball possession in contact situations. Use, for example, four tackle or shoulder bags in the 5 m area between the 22 m line and the goal-line. The ball-carrier runs from the 22 m line to the goal-line while the players with the bags try to shoulder him out of the demarcated area. The ball-carrier learns to sidestep and roll out of tackles. Expand the drill to include a ball-carrier and supporter who try to keep the ball alive between them.

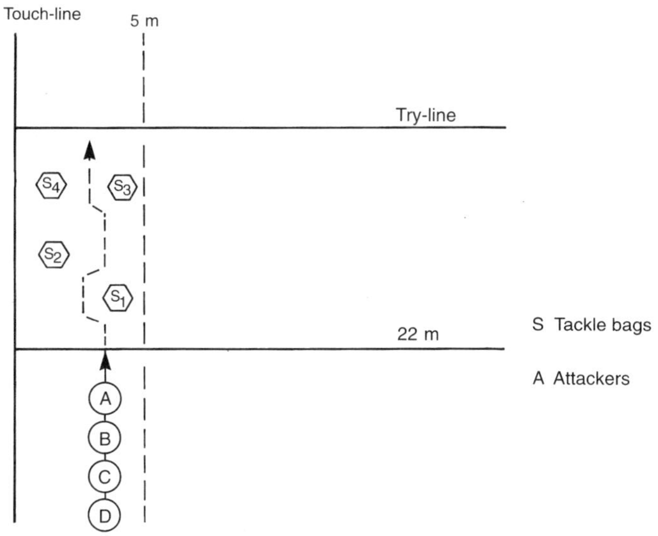

The size of the area and the number of defenders/attackers can also be increased.

Groups of five across the width of the field

These drills are first done unopposed and then in a smaller demarcated area where the player must react to the situation in front of him.

34. Handling: See the number
Five players. The players jog next to one another at a comfortable speed and pass the ball. The players on either side of the ball-carrier must be able to see the number on his jersey. (The receiver is always behind the ball; the ball is supported on either side.)

The catcher holds his furthest hand where he wants to receive the ball. (The passer has a target; the catcher has a stop hand and does not grab the ball.) The catcher looks up towards the opponents' goal-line before he passes the ball. (This helps the ball-carrier run straight before he passes the ball.)

After the ball has been passed, the passer moves a step in the direction of the ball-carrier. (He positions himself immediately to support again.) This drill can also be done with, e.g., deliberate bad passes or finger-tip passes.

35. Handling: Scissors pass on the sides
Five players. The second-last player changes the direction of play every time he passes to the last player. He does this

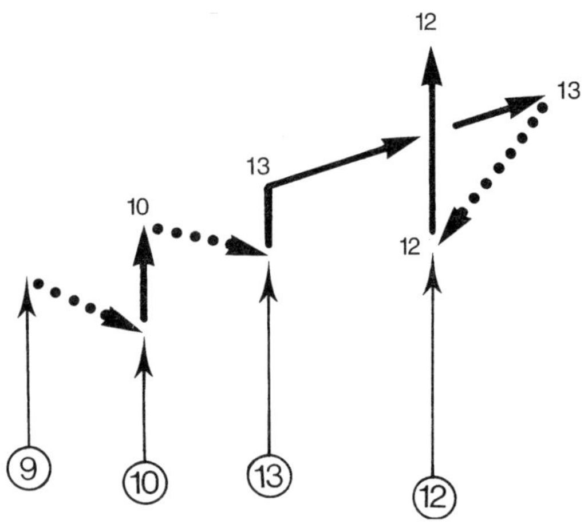

by first going straight and then diagonally across the field. (Get your opponent's attention and draw him diagonally across the field so that a gap develops for your team-mate.)

The last player initially moves as if he is going to receive the ball on the outside; slows down and waits until the ball-carrier has gone diagonally past him. (In this way the defender comes up on the wrong defensive line.)

The ball-carrier watches the receiver throughout and gives a deep back pass. (Beat the opponent with the change of direction of the pass.) Because the receiver is deep enough to see what is happening in front of him and goes straight through the gap, he does not run into the cover defence and he can play to both sides.

36. Handling: Run around and linking
Five players. No. 1 follows up behind after he has passed and gets the ball again from No. 5, etc. The ball-carrier must go straight ahead to create space on his outside. The receiver gets the ball in depth only after he has straightened his run (otherwise the movement goes diagonally across the field and the defenders push you towards the sideline). *N.B.:* Straighten before you get the ball.

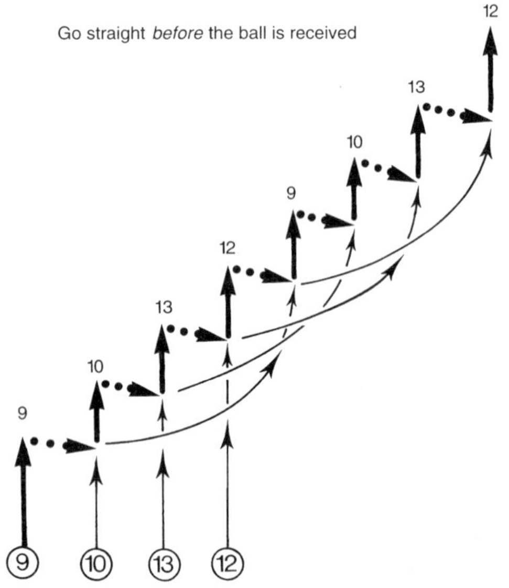

37. Pass in depth to create space for the receiver
Five players stand behind one another and start running parallel to the touch-line. The receiver moves from behind the ball-carrier and gets the ball about 3 m back and 2 m to the side. (The ball-carrier is forced to look, turn his upper body and pass deep.)

Every player concentrates only on his team-mate on the inside from whom he receives the ball. (Supporters learn to get into position in time and create space for themselves before they have the ball.)

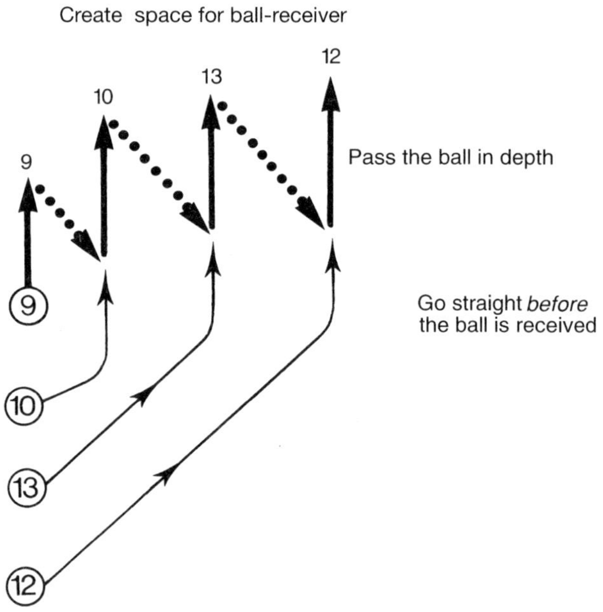

38. Follow up and link
Five players. The players pass the ball in a line. The player who passes the ball goes into an imaginary low tackle and passes the ball while going down to the ground. He then jumps up and joins again at the end. (The players learn to fall, to keep the ball available, and to follow up.)

39. Pick up the ball and make it available
Five players. The players jog in a row behind one another. The front player goes down to the ground and, while lying on his back, holds out the ball to the next player, who takes it from him. The rest repeat the process. Vary this exercise by letting the player on the ground pop up the ball with both hands to the next team-mate.

40. Avoiding direct contact
Five players. The ball-carrier sidesteps before he passes. He makes a dummy pass and sidesteps to the inside before passing. It is important for the ball-carrier to shorten his steps before an imaginary point of contact and then pass.

41. Drawing/eliminating your opponent
Five players running over the width of the field. Each of them takes it in turn to act as the opponent. The ball-carrier attacks the pass continuously and tries to take the

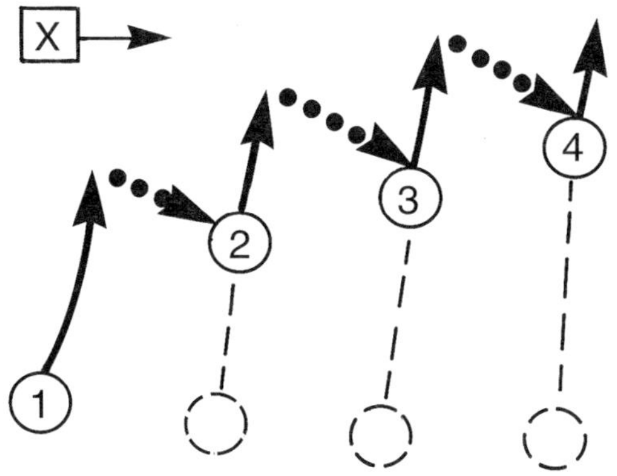

defender out of the game by going towards him before he passes. In the process he will corner the opponent in his running channel. If the opponent moves past too quickly, the ball-carrier makes a dummy pass and goes past behind the defender's back before passing.

With a full back-line, two or even three defenders can be used. Vary the number. (The players learn the meaning of channels of attack and defence.)

42. Skip and short back passes

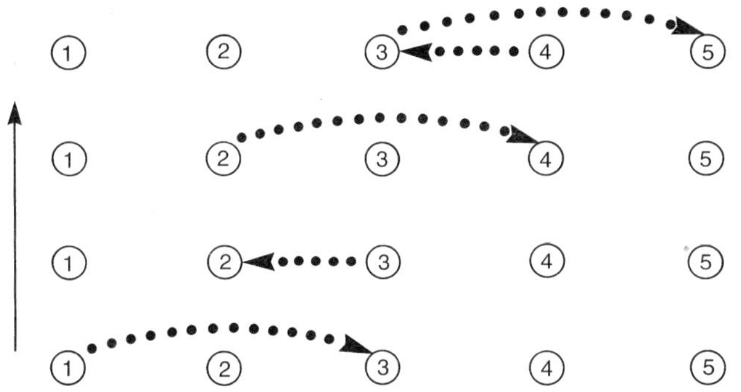

Five players. The skip should not be in depth and should virtually go through the skipped player's hands. The receiver speeds up slightly when he gets the ball. (The players learn to skip the pressure point instinctively.)

43. Skip and support in space

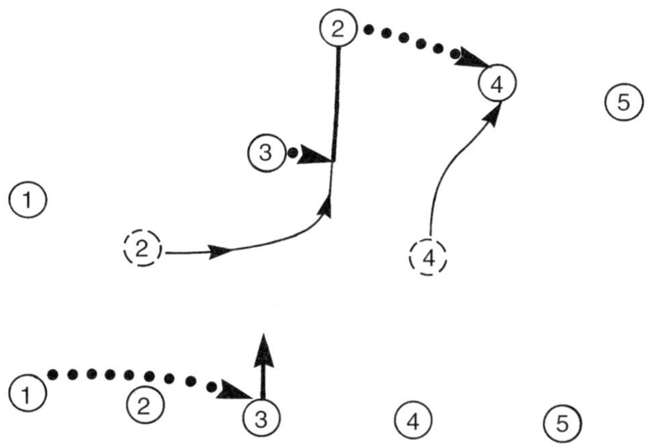

Five players. A skip pass is made and the skipped player goes round for a short pass. The skipped player runs straight into the short pass and cuts through. (The players learn to follow up and continue playing.)

44. Scissors pass

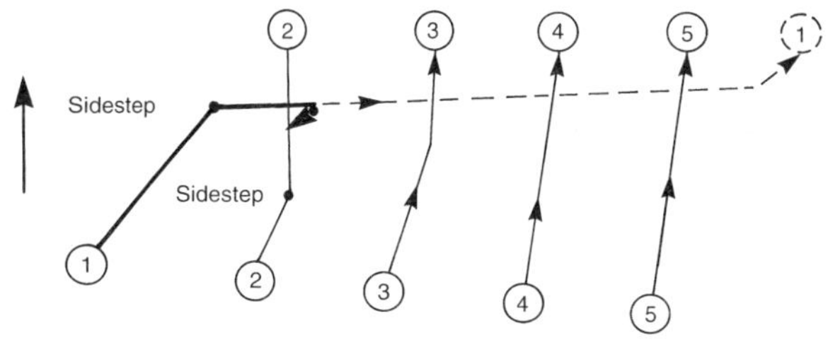

Five players. The first player changes direction, for example, to the right with a sidestep and gives a short scissors pass to the second player, who sidesteps slightly to the left, before coming through straight. The first player then moves past the group round the front and rejoins the group on the right. (The players learn about timing and running angles.)

45. Switch pass

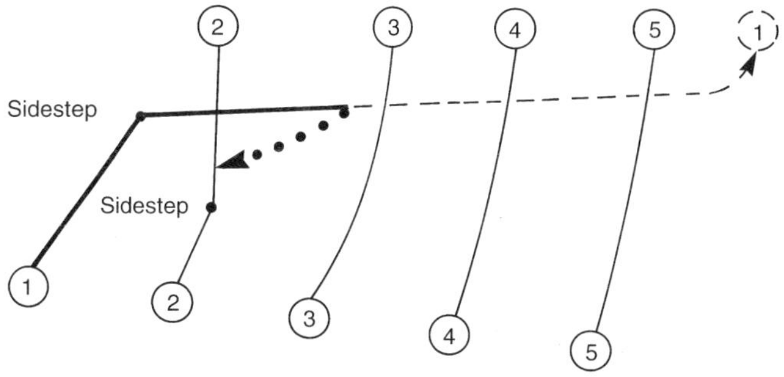

Five players. The same applies as for the scissors pass except that the pass is slightly longer and the receiver comes for the pass much later. (The players learn to create gaps, run into gaps and change the direction of attack with a pass.)

46. Short pass

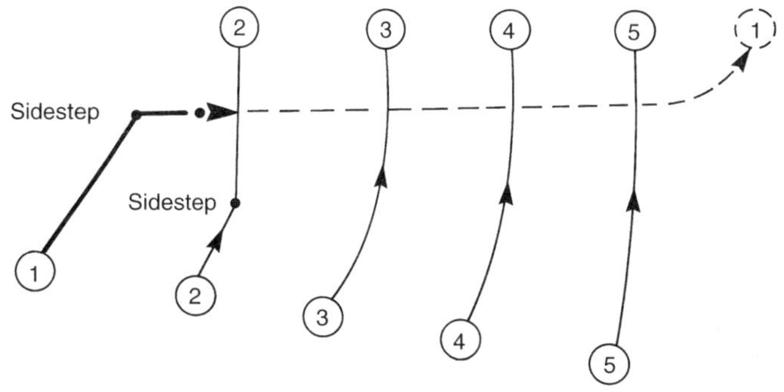

Five players. The same applies as for the scissors pass. When the first player changes direction with a sidestep, the second player comes through shallow and straight for a short pass in front of the ball-carrier. The passer goes past behind his line and joins at the furthest point. (Timing; running angles.)

47. A combination of the scissors, switch and short pass
Five players. The ball-carrier decides whether to give a scissors, switch or short pass. The supporting player's task is to run into the gap. (The players learn to react to different situations.)

48. Picking up the ball and continuity to the weak spot

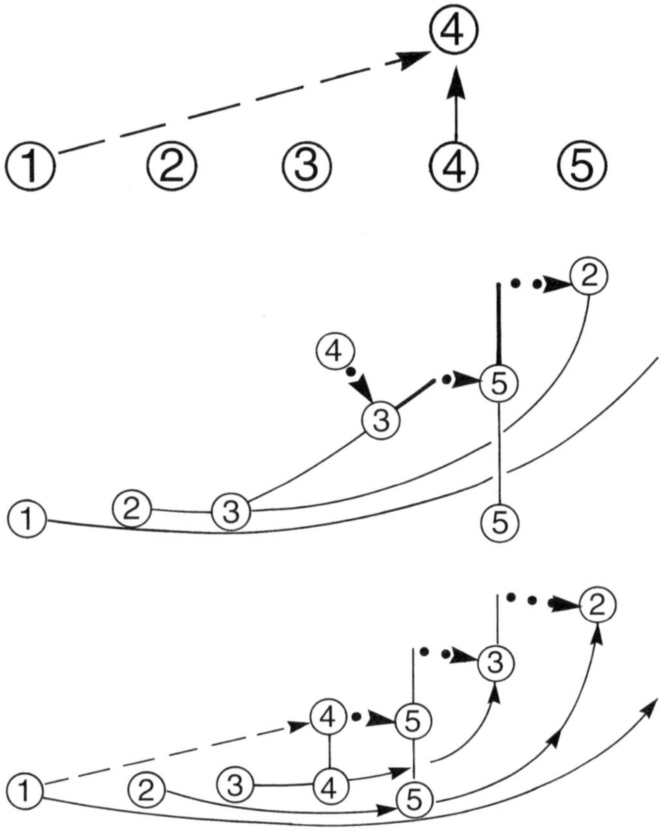

Five players. No. 1 rolls the ball diagonally in front of his group of players. The closest player - irrespective of his position in the line - picks up the ball. The other players position themselves as fast as possible on the side to which the ball was rolled, e.g., if the ball was rolled to the right, they take up position on the right side of the ball. The player who picks up the ball gives it to the first player, who comes past straight ahead. If this is not possible and the receiver runs diagonally, he immediately passes to the next player, who comes through short and straight. The players learn that one of the weak spots in defence is close to the ball. (The closest player to the ball learns to react; maintain the direction of play; uses running angles to cut the line.)

49. Picking up the ball from a team-mate who goes down on top of or with the ball and makes it available
Five players. No. 1 rolls the ball diagonally in front of his team-mates. The closest player picks up the ball and goes down as if he is being tackled. The player must keep the ball under control even if he rolls over. As soon as he stops moving he makes the ball available by placing it. The first team-mate steps over the player on the ground, squats down, picks up the ball and passes to the closest supporter, who comes through straight. This drill can be expanded so that No. 1, who rolled the ball, either acts as first opponent, who tackles (carefully!) the player who picked up the ball or acts as the second opponent/defender, who is close to the ball-carrier who went down. (Supporting players learn to assess the situation, especially in relation to the number of defenders close by, and react accordingly.)

50. Numbers/passing/running off the ball

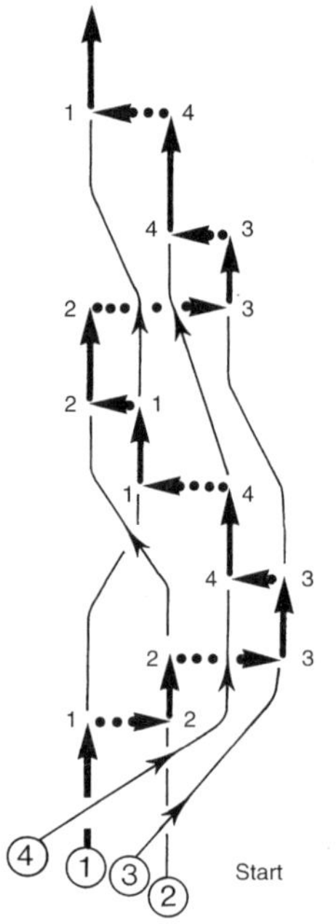

N.B. This drill can be expanded to include 15 players handling three balls
Start with balls to players 1, 6 and 10
with player 15 who gives the ball to player 1 again
Emphasise that the *ball-carrier* must go *forward*

Groups of five players numbered 1 to 5. The ball is passed consecutively and the supporters position themselves accordingly each time. The passes can vary: ordinary pass, short pass, scissors, back-flip and squat with your back to the opponent (as if you have picked up the ball, then pass to a team-mate, who comes out from deep).

These drills can first be done just across the width of the field. Then use, for example, the area between the 22 and halfway line and let six groups of five players move inside this area across the width while the groups handle the ball consecutively in each group. Although the groups start simultaneously, it is important that each group ends about 5 m to 10 m to the right of a line through its original starting point. The ball-carrier is not allowed to run

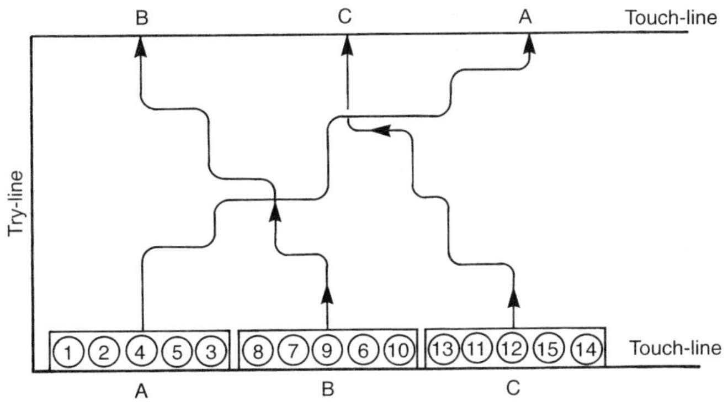

diagonally across the field. The principle is that the ball-carrier moves straight ahead and the ball is moved to the side. The players learn to concentrate in the midst of other players, to position and to handle under pressure.

When the players do number drills, the receiver must change his position continuously across the width of the field before he receives the ball. In this way he learns to beat his opponent before he gets the ball.

51. Numbers in a square
Groups with five players numbered 1 to 5. Each group passes the ball within the group consecutively from 1 to 5. Six groups move together inside a square of, say, 20 m x 20 m. The ball-carrier accelerates into the open space and the rest position themselves and join him.

52. Supporting the ball
To teach the closest player - especially the backs - to support the ball immediately.

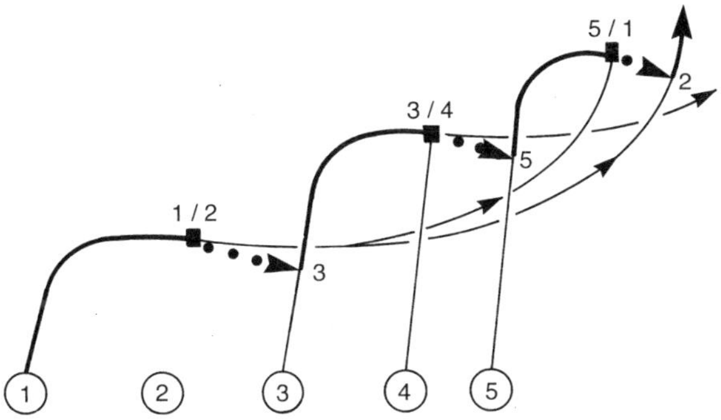

Five players. No. 1 jogs with the ball in a straight line and then suddenly changes direction to the right. No. 2 comes straight through onto the ball and rips it from No. 1. This is repeated with 2 and 3, 3 and 4, and 4 and 5.

53. Running angles
Five players. Varying running angles. The running angles are changed deliberately to break the line of defence.

No. 1 gives a relatively long pass to 2, who cuts in and passes back to 1. No. 1 then runs diagonally behind past 2 and gives a short pass to either 3 or 4, who cuts through straight. The receiver deliberately runs for the gap.

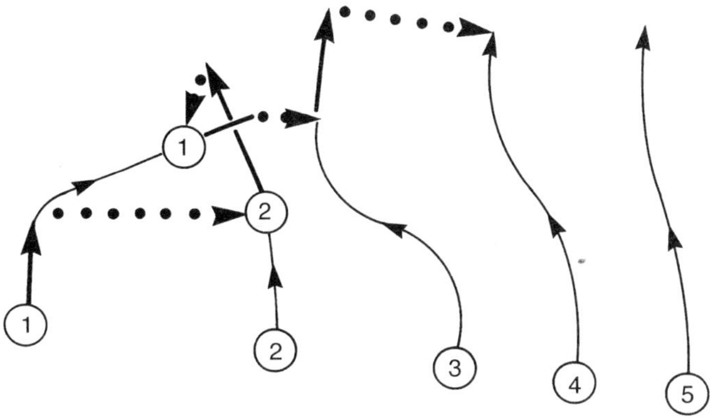

No. 1 gives a skip pass to 3, who passes back to 2. No. 2 runs diagonally behind past 3 and passes to 4 or 5, who cuts through straight.

54. Picking up the ball
Five players. Picking up the ball and making it available. Three methods are used. The player scoops up the ball and passes; the player puts one hand on top of the ball and picks it up with the other hand; and the player slides into the ball on his haunches or knees and passes the ball from that position to a team-mate, who moves close in on him.

55. Ball retention in contact. Spinning out from a tackle

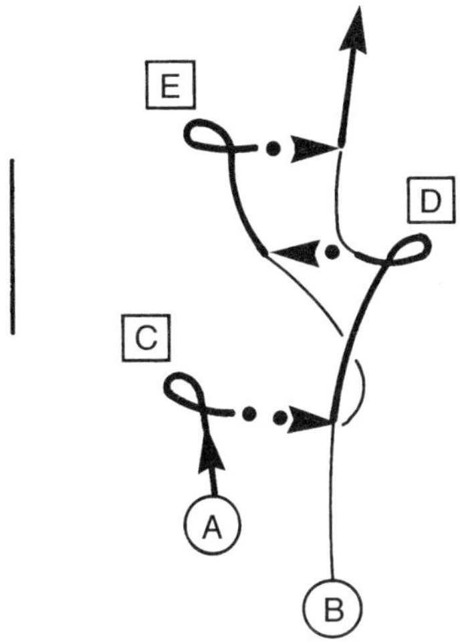

Five players. A and B are ball-carriers. C, D and E are defenders and stand apart as shown on the sketch. A goes to the right of C, hits him with his right shoulder and rolls out to the right. While rolling, he passes the ball to B. B goes to D's left, hits him with his left shoulder and rolls out to the left. While rolling, he passes the ball back to A, who repeats the process against E.

56. Decision making
Five players. To sharpen the ball-carrier's decision-making abilities when his own team has possession. A group of five players, two acting as opponents. Create the following situations:

Two opponents stand 1 m to 2 m apart. The ball-carrier's options are:
+ If they are right in front of him, to try and get through the gap with a sidestep so that the ball can go to a team-mate.
+ If they are diagonally in front of him, to try and get/draw them even more diagonally across the field so that he can beat them with a switch to his team-mate, who comes from the outside.
Two opponents stand next to or close to one another, i.e., the ball-carrier cannot go through between them. His options are:
+ To play the ball away before contact.
+ If possible, to place the ball on the ground 4 m to 5 m back for his team-mates. (*N.B.:* If you simply place the ball on the ground, the retreating opponent usually plays it first and you lose possession.)
+ If he is alone, he must try and stay on his feet for 4 to 5 seconds until help arrives. This will feel like a century in the beginning!

57. Ball retention in a tackle situation
Five players.
☐ The opponent poses no immediate threat:
No. 1 goes down as if he is being tackled, rolls over with the ball and places it. No. 2 steps over the ball and passes immediately to 3, who plays on to 4 and 5. (It is important for the supporting players to look for the weak spots/gaps and position themselves accordingly.)
☐ The opponent is close by:
No. 1 goes down as if he is being tackled and places the ball. No. 5 acts as the closest opponent and comes from the opponents' side towards No. 1. No. 2 goes over the ball and takes opponent 5 away so that 3 can play the ball to 4, who attacks the weak point.
☐ Several opponents are close by:
No. 1 still places the ball. Nos. 4 and 5 act as the opponents. Nos. 2 and 3 go over the ball and take opponents 4 and 5 away. No. 1 gets up and the drill is repeated after the ball has first been handled by everyone.

58. Ball retention when headed off against the touch-line

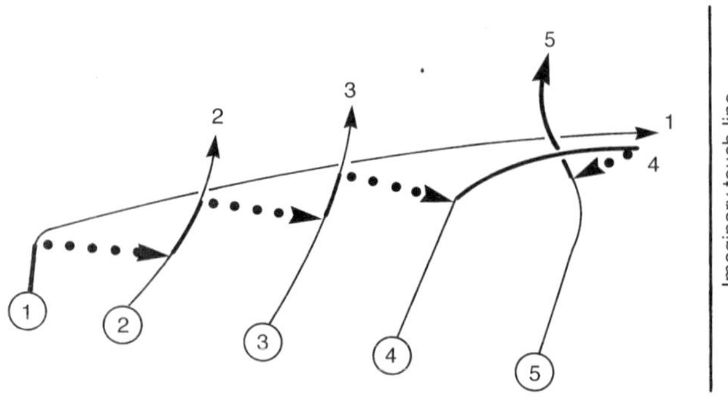

Five players. As soon as No. 1 has passed, he acts as opponent and runs diagonally across the attackers to push try out 4 into touch. No. 4 takes defender No. 1 even more diagonally across the field and gives a scissor or switch pass to 5, who comes straight through and joins his team-mates again.

59. Changing direction without a loose maul

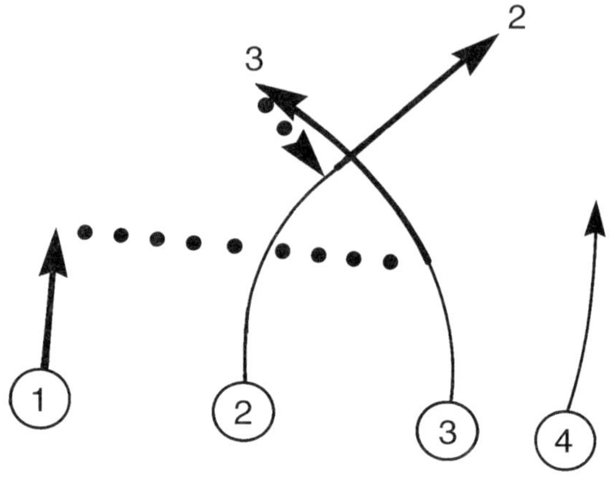

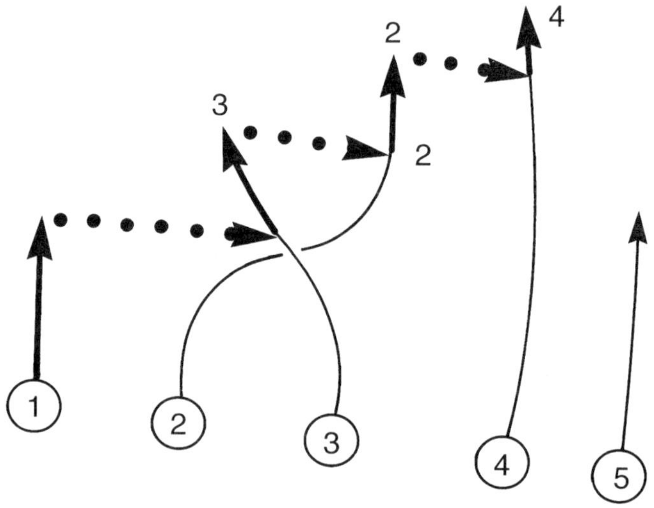

Five players. No. 1 gives a long pass to 3, who cuts in in the direction of the opponents, i.e., of the facet from which the ball is coming. On the way, he changes the direction of play with a pass away from the facet (to 2 and 1). The aim is to stop the opponents before/without contact. It is important for the supporters to move straight ahead into the ball otherwise play moves diagonally across the field.

60. Changing direction and positioning
Five players jog in a row one behind the other. The front player carries the ball. He throws the ball to himself relatively high up into the air. While the ball is in the air, the player at the back, i.e., No. 5, nominates "LEFT!" or "RIGHT!" Nos. 2 to 5 immediately position themselves to the nominated side so that the ball-carrier can immediately play the ball in that direction when he catches it. It is important for the supporters to move straight into the ball - shallow or deep.

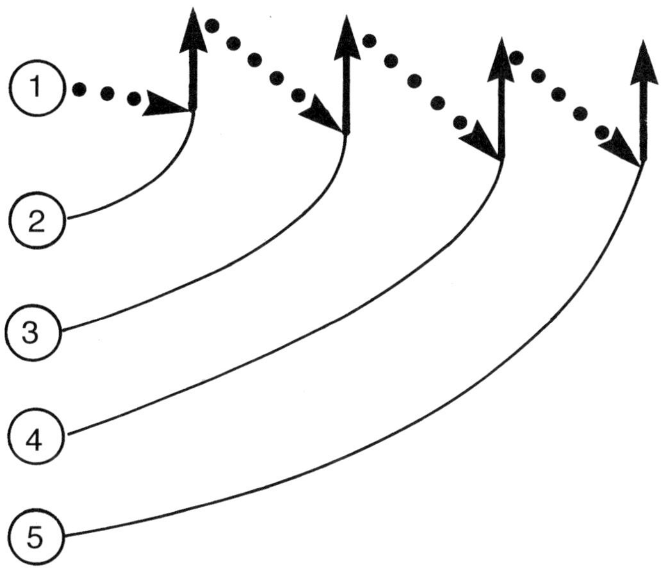

61. Handling under pressure
Groups of five. Six groups jog in the same direction in a demarcated rectangle of 25 m x 10 m. The group at the back moves forward in between the other five rows while passing uninterrupted. The ball-carrier first sidesteps either to the right or to the left in between the row in front of him before passing. (It is important that passing is uninterrupted. Players tend to run through a row first before passing.)

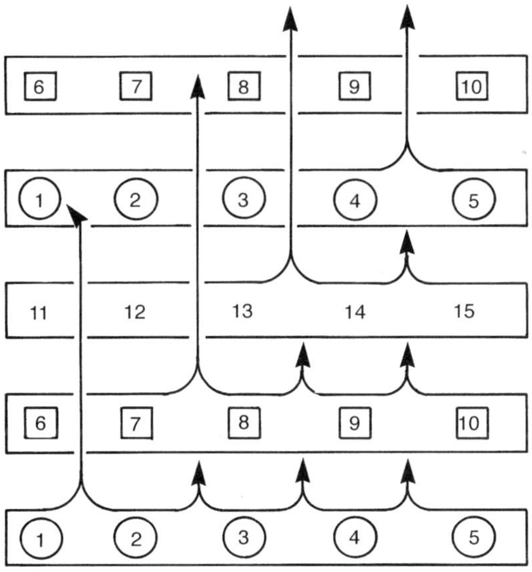

62. Handling under pressure
Groups of five. Six groups move in a demarcated rectangle of 25 m x 10 m along the length in opposite directions. The players handle normally irrespective of the running angles.
Variations: Pass as late as possible in front of the oncoming player (to improve handling speed). Pass the moment *the ball* is through the gap (the ball-carrier is still in front of or in the gap).

63. Four on four. Spotting a weakness in the defence
This exercise is carried out across the width of the field in the 22 from the 15 m to the touch-line. The coach nominates one of the four defenders to go and sit down. In this way numerous options are created for the attackers. (The attackers must constantly OBSERVE and MAKE DECISIONS.)

64. Nine backs. Spotting a weak spot in the defence; eliminating opponents

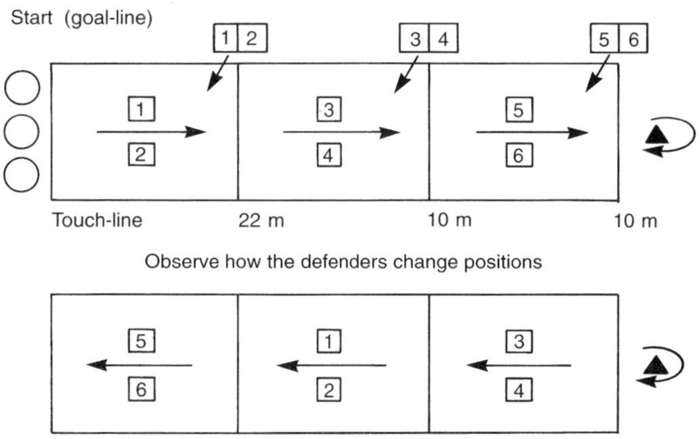

Between the 5 m and 15 m lines and from the goal-line to the second 10 m line. Three players position themselves on the goal-line with the ball. Two defenders each stand on the 22 m, the first 10 m and the second 10 m lines. As soon as the attackers start playing, the first two defenders come out to defend up to the 22 m line. The next two players defend between the 22 and the first 10 m lines. The last two defend the area between the two 10 m lines. As soon as the attackers are across the last 10 m line, they turn back and attack the two defenders waiting on the first 10 m line.

65. Sharpening observation, decision-making, reaction and support

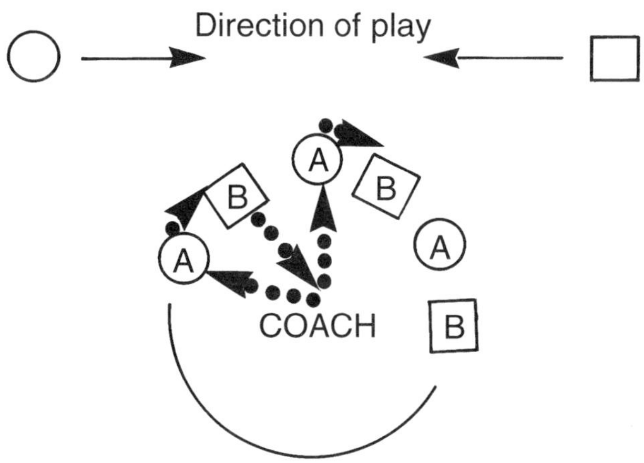

Two back-lines, A and B, against one another. The two back-lines jog together in a circle (the players from both A and B together) round the coach, who passes the ball to them (the type of pass can be varied). When a player from team A has the ball, the coach shouts "Attack!" Team A immediately attacks the predetermined goal-line while team B defends passively/normally. This works well across the width of the field between the halfway and 22 m lines.

66. Observation and decision-making

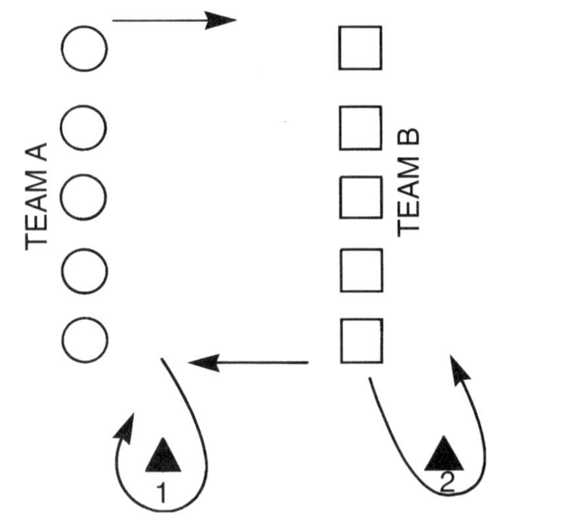

Two back-lines, A and B, against one another in the 22 area across the width of the field. Team A handles while slowly moving forward. When everyone has handled, the ball goes to B, which does the same. On the coach's command, "A", both back-lines run as fast as possible round beacons 1 and 2 and team A then attacks at full-speed while B defends. See which team is closest to its beacon before giving the command.

67. Observation and decision-making

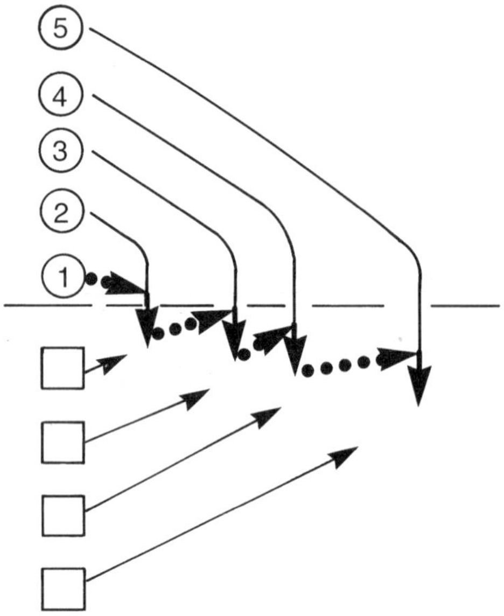

The back-line is divided into two groups of four players from the 22 m line to the goal-line.

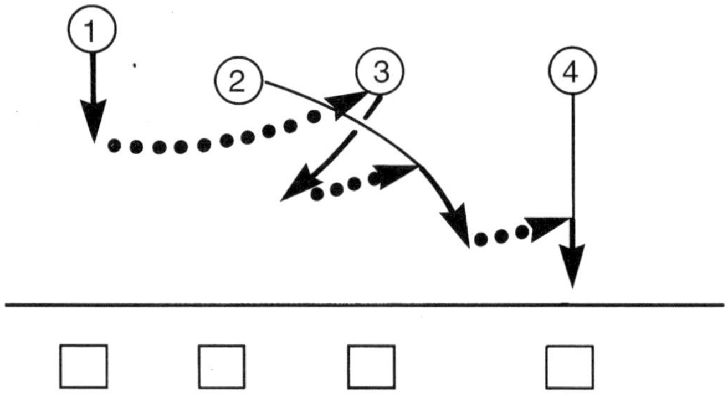

The attackers and defenders are positioned first (a) in line behind one another and then (b) across the width next to one another. On the signal, group A attacks to the right. Group B has to react fast and get into position to defend. The emphasis is on positioning and especially straightening before catching the ball. Options for attack vary continuously according to positioning. The defenders also have to organise themselves all the time. The attackers constantly look for the weak spots and penetrate them; if there are none, they create confusion in the defenders' ranks by, for example, cutting back in the direction from which the ball came and then switching direction by playing the ball away in the original direction. In the process, gaps often open up in front of the attackers.

68. Observation and decision-making
Attack from a line-out.
Three players (A, B and C) play against two others. A and B try to take the two opponents out of the game (channels) for C to go for the remaining defenders. A and B follow up quickly and support. The aim is to run straight and head off the opponent in your channel; then to follow up.

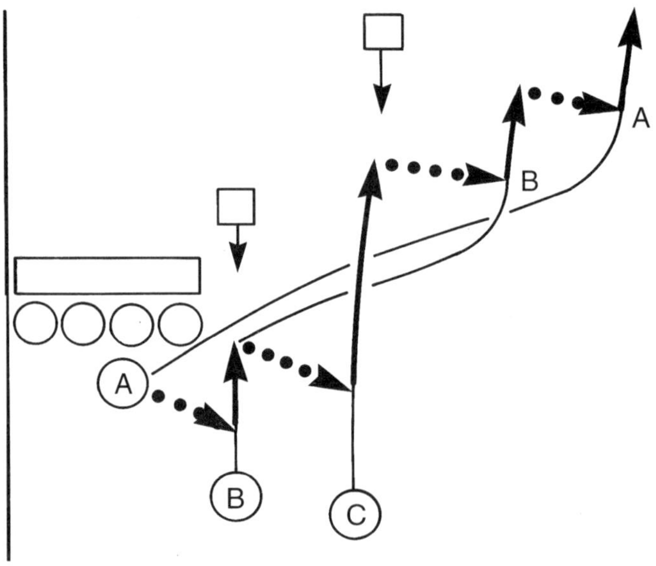

69. Observation and decision-making - continuity

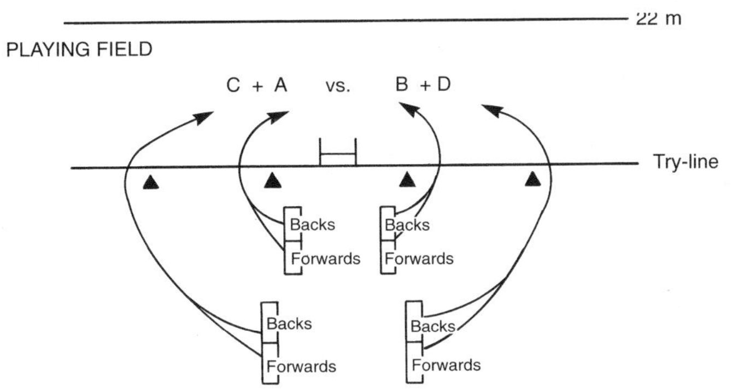

Four teams of eight players (four backs and four forwards) play across the width of the field in the 22.

A play against B, and C against D. On command, the backs of each team (A and B, for example) run round the various beacons. A have the ball and start to play against B, who defend. Their forwards follow a second or two later. Now they play as a team with their main aim being CONTINUITY AND PENETRATION. While A and B are playing, C and D rest and vice versa.

70. Observation and decision-making - attack and defence

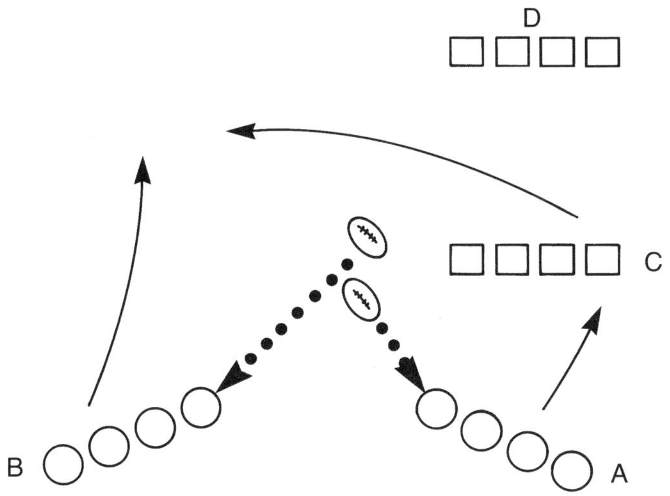

The back-line is divided into two groups of four (A and B) and plays from a centre scrum situation.

Two balls are on the field. Group A attacks to the right against four defenders, C. (The other four defenders, D, rest and do not take part in the exercise for the moment.) The coach decides when and then shouts "Second ball", on command of which group B attacks to the left with the second ball. Defenders C shoot across the field and defend against group B. (Attack, ball retention, continuity, defence, stamina.)

71. Back-line drill for three back-lines to improve decision-making during attack and defence
A plays half a length first against B and then against C; B does the same against A and C; C the same against B and A.

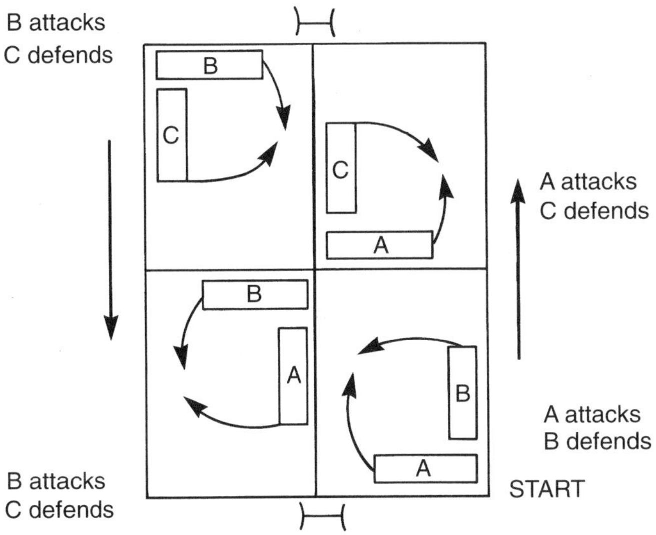

The coach decides on the positions from which to attack and which to defend. Start with, for example, deep positioning and change to wide positioning. Then create counter-attack opportunities from kicks arising out of different situations, e.g., high kicks, long kicks forward, and kicks diagonally across the field.

72. Counter-attack

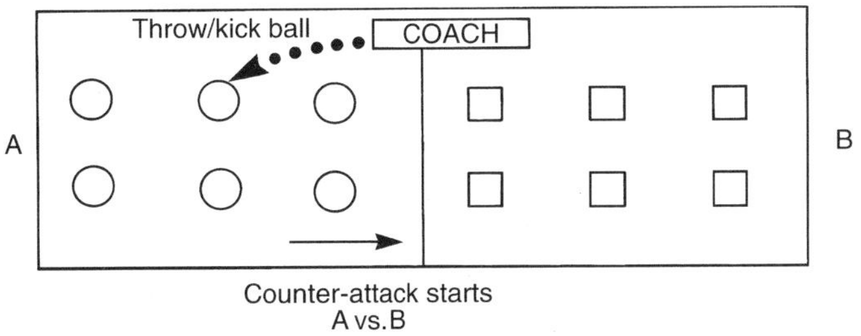

Two back-lines stand in pairs about 10 m apart behind one another along the length of a reduced field. The coach says beforehand which side is to be played to. The players then throw or kick the ball to an attacking team while the other team defends. The emphasis is on the catcher, who must first look before deciding where to play to, and on the supporters, who must drop back into ball-supporting positions. (Observation, decision-making, support of the ball.)

73. Back-line alignment and play
To teach the back-line to take up the correct starting positions as a unit, to play deep, to run straight, and to follow-up by using two beacons, A and B:

The back-line moves in the same direction throughout. Scrum possession is from beacon A; the ball goes down along the line to the right so that it is put down at beacon B. All the backs run round beacon B. Scrum possession is now from beacon B; the players take up position so that the ball can be played to the left towards beacon A. The coach decides on the length of time from the moment that the ball is put down at a beacon until the scrum-half plays it.

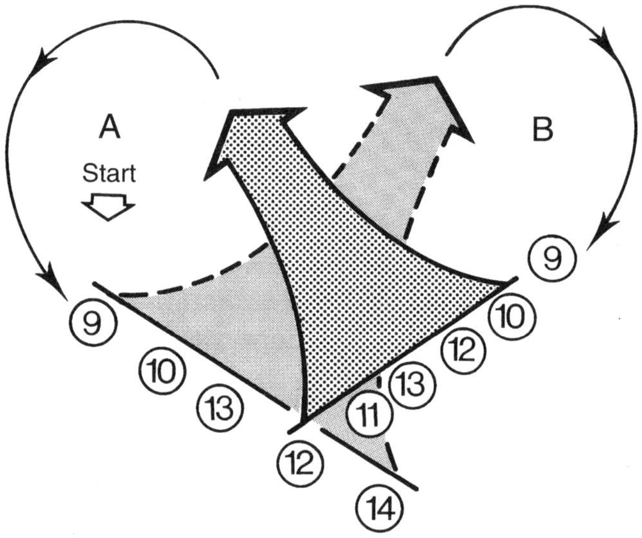

74. Decision-making for the back-line in respect of direction of play
Place a number of balls at beacons on the field and decide beforehand on the direction in which the back-line must play from each beacon. The positions of the beacons must correspond with the contact lines in the game and the directions with the most effective option.

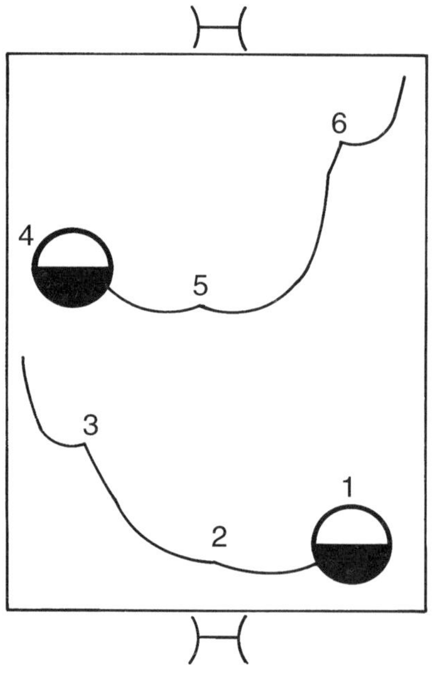

75. Kicking drill for halves and wings
The scrum-half stands on the right-hand touch-line with about 10 balls. He kicks high over the "scrum". The left winger practises catching and reacts to the type of kick. The scrum-half and left winger then change position and the scrum-half passes to the fly-half, who practises up-and-unders, etc.

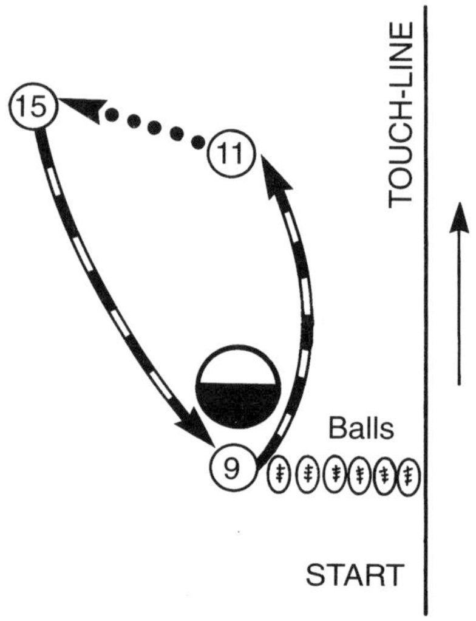

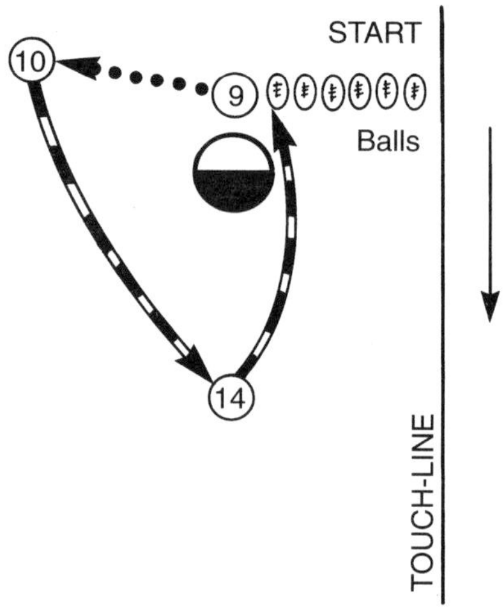

76. Defence
Five groups of three players with five tackle bags. The first player holds the bag; the second player tackles with a run of 5 m to 8 m; he immediately gets up with the bag; the third player then tackles. Do this across the width of the field. Hit the bag upward with your shoulder and fall on top of it. The tackler must get up onto his feet again as quickly as possible and get back into the game.

77. Defence
A group of four players. No. 1 holds the tackle bag, on top of which is a ball; 2 tackles; 3 picks up the ball for 4, who drives past; everyone supports for 10 m. The players then change position.

78. Defence
Place five tackle bags with balls in different places on the field, e.g., in the 22. Nominate which bags the defenders are to tackle by shouting the number. Try to make the situation as realistic as possible. In addition to this being an exhausting drill, it teaches the players to position fast.

79. Defence

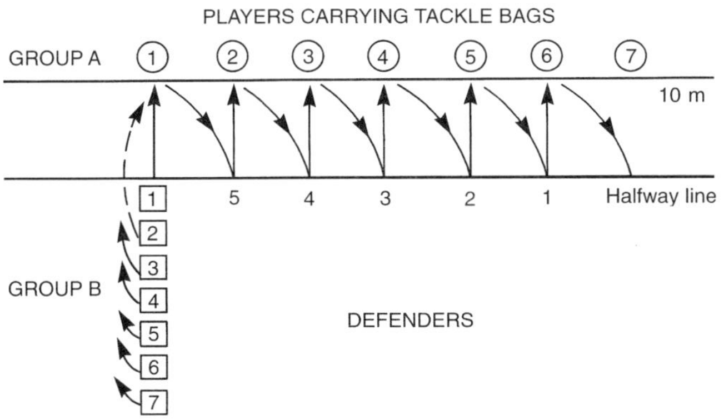

Two back-lines work against one another. Row A, each player with a tackle bag, stand on the 10 m line across the width of the field facing the halfway line. Row B stand on the centre line in a row one behind the other facing the goal-line. No. 1 of row B tackles A1, gets up and returns to the halfway line opposite A2. B2 and B1 then tackle A1 and A2 respectively. The process is repeated with one tackler from row B being added each time until all seven players from row B tackle all seven tackle bags at row A simultaneously. The tacklers are then decreased from the furthest point. The tackler opposite A1 can shout every time the defenders are to go in for the tackles.

80. Defence

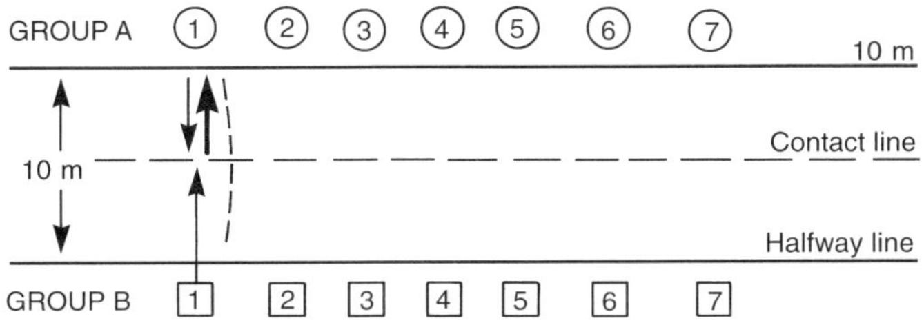

Two groups stand 10 m apart. Group A hold tackle bags on, for example, the 10 m line while group B take up position on the halfway line. The players in group B jointly give a signal - "One!" - and move forward towards group A, who meet them about 5 m forward. Group B drive with their shoulders into the bags and push the defenders back to the 10 m line. They then quickly drop back to their starting positions on the halfway line. This is repeated twelve times in one minute, with half a minute's rest while the groups change round. This done three times in a row is excellent work. (Vary this exercise by first letting the defender shoot off after the tackle about 8 m on to a beacon before he returns to his starting position.)

81. Defence and counter-attack

A team plays unopposed in one half of the field where several tackle bags are placed at specific points. The purpose of this exercise is to give the attackers different

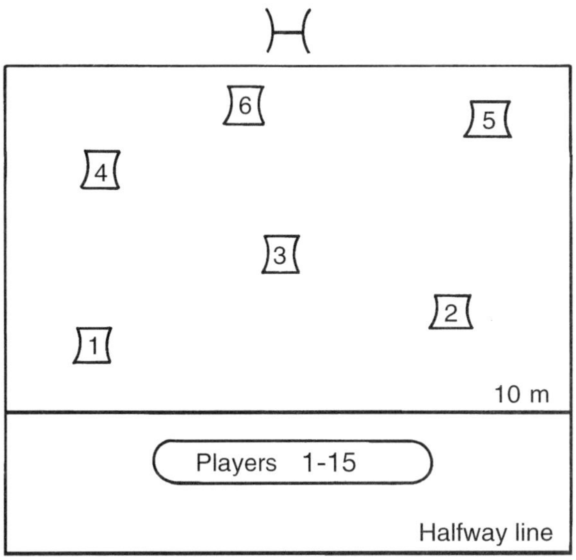

options for counter-attack and to see whether the right options are taken. The coach nominates the tackle bag; the closest player (or the nominated player) tackles, from which the team launches a counter-attack.

82. Counter-attack from kicks

The whole team must focus on counter-attacking. The full-back and wingers are the axis around which counter-attacks revolve.

The players drop back across the width of the field when the opponents kick. The first player to reach the ball should immediately know: whether he has time and space to play; whether he has support; and where on the field there is least pressure.

Kicks against the touch-line are played across the width of the field with two long passes if centre field is open; otherwise the attack is launched along the touch-line.

Kicks in centre field are played to the sides and, depending on which side there is most support, either straight or with a scissors movement in that direction.

83. Maul/driving

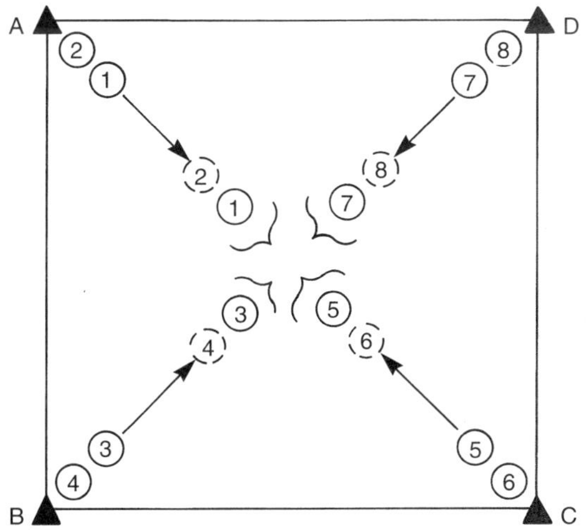

Grid situation. The first player moves from each beacon to the centre and makes contact in a squat position with his back to the others. Each group's second player then drives straight ahead onto the ball and together the two team-mates move forward in between the others to the opposite beacon. Gradually build up the number of players in the loose maul to five or six.

84. Maul - forwards and backs together

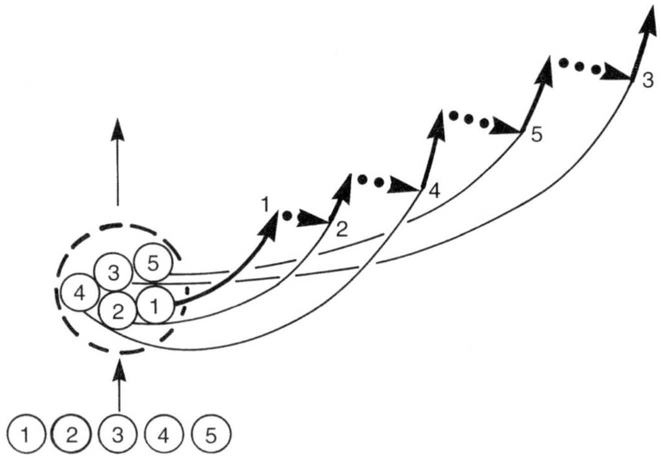

Groups of five. The whole group forms a driving maul and moves, bound together, about 5 m to 8 m. On the ball-carrier's (who becomes the scrum-half) signal, the group breaks up and plays either as forwards or as a back-line. When the ball reaches the last player the process is repeated. This teaches both forwards and backs the techniques of the loose maul, drive and back-line play.

85. Fast mauls/mini-maul

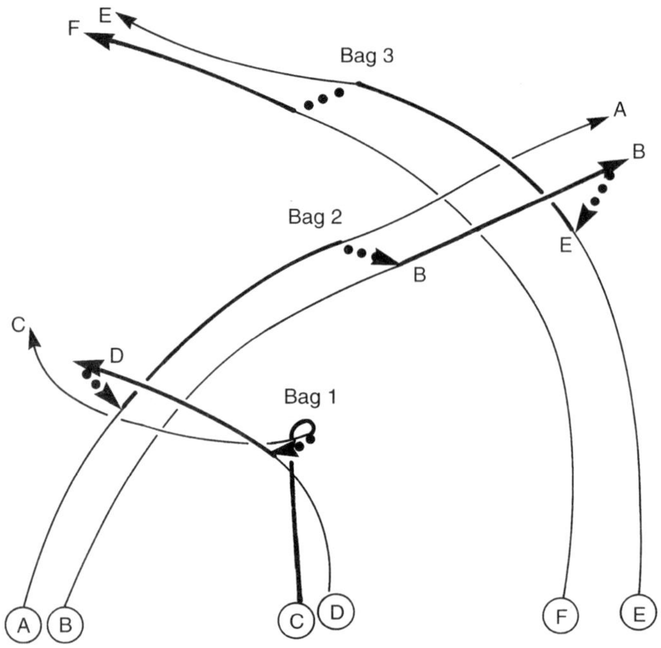

Six players form three groups - A and B, C and D, and E and F. Each group stays together the whole time.

Set up three tackle bags across the width of the field on the halfway line about 15 m apart. Group AB stands on the 10 m line, CD on the halfway line, and EF on the other 10 m line.

C goes with the ball against the first tackle bag, hits it with his left shoulder and passes to D, who runs diagonally to the left. D changes direction with a pass to A, who runs diagonally to the right and hits the second bag with his right shoulder. A then passes to B, who moves out diagonally to the right where C and D have in the meantime taken up position. B changes direction with a pass to D, who repeats the process at the third tackle bag. The process is then repeated. The emphasis throughout is on quickly making the ball available in the centre, preferably just after or before contact, and changing direction on the sides. The players have to concentrate and position themselves constantly. The number of players in each group is expanded to four but the group always plays as a unit. Two packs of forwards can be used as three groups of four that play and one group of four that holds four bags.

86. Maul/driving

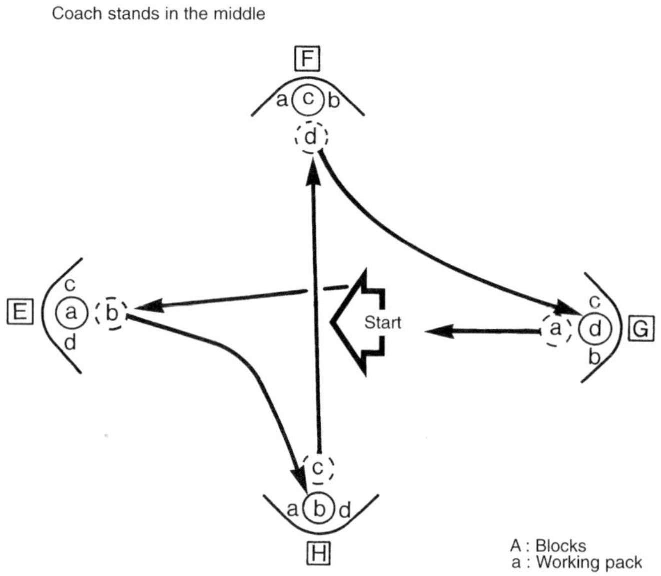

Divide the pack of eight forwards into two groups. One working group of four (A, B, C and D) and the remaining four. The latter four players stand about 10 m apart on the corners of a square and act as opponents (E, F, G and H).

A goes to E and makes contact; B immediately gets possession of the ball, while C and D bind on either side of A to protect him as ball-carrier B. (Another technique is for A to retain the ball without turning and a scrum to be built up around him, i.e., three players in front with A in the position of hooker; the rest of the "scrum" builds up behind them.) The process is repeated with F, G and H before the players change round.

The number of players can be increased until the working pack consists of eight and the defenders make up four groups of two each. This is a high-intensity drill that can be done in a small area.

87. Rucking

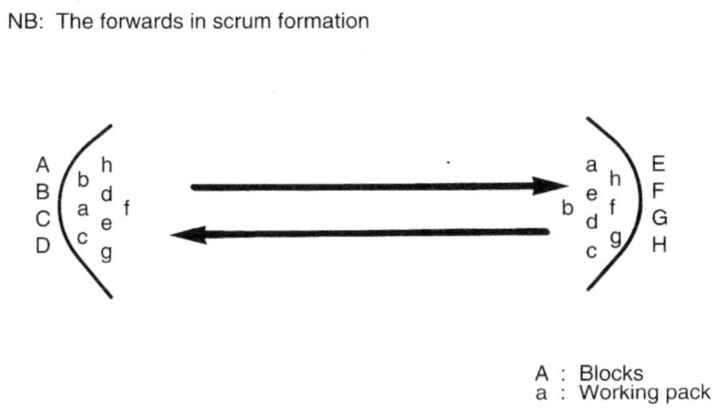

The same basic setup can be used here as for the loose maul drill, except that the ball-carrier on contact puts the ball down on the ground. The first player goes over the ball while staying on his feet; he is the "hooker" of the pack. The rest of the players join the first player so that a scrum formation develops. The main aim is for everyone, bound together, to go over the ball without touching it.

88. Rucking with seven players

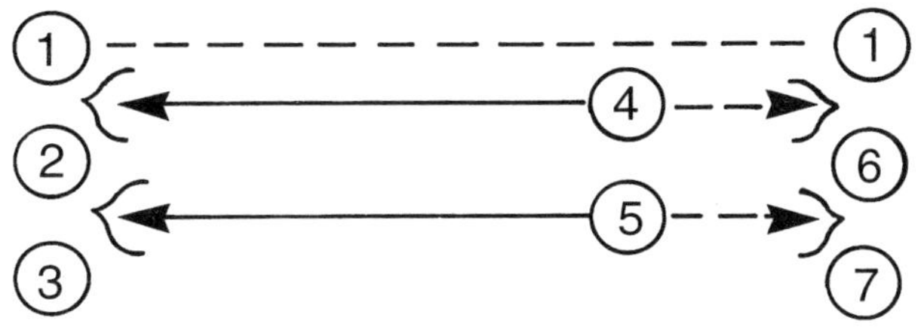

Players 4 and 5 are the working pack for one minute. They drive, bound together, from behind (like a pair of locks) into players 1, 2 and 3, who stand bound together like a front row, and push them 5 m. They then break up and run to 6 and 7, whom 1 has in the meantime joined, and repeat the process. When they have done this, 7 runs to complete the threesome with 2 and 3. This is an excellent drill for technique and stamina.

89. Rucking
All the players in groups of four per bag. One player holds the bag. The second drives against the bag and goes down with the ball. The third ignores the ball and drives over the ball-carrier against the bag. In practice this means he drives the closest opponent away from the ball so that the ball is available for the fourth team-mate. (This approach works in practice only if there are more attackers close to the ball than defenders.)

90. Rucking
One team against two sets of tackle bags. Play from a specific facet, like a scrum. The coach decides which player makes contact with the first bag. Create a loose scrum and play in the same direction until a player makes contact with the second tackle bag. Round off the movement with a try to the same side.

91. Rucking or mauling from a drive

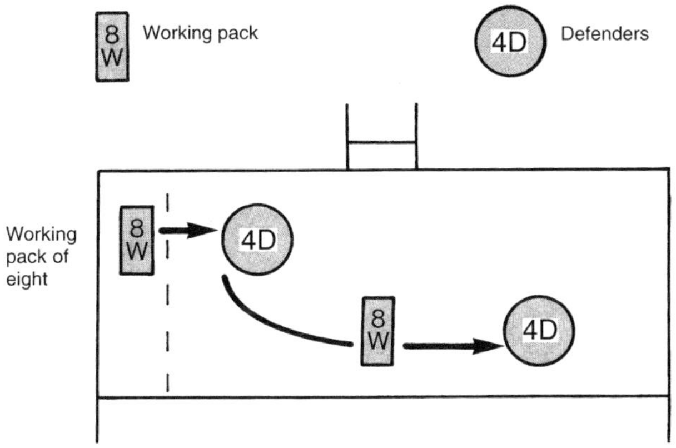

Two packs of forwards (A and B) play against one another across the width of the field between the goal-line and 22 m line. A scrum-half plays with the working pack (A) against the defending pack (B), which is divided into two groups of four players each. The working pack plays against each group of defenders separately.

The working pack stands on the touch-line, the first four defenders on the 15 m line and the second four defenders opposite the goal posts. The working pack tries to carry the ball to the other touch-line without the defenders "killing" it or taking it off.

The options of the working group are as follows:

Ball-carrier: Choose the weakest point; stay on your feet; do not become isolated; make the ball available to your first team-mate in time while still applying forward pressure; your last option is down to the ground quickly and placing the ball back.

First team-mate: Go for the ball on the furthest side of your team-mate; get control of it and drive forward together with your team-mate; if you lose momentum and/or are stopped, make the ball available to the scrum-half or next forward, who drives past.

The rest: Nos. 3 and 4 go in on either side of the first player, bind, and push straight ahead; 5 and 6 go in as locks so that the channel remains open for the ball; 7 and 8 pack as loose forwards.

The forward (No. 5, 6, 7 or 8) who wants to break away from the loose maul with the ball must tell his team-mates where he is breaking away to, otherwise he will find himself on his own.

If the ball-carrier goes down, everyone goes over the ball on their feet in scrum formation. The target is a metre past the ball!

The defenders' options are:

If the ball is open, No. 1 goes for the ball; 2 and 3 isolate the ball-carrier and rip his elbows and/or wrists apart so that 1 can take the ball off.

If the ball is protected, No. 1 has two choices: either he throws the ball-carrier down over his leg so that the ball lies on the defender's side of the ball-carrier and the defenders can win it by rucking, or he turns the ball-carrier around away from his supporters so that his team-mates can win the ball in the ensuing maul.

92. Ruck or maul from a scrum

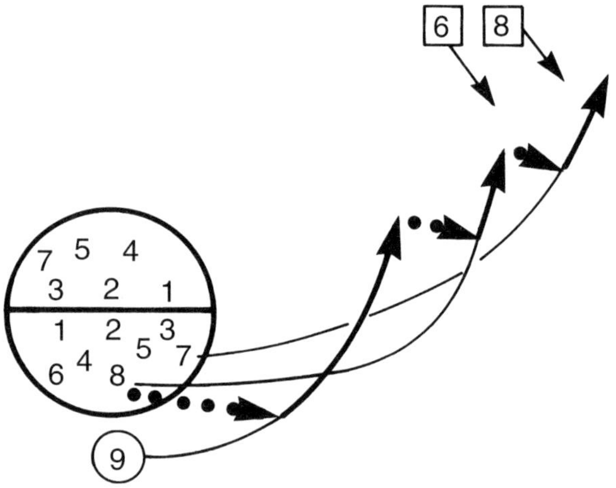

The working pack has the help of a scrum-half while the defending pack's Nos. 6 and 8 stand 5 m and 10 m respectively behind the loose-head side of the defending scrum and act as first defenders. If the attackers master the technique first add 8 and then 6 to the defending scrum.

The scrum-half puts in the ball, which should come quickly through the scrum. He then breaks to the right with the loose forwards in triangular support; the rest of the pack plays with them.

Practise all the variations between the scrum-half and loose forwards, and later add the blind-side winger and even the full-back.

93. Ruck or maul from line-out possession

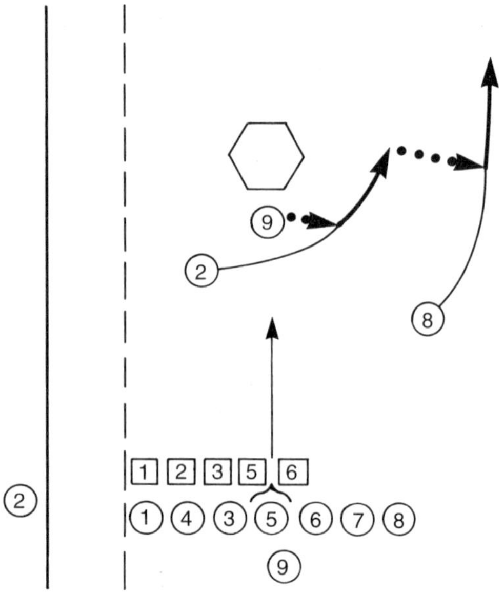

The working pack has a scrum-half while the defending pack has only four forwards opposite the point of the throw-in. The rest stand 10 m back and act as the next defensive line for the working pack. It is important for the players to know what they can do with ball possession at the front of the line-out, in the middle, at the back, and behind and over.

94. A maul or ruck in the context of a game

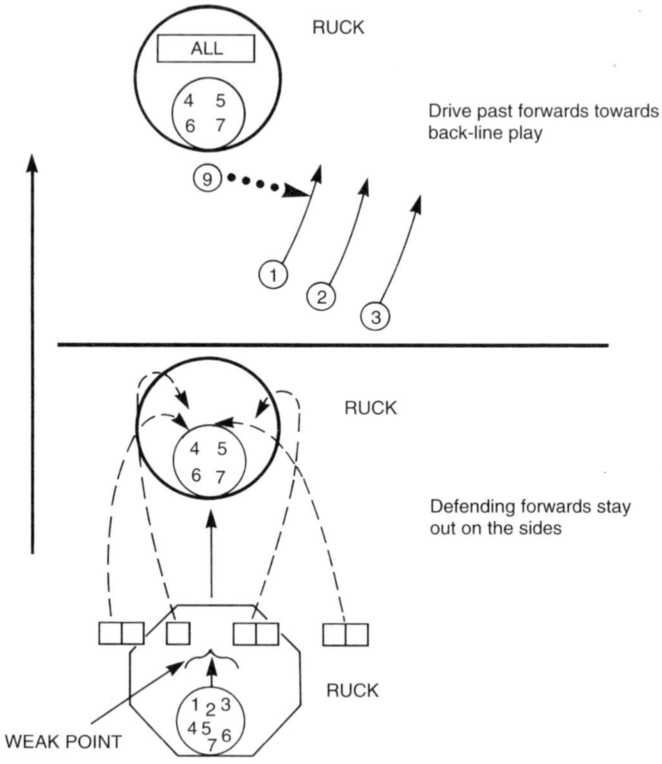

A pack of forwards driving forward in the maul situation. The maul is swung towards a weak spot and one or two players break through the defensive loose maul (not past it on the side). They drive on their feet about 5 m to 8 m forward and then form a loose scrum. (It is at this point that they are tackled by the opponents' forwards, who originally stood out on the sides.) In this loose scrum/ruck, the first forwards go over the ball and the scrum-half passes it to one or two forwards who are standing out. They drive on to the opponents' backs. (There is no sense in forwards driving onto forwards, as happens most of the time.)

95. Line-out skills
Five players stand in a circle. The group moves down the field while giving high volley-ball passes. It is important for the players to pass with their fingers and wrists and not with the palms of their hands. (Ball skills for line-outs, among other things.)

96. Short line-outs
The players know beforehand that they are going to do short line-outs in the following order: two-man, three-

man, four-man, and five-man. They keep to that order without the captain having to shout it beforehand. He simply says "Short line-out" and they then start with the two-man. If a prop goes in by mistake, he simply stays there. When this technique is mastered and done quickly, it creates great confusion among the opponents.

97. Forwards: combination drill from set phase

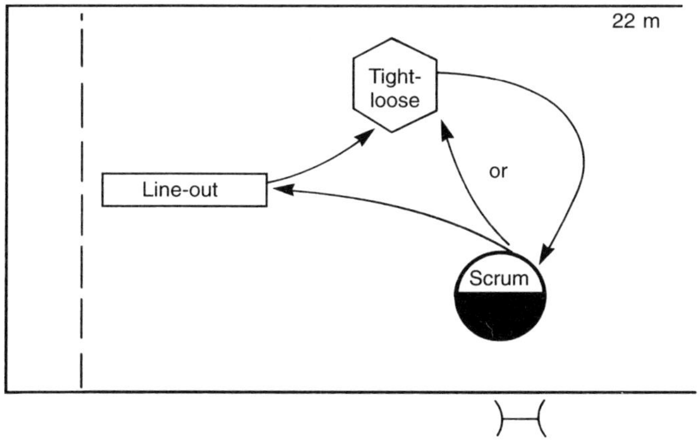

A pack of forwards moves alternately from scrumming against a machine, to tight-loose (maul or ruck), to line-out. The last two can be interchanged. Emphasise communication. The players must shout out the commands, for example, while scrumming:

Examples of scrum work:
"Pull - Now - 1, 2!" (The last-mentioned refer to the steps taken and can also be "1, 2, 3, 4" or "1, 2, 3, 4, 5".) The machine is then deliberately pushed so that it swings as follows: "Left 1, 2, 3, 4, 5" - and then immediately - "Right 1, 2, 3, 4, 5".

98. Team combination/pattern of play

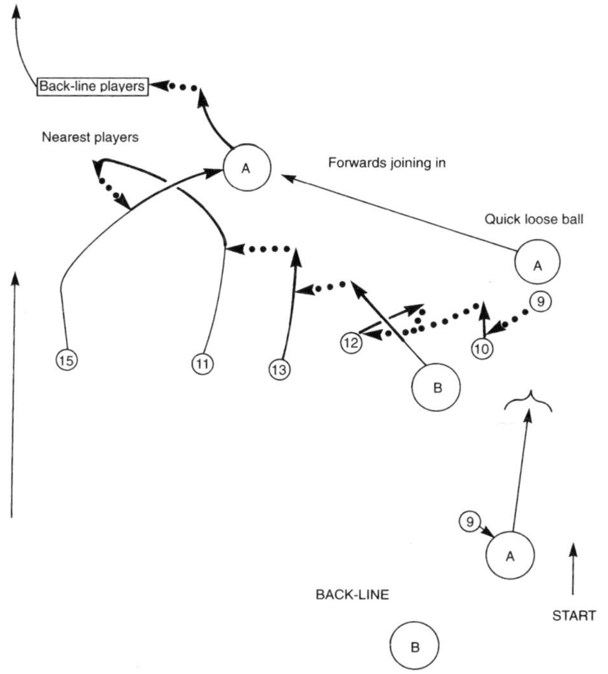

To get communication between forwards and backs and ensure continuity in the game. The tight forwards (A) stand with the scrum-half, and the loose forwards (B) stand behind the fly-half. The scrum-half passes to the left, for example, and the ball is brought to the inside with a cut-back movement by the fly-half or inside centre to the loose forwards. From them the ball goes left along the back-line. At this point, the direction is changed by winger or full-back and brought back, e.g., to the inside with an inside or switch pass, to link with the tight forwards, who continue playing to the left. Thereafter everyone plays to the left - if there is still space - on a first-come-first-serve basis. The last players form the back-line open side in case the opponents get the ball and move to that side.

99. Team drills to warm up
Any facet can slowly be worked through in a team context to bring the objective home to the players. At the same time, they also gradually warm up.

Examples:
Kick-offs followed by driving; blind-side movements with the loose forwards from scrum possession; centres and loose forwards joining after line-out possession; free kicks and penalty kicks; counter-attacks, etc.

If the players are already warmed up, facets can be practised in 10 to 15 second bursts. This ensures maximum effort and speed by every player.

100. Team drill: support/continuity

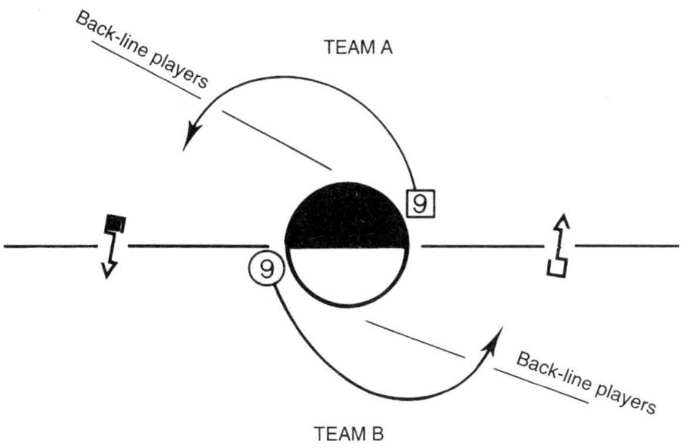

Two teams practise support from scrum possession in a competition context but with minimum contact.

Scrum in the middle of the field; every scrum-half has a ball to put in. Both back-lines take up position to the right, for example:

The scrum-halves put the balls into the scrum simultaneously and each team concentrates on its own ball. The loose forwards (and the rest of the forwards) break up to the side where their back-line is and support the ball. One maul per team is compulsory.

Which side is first across the goal-line?

In an ordinary match practice, the coach can count out loud how long the team that obtains possession retains possession. It works!

101. Team drill: observation and decision-making
The coach starts the drill with passive resistance from, say, a loose play situation, and watches whether the attackers exercise the right options. As soon as play becomes static, introduce a second ball into play so that the players have to observe, sum up and make decisions in this new situation. Repeat the process every now and then until an entire length of the field has been played. The coach has many possibilities for play from: mauls in front of or behind the forwards; the centres; the loose forwards; the full-back; the blind-side winger; against kicks (all types).

102. Three back-lines - A, B and C (see opp.) - positioned from goal post to goal post; A and C facing towards the same touch-line and B towards the other one. One scrum-half passes six balls to the three back-lines as shown on the diagram. (Quick alignment, straight running, creating space out wide.)

103. Two back-lines playing between goal-line and 22 metres. First line positioned on goal-line facing their own deadball line. Second back-line positioned in 22 m area. On command the first line turns, observes the situation and plays towards weak spots. Reaching the 22 it immediately launches a counter attack towards starting point. The coach must vary the defender's position in order to guide the attackers towards the correct decisions.

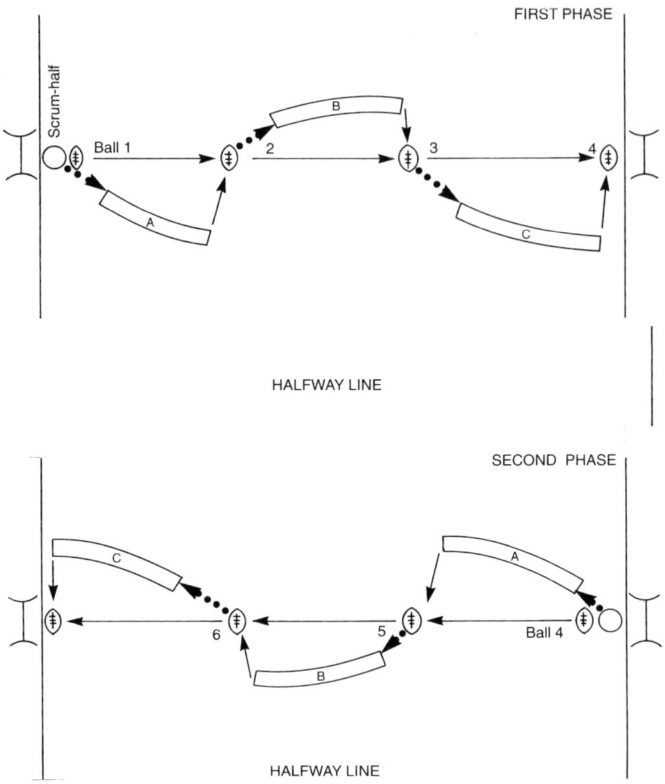

18. Drills: reference

We don't play drills, we play rugby

This outline is a shortcut for the coach/player to the drills relating to specific aspects of the game. Keep in mind that some of the drills that, for instance, will improve your handling, usually will do the same to your running technique. Drills shouldn't be seen as isolated in compartments.

Warming up
11, 12, 15, 16, 18

Running
Basic
1, 2, 5, 7, 18, 27, 30, 40, 50, 51, 61, 62
Side-step
3, 4, 18, 29, 30, 33, 40, 41, 51, 62
Running angles
53, 56, 59, 67
Support/running off the ball
25, 26, 29, 30, 33, 36, 38, 43, 50, 51, 59, 60, 64, 68
Positioning/alignment
7, 18, 26, 30, 31, 34, 36, 37, 41, 45, 46, 47, 50, 51, 58, 59, 60, 62, 64, 65, 67, 69, 70

Handling
Basic
8, 11, 12, 13, 14, 15, 16, 17, 18, 19, 21, 24, 25, 26, 27, 28, 29, 30, 33, 34, 35, 36, 37, 40, 41, 50, 51, 54, 61, 62, 95
Scissors/switch pass
35, 44, 45, 58
Wallaby pass
24
Skip passing
29, 42, 59, 60
Short pass
42, 43, 46, 51, 59, 60
Scrum-half
14

Observation
3, 7, 27, 28, 30, 33, 41, 50, 51, 58, 61, 62, 63, 64, 65, 66, 67, 68, 69, 70, 72

Reaction
5, 18, 27, 30, 41, 47, 50, 51, 56, 58, 61, 62, 64, 65, 69

Back-line
31, 59, 60, 61, 65, 66, 67, 69, 70, 71, 72, 73, 74, 102

Counter-attack
72, 81, 83

Kicking
76

Tight-loose
Contact-driving
6, 33, 41, 55, 56, 57
Rip
9, 10, 20, 23, 52
Placing the ball
22, 39, 49, 57
General
9, 10, 20, 23, 32, 33, 38, 49, 52, 55, 56, 57, 59, 69, 83, 84, 85, 86, 87, 88, 89, 90, 91, 92, 93, 94, 97

Tackle
76, 77, 78, 79, 80, 81

Line-out
95, 96

Team-drill
98, 99, 100, 101